Modes of
Public Speaking

Principles
and Practice

Modes of
Public Speaking

Principles
and Practice

Arthur B. Miller
University of Akron

Wadsworth Publishing Company, Inc.
Belmont, California

L. C. Cat. Card No.: 77–135115

Printed in the United States
of America

1 2 3 4 5 6 7 8 9 10 — 75 74 73 72 71

Preface

Modes of Public Speaking derives its meaning from the thesis that the speaker must adapt his thought to that of his hearers. Each chapter attempts to show how the speaker adapts his thought to the hearer through the *meaning* $\longrightarrow$ *identification* $\longrightarrow$ *persuasion* sequence, thus making the text an integrated whole.

Chapters 8 through 12, dealing specifically with the modes, are designed to guide the student in composing his speeches. These chapters present illustrative student speeches to enable the student to see how he may apply the format of each mode. They also present, for further study, full-length professional speeches that are also correlated with the modes, chapter by chapter.

Because the enthymeme inherently involves the hearer, and is an essential topic in discussing human communication, this book contains a full chapter on the enthymeme. Although Chapter 7 focuses on the subject, consideration of the enthymeme permeates the book.

Obviously, no book is the product of one human being. It would be impossible to acknowledge the intellectual debt owed to everyone, but I should like to mention in particular the following persons:

I should like to thank Professor Tom Willett of William Jewell College, Professor Forster Day, Miss Diane Dean, and Miss Carol

275531

Sowards, all of Park College, for their comments on selected portions of the manuscript.

For reviewing the text in its entirety, I should like to thank Professor James Rasmussen of Northern Michigan University, Professor Allan Schramm of the State University of New York–Oneonta, and Professor Hugh Seabury of the University of Iowa.

Finally, I should like gratefully to acknowledge the expertise of my wife, Lucy, in typing and proofing the manuscript. Of course, I acknowledge full responsibility for any inadequacies.

Arthur B. Miller

Contents

1
Philosophy of Human Communication   1

How the meaning ⟶ identification ⟶ persuasion sequence works . . .
its philosophical base . . . its historical continuity . . . its importance illustrated by a case of failure

2
Introduction to Adaptation   24

The basis for all human communication . . . procedure for selecting a
topic . . . procedure for formulating a statement . . . procedure for testing
a statement . . . procedure for selecting a mode . . . procedure for structuring the speech

Philosophy
of Human
Communication

In this chapter, my aim is to show you why the meaning ⟶ identification ⟶ persuasion *sequence works in helping the speaker to adapt his thoughts to the hearer. I will show that this conception is philosophically sound and that the historical continuity of the conception is rooted in the experiences of human beings. I begin my illustrative material with ancient Greece and proceed through the twentieth century.*

As you read this chapter, you should be particularly alert to the ways that speakers throughout the ages have presented ideas that constituted a meaningful basis for identification between hearers and the speaker. To reinforce this point, I end the chapter with a student's paper that analyzes how a speaker failed because he did not provide a meaningful basis for identification.

The philosophy of this book is that anyone who asks hearers to believe him should do so only if he intends to lead them into an enhancement of the meaning of their lives. This posture is based upon the threefold premise (1) that each person has essential human dignity, (2) that therefore each human being is worthy of respect, and (3) that each human being has the right to seek his own meaning.

Given the foregoing, then, the communicator's message should not be egocentric but *anthropocentric,*[1] or "man-centered." Whereas egocentric communication centers about the speaker's attempt to persuade an audience to accept *his* meaning, anthropocentric communication involves the speaker's attempt to lead the hearers to discover *their* individual and specific meanings in his conceptions. One may explain the anthropocentric transaction between speaker and hearer this way: Given that "S" (speaker) has already discovered meaning in "I" (idea) and that "S" leads "H" (hearer) to discover meaning in "I," then it is possible for "H" to identify with "S" and for "S" to be persuasive. In other words, "S" aims for multilateral identification among all the participants involved in any particular communicative dialog. The establishment of this identification provides a firm bond between the speaker and the hearers, and the effect is persuasion.[2] This process is the *meaning ⟶ identification ⟶ persuasion* sequence; man's search for meaning provides a basis for identification, and identification leads to persuasion.

A basic question arises from this thesis: "How much of a force in his life is man's quest for meaning?" Viktor Frankl, who has been called the successor to Freud, states:

> Man's search for meaning is a primary force in his life and not a "secondary rationalization" of instinctual drives. This meaning is unique and specific in that it must and can be fulfilled by him alone; only then does it achieve a significance that will satisfy his own will to meaning.[3]

Frankl further points out:

> Everyone has his own specific vocation or mission in life; everyone must carry out a concrete assignment that demands fulfillment. Therein he cannot be replaced, nor can his life be repeated. Thus, everyone's task is as unique as is his specific opportunity to implement it.
>
> As each situation in life represents a challenge to man and

---

[1] From *anthropos,* man as in mankind; man in general.

[2] From *peitho,* to use words to induce belief. Thus, persuasion is the result or effect of having been induced by words to believe.

[3] Viktor E. Frankl, *Man's Search for Meaning: An Introduction to Logotherapy* (Boston: Beacon Press, 1962), p. 99. Reprinted by permission of the Beacon Press, © 1959, 1962 by Viktor Frankl.

Chapter One

presents a problem for him to solve, the question of the meaning of life may actually be reversed. Ultimately, man should not ask what the meaning of his life is, but rather must recognize that it is *he* who is asked. In a word, each man is questioned by life; and he can only answer to life by *answering for* his own life; to life he can only respond by being responsible.[4]

If man's search for meaning is a primary force in his life, then it permeates his thought and action and must, therefore, affect human communication. Thus, the effective communicator seeks to discover ways to lead hearers into the fullest possible realization of what life expects of them. If the speaker fulfills this primary responsibility to his audience, then persuasion should occur concomitantly.

The key to anthropocentric communication lies in the positive, altruistic attitude of the speaker toward the hearer.[5] This attitude toward the hearer shows itself in the speaker's selection of the topic, in his selection and arrangement of ideas, language, and materials to support the topic, and in his delivery.[6] The obvious correlate to the speaker's attitude toward his audience is his attitude toward himself.[7] His attitude toward himself manifests itself in his communication in the same way as does his attitude toward the listener.

The major result of the strong ethical base of the anthropocentric philosophy of public address is its effectiveness. Some speeches have enabled hearers (or readers) to come to a better understanding of their lives in relation to some great principle, cause, or ideal to which they could dedicate themselves. Such speeches are the masterpieces of rhetorical literature. Although they may not have been aware of the anthropocentric philosophy of communication, most of the world's famous orators have based their remarks on its premises. This is not to suggest that all famous speakers in all places and at all times have attempted to lead hearers to discover what life expected of them and thus to find meaning for their lives. Generally, however, those orators whose speeches have endured have said something so well that it transcended the immediate occasion and led the hearers (or readers) to understand where their destinies lay.

Greece's famous orator Demosthenes constantly attempted to lead his audiences to discover that they ought to consider the welfare of Athens and their responsibilities as citizens of Athens. He appealed to Athenians to find their meaning for living in serving their state — in partic-

---

[4] Frankl, pp. 110–111.

[5] See "Tone" in I. A. Richards, *Practical Criticism: A Study of Literary Judgment* (New York: Harcourt, Brace and Company, 1929), pp. 175–176.

[6] See Chapter 2 on topic selection and Chapter 14 on delivery.

[7] From *autos*, "self," hence this attitude may be designated *autone.*

ular against their enemies. Frequently, his reasoning seemed to follow the format:[8]

> Major Premise: Athenians should think of the welfare of Athens.
>
> Minor Premise: You are Athenians.
>
> Conclusion: You should think of the welfare of Athens.

The underlying premise was that the significance of being an Athenian lay in one's relationship to Athens. Thus, implicit in this unstated premise was the idea that one lived a meaningful life centered not around himself but around the state. For example, in his introduction to "The Oration on the State of the Chersonesus," Demosthenes stated:

> It were to be wished, Athenians, that they who speak in public would never suffer hatred or affection to influence their counsels; but, in all that they propose, be directed by unbiassed reason; particularly when affairs of state, and those of highest moment, are the object of our attention. But since there are persons whose speeches are partly dictated by a spirit of contention, partly by other like motives, it is your duty, Athenians, to exert that power which your numbers give you, and in all your resolutions and in all your actions to consider only the interest of your country.[9]

Implicit in the foregoing remarks was the idea that Athenians could best serve themselves as a group by remembering that they were Athenians—by serving their state. If his hearers could find meaning in serving their country, then they would identify with the ideas of Demosthenes, and with their country.

Cicero was Rome's most famous orator. Some of Cicero's finest orations were addressed to Lucius Catiline, who had been an unsuccessful competitor of Cicero's for the consulship of Rome and who was openly plotting to kill Cicero and to take over Rome. Cicero, having full knowledge of the plot, summoned the Senate to meet in the temple of Jupiter in the Capitol. When Catiline had the audacity to attend this meeting, Cicero was so incensed that he departed from any formal business and delivered the invective now known as "The First Oration against Catiline." Cicero's interest in the welfare of the people and in democratic government is evident in the following passage from that oration:

---

[8] See Chapter 3 on the general modes of proof.

[9] Thomas Leland, tr., *The Orations of Demosthenes*, Vol. 1 (New York: J. & J. Harper, 1831), p. 121.

As, then, this is the case, O Catiline, continue as you have begun. Leave the city at last: the gates are open; depart. That Manlian camp of yours has been waiting too long for you as its general. And lead forth with you all your friends, or at least as many as you can; purge the city of your presence; you will deliver me from a great fear, when there is a wall between me and you. Among us you can dwell no longer—I will not bear it, I will not permit it, I will not tolerate it. Great thanks are due to the immortal gods, and to this very Jupiter Stator, in whose temple we are, the most ancient protector of this city, that we have already so often escaped so foul, so horrible, and so deadly an enemy to the republic. But the safety of the commonwealth must not be too often allowed to be risked on one man. As long as you, O Catiline, plotted against me while I was the consul elect, I defended myself not with a public guard, but by my own private diligence. When, in the next consular comitia, you wished to slay me when I was actually consul, and your competitors also, in the Campus Martius, I checked your nefarious attempt by the assistance and resources of my own friends, without exciting any disturbance publicly. In short, as often as you attacked me, I by myself opposed you, and that, too, though I saw that my ruin was connected with great disaster to the republic. But now you are openly attacking the entire republic.[10]

Both Cicero and Demosthenes premised some of their major arguments on the implicit assumption that a governmental system meaningful for its citizens would provide a basis for identification by the citizens with the conceptions of the two orators. In other words, because the idea of democratic government involved a political structure that was outside of the persons of Cicero and Demosthenes and outside of the persons of the hearers—but an idea with which the hearers could identify individually—it became a focal point for finding meaning, and thus for identification by the hearers.

Of course, the identification with liberty was not limited to the ancient Greeks or Romans. The eighteenth century saw more than one struggle for freedom and justice under law. This struggle provided the focal point of identification between hearer and speaker on March 23, 1775, before the Second Revolutionary Convention of Virginia, when Patrick Henry made his "Give Me Liberty or Give Me Death" speech.

The question before the House is one of awful moment to this country. For my own part, I consider it as nothing less than a question of freedom or slavery; and in proportion to the magnitude of the subject ought to be the freedom of the debate. It is only in this way that we can hope to arrive at truth, and fulfil the great responsi-

---

[10]Charles Duke Yonge, tr., *Orations of Marcus Tullius Cicero,* rev. ed. (New York: Colonial Press, 1900), pp. 8–9.

---

bility which we hold to God and our country. Should I keep back my opinions at such a time, through fear of giving offense, I should consider myself as guilty of treason toward my country, and of an act of disloyalty toward the Majesty of Heaven, which I revere above all earthly kings.[11]

Later on, Henry added:

Sir, we are not weak if we make a proper use of those means which the God of nature has placed in our power. Three millions of people armed in the holy cause of liberty, and in such a country as that which we possess, are invincible by any force which our enemy can send against us. Besides, sir, we shall not fight our battles alone. There is a just God who presides over the destinies of nations, and who will raise up friends to fight our battles for us. The battle, sir, is not to the strong alone; it is to the vigilant, the active, the brave. Besides, sir, we have no election. If we were base enough to desire it, it is now too late to retire from the contest. There is no retreat but in submission and slavery! Our chains are forged! Their clanking may be heard on the plains of Boston! The war is inevitable — and let it come! I repeat it, sir, let it come![12]

A perusal of these excerpts of Henry suggests that, at least in his mind, there may have been a hierarchy of meaning. For example, Henry mentioned God in a prominent position in the phrase, "to God and our country." In addition, he implied that arriving at truth was being responsible (1) to God and (2) to country. If his hearers could find meaning in searching for truth, then perhaps they could identify with the purposes (1) of God and (2) of their country. Again, the segment, "and of an act of disloyalty toward the Majesty of Heaven, which I revere above all earthly kings" suggests that Henry believed that God was on the side of freedom and that the king of Great Britain was on the side of slavery. Further, Henry's statement that "There is a just God who presides over the destinies of nations" is quite obvious in its implication.

All of the foregoing suggest that Henry argued from this position: "If you as men find meaning in the purposes of a just God, then you will find meaning in liberty and should identify with our resolution."

At approximately the same time that Henry and other colonists in America were urging liberty, Henry Grattan was urging rights for Ireland. On April 19, 1780, Grattan delivered to the Irish Parliament his famous speech, "Declaration of Irish Rights." Grattan reasoned along these lines:

---

[11] William Jennings Bryan, ed., *The World's Famous Orations,* Vol. 8 (New York: Funk and Wagnalls Co., 1906), pp. 62–63.

[12] Bryan, p. 66.

Chapter One

Premise: (In hearer's mind) Because only the recipient of a right from God has the power to resign that right,

Premise: And, because Irishmen received their liberty from God,

Premise: And, because Irishmen are not going to resign their right to liberty,

Conclusion: Therefore, Irishmen should declare their rights.

It would be difficult to conceive of a member of the Irish Parliament in 1780 who could not find his life's meaning in serving God and in working for Irish rights. Inasmuch as Grattan told the members about his own meaning in those same terms, it would seem reasonable that the members had a basis upon which to identify with him.

Early in his speech, Grattan united the three symbols of identification—country, liberty, and God.

> Turn to the growth and spring of your country, and behold and admire it; where do you find a nation who, upon whatever concerns the rights of mankind, expresses herself with more truth or force, perspicuity or justice? not the set phrase of scholastic men, not the tame unreality of court addresses, not the vulgar raving of a rabble, but the genuine speech of liberty, and the unsophisticated oratory of a free nation.
>
> See her military ardour, expressed not only in 40,000 men, conducted by instinct as they were raised by inspiration, but manifested in the zeal and promptitude of every young member of the growing community. Let corruption tremble; let the enemy, foreign or domestic, tremble; but let the friends of liberty rejoice at these means of safety and this hour of redemption. Yes; there does exist an enlightened sense of rights, a young appetite for freedom, a solid strength, and a rapid fire, which not only put a declaration of right within your power, but put it out of your power to decline one. Eighteen counties are at your bar; they stand there with the compact of Henry, with the charter of John, and with all the passions of the people. "Our lives are at your service, but our liberties—we received them from God; we will not resign them to man." Speaking to you thus, if you repulse these petitioners, you abdicate the privileges of Parliament, forfeit the rights of the kingdom, repudiate the instruction of your constituents, bilge the sense of your country, palsy the enthusiasm of the people, and reject that good which not a minister, not a Lord North, not a Lord Buckinghamshire, not a Lord Hillsborough, but a certain providential conjuncture, or rather the hand of God, seems to extend to you.[13]

---

[13] Daniel Owen Madden, *The Speeches of the Right Hon. Henry Grattan* (Dublin: James Duffy, 1867), pp. 40–41.

Early in the next century, on December 8, 1837, the Boston abolitionist Wendell Phillips delivered what remains as one of the classics of American public address—his speech on "The Murder of Lovejoy." Phillips attended a meeting called in Faneuil Hall, Boston, to consider resolutions condemning the action of the Alton, Illinois, mob that killed the Rev. Elijah P. Lovejoy for printing abolitionist views. The Rev. William Ellery Channing, followed by B. F. Hallett and G. S. Hillard, spoke in favor of the resolutions. The Hon. James T. Austin, Attorney-General of the Commonwealth, then gave a bitter, insulting speech opposing Channing and the resolutions. At the conclusion of Austin's speech, Wendell Phillips stepped forward and delivered his famous reply. In the following excerpt, Phillips stated his thesis that law must ensure freedom of the press and freedom of speech. Austin had made the charge that Lovejoy had been imprudent in defending his right to print abolitionist literature. Phillips replied as follows:

> *Presumptuous* to assert the freedom of the press on American ground! Is the assertion of such freedom before the age? So much before the age as to leave one no right to make it because it displeases the community? Who invents this libel on his country? It is this very thing which entitles Lovejoy to greater praise. The disputed right which provoked the Revolution—taxation without representation—is far beneath that for which he died. [Here there was a strong and general expression of disapprobation.] One word, gentlemen. As much as *thought* is better than money, so much is the cause in which Lovejoy died nobler than a mere question of taxes. James Otis thundered in this Hall when the King did but touch his *pocket*. Imagine, if you can, his indignant eloquence, had England offered to put a gag upon his lips. [Great applause.]
>
> The question that stirred the Revolution touched our civil interests. *This* concerns us not only as citizens, but as immortal beings. Wrapped up in its fate, saved or lost with it, are not only the voice of the statesman, but the instructions of the pulpit, and the progress of our faith.[14]

Measuring the effect of any given speech is difficult at best. This case is no exception. However, in his rhetorical study of Phillips, W. H. Yeager states that Phillips' speech had no small share in bringing about the passage of the resolutions.[15]

When Phillips talked about freedom of the press and freedom of speech, he was talking about a concept with which the residents of

---

[14]Wendell Phillips, *Speeches, Lectures, and Letters,* First Series (Boston: Lee and Shepard, 1894), p. 9.

[15]See Willard Hayes Yeager, "Wendell Phillips," in *A History and Criticism of American Public Address,* ed. William Norwood Brigance, Vol. 1 (New York: McGraw-Hill Book Co., 1943), p. 338.

Chapter One

Boston could identify. Further, Faneuil Hall—as his hearers knew, and as he reminded them—was a long-standing symbol of freedom. Early in his speech he said:

> We have heard it asserted here, in Faneuil Hall, that Great Britain had a right to tax the Colonies, and we have heard the mob at Alton, the drunken murderers of Lovejoy, compared to those patriot fathers who threw the tea overboard! [Great applause.] Fellow-citizens, is this Faneuil Hall doctrine? ["No, no."][16]

If applause was any indication, then a number of persons in attendance identified with Faneuil Hall as a symbol of freedom. Therefore, those persons should have been able to identify with Phillips.

In ending his speech, Phillips again identified his ideas with Faneuil Hall.

> I am glad, Sir, to see this crowded house. It is good for us to be here. When Liberty is in danger, Faneuil Hall has the right, it is her duty, to strike the key-note for these United States. I am glad, for one reason, that remarks such as those to which I have alluded have been uttered here. The passage of these resolutions, in spite of this opposition, led by the Attorney-General of the Commonwealth, will show more clearly, more decisively, the deep indignation with which Boston regards this outrage.[17]

Out of this same period of American history came the speeches of Abraham Lincoln. Although he delivered a number of excellent speeches, his address at Gettysburg is his best known. At the beginning of this address, he related a government of liberty to the inherent equality of man. In his conclusion, he related freedom to "government of the people, by the people, and for the people." Thus, by identifying himself with free government and with the equality of mankind, Lincoln expressed attitudinal beliefs that his audience should have found meaningful. Certainly, subsequent generations have found Lincoln's conceptions meaningful, and, thus, have identified with him and with these conceptions.

The nineteenth century provided yet another speaker, Robert Green Ingersoll, whose oratory was premised upon leading the hearer to discover a transcendent meaning. Ingersoll emphasized his belief that each human being possessed an inherent dignity and that each individual had the right to freedom. His dedication to the happiness and interests

---

[16] Phillips, p. 2.
[17] Phillips, p. 10.

---

of others was evident in his "Funeral Oration at His Brother's Grave." In concluding the eulogy, Ingersoll said of his brother:

> He added to the sum of human joy, and were every one for whom he did some loving service to bring a blossom to his grave he would sleep to-night beneath a wilderness of flowers. Life is a narrow vale between the cold and barren peaks of two eternities. We strive in vain to look beyond the heights. We cry aloud, and the only answer is the echo of our wailing cry. From the voiceless lips of the unreplying dead there comes no word; but in the night of death hope sees a star and listening love can hear the rustle of a wing. He who sleeps here, when dying, mistaking the approach of death for the return of health, whispered with his latest breath, "I am better now." Let us believe, in spite of doubts and dogmas and tears and fears that these dear words are true of all the countless dead. And now, to you who have been chosen from among the many men he loved to do the last sad office for the dead, we give his sacred dust. Speech cannot contain our love. There was—there is—no gentler, stronger, manlier man.[18]

When one considers the great English-speaking orators of the twentieth century, he thinks, first of all, of Sir Winston Churchill. Some of Churchill's finest oratory came out of the war years, 1939–1945, when he served as Prime Minister of Great Britain. On December 26, 1941, before a joint session of the Congress of the United States, less than three weeks after Japan had attacked Pearl Harbor, Churchill delivered one of his most important addresses. He argued the thesis that, together, the United States and Great Britain could defeat tyranny. The key word—"together"—implied identification. Churchill began by introducing a series of identifications that should have been meaningful for his hearers. First of all, he identified himself with the United States through his relatives in the United States:

> The fact that my American forebears have for so many generations played their part in the life of the United States, and that here I am, an Englishman, welcomed in your midst, makes this experience one of the most moving and thrilling in my life, which is already long and has not been entirely uneventful. [Laughter.][19]

Churchill then moved into a more personal kind of identification with his audience.

---

[18] Robert Green Ingersoll, *Great Speeches of Col. R. G. Ingersoll* (Chicago: Rhodes & McClure Publishing Co., 1885), p. 67.

[19] *Memorial Addresses in The Congress of the United States and Tributes in Eulogy of Sir Winston Churchill*, 89th Congress, 1st Session, House Document No. 209 (Washington: U.S. Government Printing Office, 1965), p. 227.

Chapter One

> By the way, I cannot help reflecting that if my father had been
> American and my mother British, instead of the other way round, I
> might have got here on my own. [Laughter and applause.] In that
> case, this would not have been the first time you would have heard
> my voice. In that case, I should not have needed any invitation;
> but, if I had, it is hardly likely that it would have been unanimous.
> [Laughter.][20]

The laughter and applause of his fellow public servants suggest
that they identified with him. After proceeding to strengthen his identification by citing the common language of speaker and hearers, he identified himself with the democratic legislative process. He reminded them:

> I was brought up in my father's house to believe in democracy.
> "Trust the people"—that was his message. I used to see him cheered
> at meetings and in the streets by crowds of workingmen away back
> in those aristocratic Victorian days when, as Disraeli said, the world
> was for the few, and for the very few. Therefore I have been in full
> harmony all my life with the tides which have flowed on both sides
> of the Atlantic against privilege and monopoly and have steered
> confidently toward the Gettysburg ideal of "government of the
> people, by the people, for the people." [Applause.][21]

The congressmen listening could, of course, find meaning in the above
and could identify with Churchill and with his beliefs.

Next, Churchill confirmed himself as a servant of the state, a concept familiar to every one of his listeners. Thus, this particular identification between the Congress and Churchill should have brought them closer
together in a special context—the conduct of the public business on
behalf of their constituents. Everyone should have understood that
identification between the elected representatives of the people of both
nations was important to survival. Churchill affirmed:

> I owe my advancement entirely to the House of Commons,
> whose servant I am. In my country, as in yours, public men are
> proud to be the servants of the state, and would be ashamed to be
> its masters. On any day, if they thought the people wanted it, the
> House of Commons could by a simple vote remove me from my
> office. But I am not worrying about it at all. [Laughter.][22]

He then continued to provide bases for identification by openly
admiring courage and by complimenting the legislators for having the

---

[20] *Ibid.*

[21] *Ibid.*

[22] *Memorial Addresses,* p. 228.

Philosophy of Human Communication

essential fortitude. After saying that one not knowing the United States might have expected to find "an excited, disturbed, self-centered atmosphere," he stated:

> But here in Washington, in these memorable days, I have found an Olympian fortitude which, far from being based upon complacency, is only the mask of an inflexible purpose and the proof of a sure and well-grounded confidence in the final outcome. [Applause.][23]

Churchill spent considerable time in his introduction, or *exordium*,[24] first, because the survival of both nations was at issue, and, second, because the Congress alone could provide the funds necessary to buy "guns and butter" for Great Britain. Churchill needed to establish rapport, a function of an *exordium*.

After completing his *exordium*, Churchill stopped relating the bases of identification that were particularly apropos to communication among legislators and proceeded to identify primarily with philosophical meanings. In the following excerpt, he talked about truth, hearths, homes, and "the cause of freedom in every land."

> Our peoples would rather know the truth, somber though it be; and, after all, when we are doing the noblest work in the world, not only defending our hearths and homes but the cause of freedom in every land, the question of whether deliverance comes in 1942 or 1943, or 1944, falls into its proper place in the grand proportions of human history. [Applause.][25]

Then, in almost the same breath, Churchill said:

> As long as we have faith in our cause and unconquerable will power, salvation will not be denied us. In the words of the Psalmist: "He shall not be afraid of evil tidings: his heart is fixed, trusting in the Lord."[26]

The two foregoing bases of identification: "our cause" [freedom], and "trusting in the Lord," rounded out rather well the philosophical bases for identification in this segment of Churchill's address. By the time that he had arrived at the conclusion, or *peroratio*,[27] of his address,

---

[23] *Ibid.*

[24] See Chapter 12.

[25] *Memorial Addresses*, p. 230.

[26] *Ibid.*

[27] See Chapter 12.

he had advanced numerous bases of identification. Only then did Churchill appear to be confident that the legislators were "together" with him. At the beginning of his conclusion, he said:

> Here we are together, facing a group of mighty foes who seek our ruin. Here we are together, defending all that to freemen is dear. Twice in a single generation the catastrophe of world war has fallen upon us; twice in our lifetimes has the long arm of Fate reached out across the oceans to bring the United States into the forefront of the battle. If we had kept together after the last war; if we had taken common measures for our safety, this renewal of the curse need never have fallen upon us. [Applause.][28]

Churchill continued to dwell upon the theme "together," ending with this final statement:

> It is not given to us to peer into the mysteries of the future; still I avow my hope and faith, sure and inviolate, that in days to come the British and American peoples will for their own safety and for the good of all, walk together side by side in majesty, in justice, and in peace. [Applause, the Members rising.][29]

In twentieth-century America, one of the most able communicators was President John F. Kennedy. His Inaugural Address, January 20, 1961, was probably his best known and certainly his most often quoted speech.[30] Kennedy began his address by identifying himself with freedom, rather than with political victory. His statement that "we observe today not a victory of party, but a celebration of freedom" may not have converted the opposition; but it marked him as a fair-minded man, and it set the tone for the speech. Next, he affirmed his belief that the rights of man come from the hand of God, not from the state. Persons who shared Kennedy's religious belief in God should have been able to identify to some degree with the meaning of the phrase "rights of man." The new president then moved quickly to the statement of his address—that the torch has been passed to a new generation in America that was committed at home and abroad to the realization of those rights. Kennedy's concept of a "new generation" connotatively designated meanings as different as those millions of people who heard the president use it. However, regard-

---

[28] *Memorial Addresses*, p. 234.

[29] *Memorial Addresses*, p. 235.

[30] The following citations from that address are from John F. Kennedy, "Inaugural Address," January 20, 1961, in *Inaugural Addresses of the Presidents of the United States from George Washington 1789 to Lyndon Baines Johnson 1965*, 89th Congress, 1st Session, House Document No. 51 (Washington: U.S. Government Printing Office, 1965).

---

less of the hearers' associations with the concept, it would be unlikely that any substantial number of them would wish to exclude themselves from this "new generation."

After pledging the United States "to assure the survival and the success of liberty," Kennedy then pledged to help faithful friends, new states, poor nations, Latin American republics, and the United Nations. Following these pledges — with which Americans in general could identify — he then requested "those nations who would make themselves our adversary" to explore with the United States the problems in the areas of arms control, science, and freedom.

Having identified himself with the cause of freedom in relation to the rights of man, the president began his conclusion with a direct appeal, "But, let us begin." He asserted that the success of the quest for the fulfillment of the rights of man was dependent primarily upon his fellow-citizens. With this beginning of the conclusion, Kennedy shifted the emphasis from a general commitment to freedom and the rights of man to a personal commitment. He told his hearers that "Now the trumpet summons us again . . . to bear the burden of a long twilight struggle [against] tyranny, poverty, disease, and war itself." In pursuing further his "communication of personal involvement," the president asked: "Will you join in that historic effort?"

At this point in his speech, Kennedy employed the following line of reasoning:

> Premise 1: The present generation has been granted the role of defending freedom in its hour of maximum danger.
>
> Premise 2: (In hearer's mind) If we have been granted that role, then we ought to accept the responsibility.
>
> Premise 3: "I do not shrink from this responsibility — I welcome it."
>
> Conclusion: *"And so, my fellow Americans, ask not what your country can do for you: Ask what you can do for your country."*

Thus, President Kennedy's speech centered upon the attainment and maintenance of freedom through individual responsibility to the ideals of democracy. His communication thus provided his hearers with an opportunity to find meaning in their lives.

Unquestionably one of the most effective speakers of the twentieth century was Martin Luther King, Jr. Perhaps his most often quoted speech is "I Have a Dream," which he delivered on August 28, 1963, to a racially mixed audience of more than 200,000 at the Lincoln Memorial in Washington, D.C.[31] Even before Dr. King began his speech, his

---

[31] See Wil A. Linkugel, R. R. Allen, and Richard L. Johannesen, *Contemporary American Speeches: A Sourcebook of Speech Forms and Principles*, 2nd ed. (Wadsworth Publishing Co.: Belmont, Calif. 1969), p. 290.

audience had symbolically indicated that they had found meaning in his leadership and beliefs by marching with him between two important American shrines – the Washington Monument and the Lincoln Memorial. Thus, the psychological scene had been set.

Dr. King set his theme of freedom and justice by referring to Lincoln and the Emancipation Proclamation. The speaker's point was that all men were entitled to the constitutional right to life, liberty, and the pursuit of happiness, but that the Negro had been given a "bad check." "So" the speaker said, "we have come to cash this check – a check that will give us upon demand the riches of freedom and the security of justice."[32] If response to a speech is one reasonably accurate indicator of the speech's persuasiveness, then his hearers thought that freedom would enable them to find meaning in their lives; they identified with freedom and rejected injustice.

Throughout his brief speech, Dr. King constantly identified with freedom and justice, or with their equivalents. He related his faith to God and to the Scriptures. He referred to the American dream as his dream, thus identifying with the nation and the Constitution. He also identified with dignity and discipline and renounced physical violence. He identified with soul force as opposed to physical force.

Near the conclusion of his speech, Dr. King tied together all the basic meanings with which he identified and with which, directly or indirectly, he urged his hearers to identify.

> With this faith we will be able to work together, to pray together, to struggle together, to go to jail together, to stand up for freedom together, knowing that we will be free one day. This will be the day when all of God's children will be able to sing with new meaning – "my country 'tis of thee; sweet land of liberty; of thee I sing; land where my fathers died, land of the pilgrim's pride; from every mountain side, let freedom ring" – and if America is to be a great nation, this must become true.[33]

Of course, not everyone in the United States identified with Dr. King, any more than everyone identified with Lincoln. Neither is it the point that probably the preponderance of his immediate audience *did* identify with him. Rather, the question is, considering the hearers, occasion, and his thought, did Dr. King do the best possible job of adapting his thought to the thinking of his hearers? The answer would seem to be, first, that he provided the strongest bases for identification known to his hearers. Second, it seems a fair statement that, in general, Dr. King did not identify with conceptions that would cause his hearers to divide from him. It appears, then, that under the circumstances, the speaker did

---

[32] Linkugel et al., p. 291.

[33] Linkugel et al., p. 294.

employ the best possible means to adapt to his hearers. It should be no surprise that "I Have a Dream" has entered the portals of rhetorical[34] literature.

Thus far, this chapter has considered successful speakers and has attempted to illustrate some of the principles they employed. Another way to measure the significance of these principles is to examine the case of a speaker who violated them. The following student speech of criticism argues that Eugene V. Debs was a *rhetorical* failure because he failed to adapt to hearers by employing "stylistic identifications."[35] This paper amply explicates the point that without meaning there is no identification, and without identification there is no persuasion.

---

[34] Rhetoric may be defined as the theory and practice of communicative behavior.

[35] See Kenneth Burke, *A Rhetoric of Motives* (New York: George Braziller, 1955), p. 46.

Eugene V. Debs—
A Case of
Rhetorical Failure*

Eugene V. Debs, spokesman for revolutionary socialism, was a rhetorical failure. Because he failed to employ stylistic identifications in his attempts to persuade, he did not adapt to audiences in general. Professor Bernard Brommel, in his doctoral dissertation, notes that during Debs' speaking career, which spanned nearly one-half century, he made over six thousand speeches.[1] Before 1897 he spoke for organized labor and industrial unionism; after 1897 he was an active campaigner for revolutionary socialism. He was the party's candidate for president five times.[2]

Perhaps Debs' failure to adapt stemmed from his emphasis on class struggle. According to Ray Ginger, his biographer, he approached every issue from the standpoint of class question.[3] During Debs' speaking career as a revolutionary Socialist, he based his remarks on the premise that there were two classes of society—capitalists and wage slaves. Capitalists exploited the wage slaves;

---

*This student speech of criticism was presented originally at the Cal State Conference in Rhetorical Criticism, Hayward, California, May 10, 1969, by Verna L. Quirin, a student at Park College, Kansas City, Missouri. The paper is printed here with the permission of both Mrs. Quirin and the Conference, California State College at Hayward.

[1] See the unpublished dissertation (Bloomington, Ind., 1963) by Bernard J. Brommel, "Eugene V. Debs: Spokesman for Labor and Socialism," Preface.

[2] 1900, 1904, 1908, 1912, 1920.

[3] Ray Ginger, *The Bending Cross* (New Brunswick, N. J., 1949), p. 258.

therefore, capitalism was responsible for all evil in the world. Socialism would eliminate capitalism; therefore, wage slaves should unite in political action to overthrow capitalism.

By his insistence on his philosophy of class struggle he made it difficult, if not impossible, for many persons to identify with him. For instance, in 1899 Debs made a speech to the exclusive Nineteenth Century Club in New York City on "Prison Labor, Its Effects on Industry and Trade." Debs said:

> I must confess that it would have suited my purpose better had the subject been transposed so as to read: "Industry and Trade, Their Effect on Labor," for, as a Socialist, I am convinced that the prison problem is rooted in the present system of industry and trade. . . .
>
> It is therefore with the economic system, which is responsible for, not only prison labor, but for the gradual enslavement and degradation of all labor, that we must deal. . . .[4]

First of all, twisting the topic around to his favorite theme probably did nothing to promote identification with Debs' cause. In addition, the audience should have been expected to have difficulty identifying with conditions with which the members had had little or no experience. Finally, his hearers might have had considerable difficulty identifying with the picture Debs painted of themselves in the role of capitalist oppressors. Apparently, Debs' performance contrasted sharply with Aristotle's dictum that in political oratory "it adds much to an orator's influence that . . . he should be thought to entertain the right feelings towards his hearers. . . ."[5]

As the Socialist candidate for president in 1904, Debs had shown no effort to adapt to audiences in general. In his opening speech he stated:

> The twenty-five millions of wage-workers in the United States are twenty-five millions of twentieth-century slaves. . . .
>
> They who buy and they who sell in the labor market are alike dehumanized by the inhuman traffic in the brains and blood and bones of human beings.[6]

Although Socialists could identify with his words because these were party doctrines mouthed over and over by the members themselves, non-Socialists could hardly see themselves as slaves.

---

[4]Eugene V. Debs, *Debs: His Life, Writings and Speeches* (St. Louis, 1908), pp. 346–347.

[5]Aristotle, *Rhetoric*, trans. W. Rhys Roberts; *Poetics*, trans. Ingram Bywater (New York, 1954), 1377b 27–28.

[6]Debs, p. 357.

They had the vote, they could go anywhere they pleased, and they did not get off the sidewalk when the boss walked by. If the revolutionary Socialists in particular could identify with Debs, then it would appear that both Democrats and Republicans would divide from him.

But Debs also experienced difficulty adapting to organized labor. By identifying with the revolutionary Industrial Workers of the World,[7] he isolated himself from the larger membership of the American Federation of Labor who were followers of reform movements. In his speech to the IWW in 1905, Debs stated that "the Industrial Workers . . . ultimate object is to entirely abolish the capitalist system. . . ."[8]

In contrast to Debs, Samuel Gompers, leader of the AFL, opposed the theory that labor should fight for socialism or for any other ultimate goal. His program was based on: "More: Here: Now."[9] According to H. Wayne Morgan, author of *Eugene V. Debs: Socialist for President*, Gompers once said to Debs: "I am not only at variance with your doctrines, but with your philosophy. Economically you are unsound; socially you are wrong; industrially you are impossible."[10] Debs' revolutionary aims, therefore, instead of uniting labor, divided it and delivered the largest organized labor group,[11] the trade unions, into the reform camp.

In 1908 Eugene Debs was given the party nomination for president for the third time. He opened his campaign in the quiet little town of Girard, Kansas. Debs told his listeners:

> In this system we have one set who are called capitalists, and another set who are called workers; and they are at war with each other. . . .
>
> Eighty per cent of the people of the United States have no property today. A few have got it all. They have dispossessed the people, and when we get into power we will dispossess them.[12]

Furthermore, in speaking of farmers, Debs told his Girard audience:

> After his hard day's work is done, here he sits in his little shack. He is fed, and his animal wants are satisfied. . . .

[7]See Ginger, p. 242.

[8]Debs, p. 395.

[9]Ginger, p. 257.

[10]H. Wayne Morgan, *Eugene V. Debs: Socialist for President* (New York, 1962), p. 61.

[11]Bureau of the Census, *Historical Statistics of the United States, Colonial Times to 1957* (Washington, 1960), D735–740, p. 97.

[12]Debs, pp. 488–489.

He knows nothing about poetry or art. Never rises above the
animal plane upon which he is living. . . . That is life under the
present standard.[13]

However, census records show that farming in Girard and the surrounding areas of Crawford County, Kansas, had taken a sharp upward swing in the decade between 1900 and 1910. Farm property,
including land, buildings, livestock and machinery, had more than
doubled in value in those ten years. Between eighty and ninety
percent of farm land in Crawford County was above average in
quality and value.[14]

Mr. Henderson Martin, chairman of the Democratic State
Committee for Kansas, stated after the Republicans won the 1908
election that "I believe the prosperity argument was the most potent
one against us in Kansas. It appealed to the farmer with such force
as to persuade him to overcome his admiration for Bryan, his fear
of Wall street domination and vote the Republican ticket."[15] Since
farmers in general around the area did not fit Debs' description, it
is difficult to see how very many could have found meaning, and
thus identification, in his cause.

The campaign of 1908 featured the Red Special, a chartered
train, decked with red bunting and loaded with Socialist literature.
In sixty-five days,[16] as the train traveled from coast to coast, Debs
spoke to 500,000 persons.[17]

As the band played the "Marseillaise"[18] and the crowd waved
red flags[19] passed out to them by the Socialist workers, Debs
mounted the platform and preached the overthrow of capitalism.
The music and the red flags identified him with European socialism
before he even began to speak. It is highly probable that the audience could have identified more readily with him if he had associated himself with "The Star-Spangled Banner" and the American
flag. In the same manner the words "masses, proletariat, revolution,
overthrow, comrade, and bourgeoisie" all had European conno-
tations.

In California, Debs encountered his strongest opposition.
Here, too, Debs did not say much to promote identification with his
cause. For instance, Brommel relates that in Berkeley a member of
the audience asked: "If socialism went into effect . . . how would it
affect the Supreme Court and the Constitution of the United

---

[13] Debs, p. 484.

[14] Department of Commerce and Labor, Bureau of the Census, *Thirteenth Census
of the United States Taken in the Year 1910*, Vol. 6, Agriculture (Washington,
1913), pp. 554–556.

[15] "Prosperity Won in Kansas—Democratic Chairman Admits It Was an Invincible Argument," Kansas City *Journal*, November 5, 1908, p. 4.

[16] Brommel, p. 106.

[17] Ginger, p. 283.

[18] Morgan, p. 103.

[19] Morgan, p. 106.

States?" Debs answered that "If socialism went into effect . . . we would not be ruled by a Constitution a hundred and twenty years old, or governed by the dead."[20] It is fairly safe to assume that Americans who had long revered the Constitution as the next thing to holy writ would not be inclined to identify with either Eugene Debs or socialism.

In view of the Socialist prediction of one and one-half million votes, the election of 1908 was a disappointment. The Socialist total of 420,793 was only four percent higher than that of 1904, 402,283,[21] and less than three percent of the total vote cast. The total vote cast in the United States in 1908 was up ten percent over that of 1904, indicating that the four percent rise in the Socialist vote fell far short of their reasonable share of the increase.

In retrospect, David A. Shannon, author of *The Socialist Party of America*, observes in relation to the Socialist election campaigns, that "If all the people who subscribed to the *Appeal to Reason* to read Debs' editorials, and who paid their money to hear Debs speak, had voted for Debs as they cheered for Debs, his percentage of the popular vote would have been considerabley higher than it ever was."[22]

Perhaps one can gain some insight into Debs' failure by noting Kenneth Burke's statement that the rhetorician who wants to change his audience's opinion in one respect can only succeed insofar as he yields to his audience's opinions in other respects.[23] Debs yielded to nothing except his own conscience. According to Ginger, "His conscience was the Great Umpire, and Debs was the only spectator near enough to hear the umpire's decisions."[24] One who identifies with rigidity divides from adaptation. Brommel says that, in 1911, "Debs cautioned his followers to keep out of the party those who would not endorse socialism as a working class revolutionary enterprise. He feared that the party might become 'permeated and corrupted with the spirit of bourgeois reform to an extent that would practically destroy its virility and efficiency as a revolutionary organization.'"[25]

As the war years loomed, Debs found another evil to blame on capitalism. The culmination of his anti-war speaking came in Canton, Ohio, on June 16, 1918. He maintained:

> Wars throughout history have been waged for conquest and plunder. . . . The feudal barons of the Middle Ages, the economic predecessors of the capitalists of our day, declared

---

[20]Brommel, pp. 88–89. Brommel's source is the Berkeley *Independent*, September 12, 1908, p. 1.

[21]*Historical Statistics*, Y27–31, p. 682.

[22]David A. Shannon, *The Socialist Party of America* (New York, 1955), p. 263.

[23]Kenneth A. Burke, *A Rhetoric of Motives* (New York, 1955), p. 56.

[24]Ginger, p. 261.

[25]Brommel, p. 109.

all wars. And their miserable serfs fought all the battles. . . .
The master class has always declared the wars; the subject
class has always fought the battles.[26]

Debs was arrested four days after this speech and charged on
four counts with violating the Espionage Act. His trial was held
September 11, 1918, in the Federal Court at Cleveland, Judge
Westonhaver presiding.[27] Debs appeared as the only witness for
the defense. His audience was a very select group, each of the
twelve jurors being about seventy-two years of age and worth from
fifty to sixty thousand dollars each. All were retired from business;
seven were former merchants or farmers.[28] Debs made no apparent
attempt to adapt to his jury.

I admit being opposed to the present social system. I am
doing what little I can . . . to bring about a change that shall do
away with the rule of the great body of the people by a relatively small class and establish in this country an industrial and
social democracy.[29]

Although no one knows what decision the jury would have
brought in had Debs adapted to them, it is equally clear that his
failure to adapt counted against him. The New York *Times* reports
that Judge Westonhaver in passing sentence stated: "I appreciate
defendant's sincerity, I may admire his courage, but I cannot help
wishing he might take better note of facts as they are in the world
at the present time."[30]
Clearly, Debs, the apostle of revolutionary socialism, failed to
adapt his message to audiences in general. His unyielding commitment to class struggle made his task of persuasion extremely difficult. In his analysis of American socialism, Shannon[31] has pointed
out that there was no feudal tradition in America, no aristocracy
based on birth against which the middle class needed to revolt. The
citizen had always had the vote, which left only social and economic
lines between him and propertied men. The abundance of cheap land
made property ownership possible to a large number of people. The
growth of the economy made possible a high degree of class mo-
bility. The able and ambitious made the rags-to-riches transition a
visible fact. The relative success of American capitalism produced

[26]A. M. Schlesinger, Jr., ed., *Writings and Speeches of Eugene V. Debs* (New
York, 1948), p. 425.
[27]Houston Peterson, ed., *A Treasury of the World's Great Speeches* (New York,
1954), p. 722.
[28]Ginger, p. 364.
[29]Schlesinger, p. 434.
[30]New York *Times*, September 23, 1918, p. 7.
[31]See Shannon, pp. 264–268.

a better standard of living for each generation that was just a little bit better than the last. In addition, Americans held "a pragmatic view of life" that demanded "visible and practical results, and the quicker the better." They rejected the vague promises of the revolutionary Socialist in favor of the "half-a-loaf" offered at the time by the reform and progressive parties.

Debs was a man following the path he set for himself—looking neither to right nor left. He appeared to be so rigid in his thinking that he was unable to adapt satisfactorily to audiences.

Conclusion

Based upon the practice of communication by successful speakers, the following minimal suggestions appear to be in order:

1. The speaker should treat each hearer with respect as a human being.
2. The speaker should have the proper attitude toward his audience (tone).
3. The speaker should have the proper attitude toward self (autone).
4. The speaker should believe that his point is in itself worth making.
5. The speaker should believe that his speech would in some way lead hearers to discover or to fulfill the meanings of their lives.
6. The speaker should provide concepts that symbolize meaning for listeners; for example, freedom of speech, or the right to own property.
7. The speaker should select illustrations with which the communicatees can identify.

Suggested Readings

Baird, A. Craig. *Rhetoric: A Philosophical Inquiry*. New York: Ronald Press Co., 1965. Chap. 1, "Boundaries and Applications." This chapter should prove useful to those students interested in speculating about rhetoric.

Colburn, C. William. "Fear-Arousing Appeals." *Speech Communication: Analysis and Readings*, eds. Howard H. Martin and Kenneth E. Andersen. Boston: Allyn and Bacon, 1968. Pp. 214–226. This essay should help the student understand the role that fear can have in causing arguments to be meaningful to the hearer.

Chapter One

Frankl, Viktor E. *The Doctor and The Soul: From Psychotherapy to Logotherapy.* New York: Alfred A. Knopf, 1965, "Introduction."

Frankl, Viktor E. *Man's Search for Meaning: An Introduction to Logotherapy.* New York: Washington Square Press Edition, 1963. Pp. 151–177. Both of these references by Frankl explicate his conception of man's search for meaning. Both books are fascinating reading.

Suggested Assignments

1. Evaluate the potential of fear-arousing appeals in leading the hearer to find meaning in the message of the speaker.

2. With regard to William Jennings Bryan's "Cross of Gold" speech, what were the major ideas that he attempted to communicate? Were these ideas apt to be meaningful to his hearers?

3. Select a speech for which there is a printed text and evaluate it to determine whether it measured up to the criterion of meaningfulness for the *hearers*.

4. In regard to assignment 3, evaluate its meaningfulness for *readers* of the speech.

5. Discover an instance of rhetorical failure and explain how the communicator failed to make his speech meaningful to his audience.

Introduction
to Adaptation

This chapter will give you an overview of the total process of adapting your thought to the thinking of your hearer. I discuss this process in terms of five stages that are necessary in preparing to communicate.

As you read this chapter, pay particular attention to the question: "Why do I want this audience to believe this specific point?" I have found that answering this question has made it much easier for students to develop reasoning that provides the audience with a meaningful basis for identification.

Finally, you should note very carefully the section "Selecting a Mode." In this discussion, I introduce the concept of the modes and their relationship to adapting thought to hearers.

All human communication is based on the proposition that "I want you to believe what I am saying." Regardless of whether the communicator is speaking informally or making a formal presentation, he still has the overriding desire to be believed by his audience. And, if the hearers are to believe what the communicator says, then he must adapt his message to them.[1] As discussed in Chapter 1, one adapts through the *meaning* ⟶ *identification* ⟶ *persuasion* sequence.

A speaker can persuade his audience only in relation to a specific proposal. In preparing to adapt to his audience, the speaker should employ five stages: (1) selecting a topic; (2) formulating a statement by completing the assertion "I want my audience to believe that . . ."; (3) testing the statement by answering the question "Why do I want this audience to believe this specific point?"; (4) selecting a mode of communication by answering the question "What mode of communication would best enable me to adapt my specific thought to this group of hearers?"; and (5) structuring the speech.

Selecting a Topic

With an eye toward adaptation, the speaker should select his topic by using the following process:

Step 1: The speaker should choose a point about which he has convictions. In the first place, if one has no vital interest in a topic, he has no right to ask the hearers to listen to him. In the second place, the speaker's lack of conviction most assuredly will communicate to the hearers; for conviction reveals itself in idea selection, word selection, pitch, rate, intonation, and in physical movement.

Step 2: The speaker's point should be generally applicable. The point must not be unique in its applicability to the speaker but should be applicable at least to the specific audience, and preferably to audiences generically related to the specific audience. A speaker who urges an audience to adopt a solution to a problem unique to him is going to be faced, at the very least, with great difficulty in showing the applicability of his point. However, if the speaker talks of a problem affecting the group, then he probably can communicate effectively because the problem will have meaning for the hearers. If the speaker also wishes his communication to have rhetorical literary merit, he must construct his communication so that it can be applicable, with but slight modification, to wider, generically related audiences. For example, if a sermon is to have rhetorical literary

---

[1]See Aristotle, *Rhetoric*, trans. W. Rhys Roberts; *Poetics*, trans. Ingram Bywater (New York: Random House, 1954), 1356a1–20. The Aristotelian concept of persuasion centers about belief. When the *hearer* believes the assertions of the speaker, then to him they become proof. At the moment of belief the effect is persuasion. See also the chapters on proof and the enthymeme.

merit, it should be able to be adapted, with slight changes, to any congregation within a theological grouping.

The speaker who selects a point that is of universal concern or that can be made to be the subject of universal concern is likely to produce a speech that is at once (1) the easiest to adapt to the audience in terms of interest and (2) the most promising in its potential for being rhetorical literature. To refer again to the familiar speech of Phillips on "The Murder of Lovejoy,"[2] although the speech was a model of technique, particularly of refutation, the subject of his speech—freedom of communication—continues to elicit universal identification with freedom of the press, a concept that is dear to the lovers of freedom everywhere. Phillips' speech transcended the immediate occasion. Although universality of appeal may not be sufficient in itself to produce masterpieces of rhetorical literature, nevertheless one would find it difficult to produce a masterpiece *without* it.

Step 3: The speaker's topic should be appropriate. Propriety is inherently related to the specific audience of the speaker. In attempting to discover what is appropriate to a specific audience, one should consider the following: (1) the general age of the audience, (2) the sex of the audience, (3) the social interests of the audience, (4) the intellectual interests of the audience, (5) the professional-vocational interests of the audience, (6) the political interests of the audience, (7) the religious-philosophical interests of the audience, and (8) the unusual or atypical characteristics of the audience.

The topic must also be appropriate *to the speaker.* First of all, the speaker should know what he is talking about. Second, the speaker must have an interest in his topic. If the speaker falters on either one of these requirements, then he is not apt to interest his listeners.

Finally, the speaker should consider whether his point is appropriate to the occasion. If it is not, his audience will consider him to be lacking in judgment, and his effort to adapt his idea to his hearers may falter. If the occasion is a special one, the speaker should be aware of its significance to his hearers and should select a topic that develops the occasion's meaningfulness for them. If the occasion is a regular luncheon meeting of, say, the local Rotary, the speaker should know that and be prepared to adapt his presentation accordingly.

The author once heard a speech that violated the requirement of propriety for both the audience and the occasion. The speaker's area of competence was constitutional law. During the year preceding the speech, the speaker had been a Fullbright lecturer in a country in whose system of justice he had a professional interest. The occasion of the speech was the commencement exercises in the gymnasium-auditorium

[2] Wendell Phillips, *Speeches, Lectures, and Letters,* First Series (Boston: Lee and Shepard, 1894), pp. 1–10. See also Chapter 1 of this work.

at a small town high school. The audience consisted of the high school graduates, numbering between 40 and 50, and perhaps 250 to 300 relatives and friends of the graduates. The industry in the town centered about small diversified farming operations and logging; thus, the members of the audience largely were interested in those activities.

But although the speaker taught in a university less than 100 miles from the site of the commencement, he chose to speak on a subject dealing with the idiosyncracies of country "X's" system of justice. Thus, the speaker selected a topic that missed the audience's intellectual and pro-fessional-vocational interests. In addition, after selecting a topic that had little or no inherent meaning for the audience, he made no attempt to *make* it meaningful to them. Considering the atypical characteristics of his audience, if the speaker had been able to relate law in country "X" to education, logging, or farming—all meaningful topics to them—then he would have had a better chance to adapt his thought to his hearers.

Step 4: The speaker should consider the time available and the adequacy of available materials. Sometimes, a speaker will select a topic meeting the other criteria, but then he will discover that he needs supplementary factual or authoritative materials which are not readily obtainable in existing facilities and/or in the time available. In particular, the student speaker may encounter this difficulty because he must usually work under the pressure of time. Therefore, the student speaker, especially, should complete a reconnaissance of the materials available to him before he decides on a topic.

Formulating a Statement

Now that the speaker has selected his topic, he must proceed to formulate his statement. In deciding, first of all, upon the explicit thought[3] he wishes the hearer to believe, the speaker structures his thought into propositional form. A *proposition* is an assertion in which something is affirmed or denied. Each proposition consists of two parts: a subject and a predicate. The *subject* is that of which something is affirmed or denied. The *predicate* affirms or denies something of the subject. The communicator *must* be able to write out in propositional form the thought he wishes his audience to believe; for if he cannot find words for this proposition, then he does not have, indeed *cannot* have, a precise notion of what he wants to lead the audience to believe.

[3] For information about deciding the explicit thought to talk about, see "Selecting a Topic" in this chapter.

The proposition becomes the *statement* of the speech.[4] Because the statement contains the germ of the speech, *the entire configuration of the speech has its inception in the statement, particularly in the predicate of the statement.* For example, in relation to making a narrative speech about vacationing in Yellowstone National Park, one might be developing the following thought:

subject   predicate

Anyone considering a vacation // should consider visiting Yellowstone.

Or, when talking about a proposal to enact a federal personal income surtax, one might focus on this statement:

subject   predicate

Enactment of an income surtax // would bring about certain benefits.

Similarly, in relation to urging a change in the voting age, one probably would suggest:

subject   predicate

The voting age // should be lowered to age 18.

The speaker may best accomplish his objective of formulating a statement by adhering to these criteria:

1. *The statement must always be a declarative sentence.*

 Wrong: Should the United States renounce the Monroe Doctrine?

 Right: The United States should renounce the Monroe Doctrine.

Although the speaker may introduce rhetorical questions during his speech to focus the hearer's attention, he should avoid them in statements, since one's purpose in composing his statement is to formulate as clearly as possible the focus of the speech.

2. *The statement must have a predicate consisting of no coordinate elements.*

 Wrong: The United States should withdraw from SEATO *and* from NATO.

---

[4]The statement is the original proposition. Therefore, the statement controls the development of the proof in support of the statement.

Right: The United States should withdraw from SEATO.

Right: The United States should withdraw from NATO.

If a person were to attempt to prove in *one* argument that the United States should withdraw from both SEATO and NATO, he would soon discover that because SEATO and NATO are unique, he would need different reasons for each organization. Apart from the difficulty of the speaker in argumentation, the *hearer* would also experience difficulty in sorting out the speaker's argument and evidence.

3. *The statement must have a subject consisting of no coordinate elements.*

Wrong: The federal *and* state governments should initiate programs to preserve the natural resources of the United States.

Right: The federal government should initiate a program to preserve the natural resources of the United States.

Right: The state governments should initiate programs to preserve the natural resources of the United States.

For some reason, a good many persons neglect the subject of a proposition and, in particular, fail to take steps to prevent a bifurcated subject. If one were to attempt to prove that *both* federal and state governments should take an action, as above, he would find it difficult, if not impossible, to support such a proposition in a single argument. In addition, since each predicate should relate uniquely to its subject, a predicate that would relate to federal government would not relate to state government and vice versa.

4. *The speaker should avoid framing a negative statement*[5] *when dealing with policy questions.*

Wrong: The United States should *not* abolish protective tariffs.

Wrong: The United Nations should *not* control the utilization of the planets of our galaxy.

The major difficulty with proving a negative statement is that the word "not" or its equivalent is timeless; the statement is not limited to rejection of a specific proposition. Who knows but what the time may come when the United States "should" abolish protective tariffs or when the United

---

[5] "Negative statement" as here employed refers to a universal negative as contrasted with a "statement of opposition," in which one opposes a proposal.

Nations "should" control the development of space. Although "not" is absolute — timeless — man, of course, is finite; he cannot know the future. Someone has said that not even hindsight is 20-20. How much less, then, must be the acuity of foresight! For example, there were persons who argued in effect that the "United States should *not* purchase Alaska" and that the "United States should *not* purchase Louisiana."

5. *If the speaker wishes to oppose a course of action, he should frame a statement of opposition.* The verb in the predicate of such a proposition is "should reject" or its equivalent.

> Wrong: The Congress of the United States should not abolish protective tariffs.
>
> Wrong: The Congress of the United States should not admit Puerto Rico as a state.
>
> Right: The Congress of the United States should reject H. R. ___ providing for the abolition of protective tariffs.
>
> Right: The Congress of the United States should reject S. ___ providing for admitting Puerto Rico as a state.

In general, if one can show that, in all likelihood, evils would result from the adoption of a proposal and that these evils would outweigh (counter) any probable advantages, then he may construct a statement of opposition.

Testing the Statement

After the communicator has completed the assertion "I want my audience to believe that . . . ," he must obtain a rational answer to the question "Why do I wish this specific audience to believe this specific point?" *If he cannot obtain a rational answer, then he would have no reason to believe that his hearers would be any more successful than he in finding meaning in the topic.* And if the hearers were to see no meaning for them in the topic, they would have no basis for identifying with the topic and with the speaker. The net effect would be that the communicator could not adapt his thought to his audience. Thus, if the speaker does not find a satisfactory answer to his question, he should look for another topic. Communication occurs when one human being asserts an idea that is meaningful[6] to another; therefore, the communicative act involves (1) the communicator, (2) a meaningful message, and (3) the hearer. If the communicator's message is to be meaningful, the communicator must be more than a person with a voice and the hearer must be more than a person with ears. Both must be purposive perceivers. In the first instance, the speaker must have a precise conception of the meaning that he intends to communicate. Obviously, no one can clearly communicate an idea about which he has only the foggiest notion. In the second place, assuming that the speaker does have a precise meaning in his mind, then he must determine how to lead the *hearer* to perceive the thought clearly when it is communicated. To do that, the speaker must understand something about meaning.

Meaning is tied to purpose;[7] the act of symbolizing one's conceptions is, in itself, purposeful behavior. The primary purpose of a particular communication lies in the answer to the question "Why do I want my hearers to believe this thought?" The answer to the question should assist the speaker to determine whether he has symbolized his purpose as he intended. The answer should also assist the speaker in examining the speeches of successful speakers and learning how they symbolized their purposes.

To use a hypothetical illustration, if the Department of Defense were to request "X" dollars for adding "Y" number of personnel for the armed forces, then it should relate the request to something meaningful for its audience, the Congress. The proposal (statement) would be "The Department of Defense needs "X" dollars for adding "Y" number of personnel to the armed forces." The department might then argue that it needed to add "A" number of personnel to the Army and "N" number of personnel to the Navy, because the Army was 100,000 men below strength, and the Navy was 100,000 men below strength.

Strictly in terms of argument, the two foregoing arguments might have formal validity, because a lack of 100,000 men would constitute an argument for procurement of additional personnel. However, such arguments may lack meaning for hearers.

If, on the other hand, the department were to show that present personnel levels in the various branches of service were inadequate for defending an attack against the United States, then the request would be meaningful — and the more desperate the condition, the more meaning-

---

[6]See Chapter 1 for a discussion of man's quest for meaning. In addition, for an interesting and useful comparison, see Aristotle's statement (*Rhetoric*, 1360b1–1360b7) that one argues about measures on the basis that all men seek happiness and its constituents.

[7]See the discussion of "Intention" in I. A. Richards, *Practical Criticism: A Study of Literary Judgment* (New York: Harcourt, Brace and Company, 1929), p. 176. For information regarding "purposive (hormic) psychology," see William McDougall's pioneer work in social psychology, *An Introduction to Social Psychology* (Boston: J. W. Luce, 1909).

---

ful. The assumed premise is that human beings in general need to feel secure from personal destruction. Thus, the purpose of the speaker in wanting his hearers to believe a certain point should center about leading his hearers into activity meaningful to them. For example, during World War II, the peoples of many nations found it very meaningful to identify with the cause of freedom, even at the risk of loss of life.

Selecting a Mode

After the speaker has determined the specific thought that he wishes the audience to believe, and after answering the question regarding reasons why he wants the hearer to believe that thought, he then should inquire as to what mode of communication[8] would be best suited for adapting his thought to his audience. The purpose of every speech is adapted through a mode of communication. Since the aim of communication is to enable the speaker to lead the hearers to believe him, *the relationship between the speaker's thought and his audience primarily determines the mode of communication.* The question is "How can I best cause *my* meaning to be meaningful to the *hearer*?"

The speaker may employ one of several modes of communication: *narration,*[9] *exposition,* or one of the modes of *argumentation.* The premise here is that what *is* important is whether the hearer accepts what the speaker asserts—not whether the speaker *narrates* the point, *explains* the point, or *argues* the point. Persuasion is the primary function of the modes of communication. If, in a given case, the narrative mode is the best one to effectuate persuasion, the speaker would be foolish to use either the expository or one of the argumentative modes. The speaker should be on guard against the error of thinking that the one true way to bring about persuasion is through one of the argumentative modes.

If, for example, a speaker wishes to persuade hearers to take a vacation trip to the Finger Lakes country of New York state, then he would probably employ a narrative structure. For one reason, a trip has a beginning and an end in time, and it would easily lend itself to the narrative mode. But perhaps more important, the narrative structure would suit the nature of the topic, and the development would be natural and unobtrusive. As a result of the speaker's narration about his trip, the hearers would be able to sense the trip in such a way as to have meaning for them

---

[8] A mode of communication is a specific approach to adapting the thought of the speaker to the mind of the hearer. See further discussion on the various modes in later chapters.

[9] Description is included under this mode.

and, therefore, to inspire them to experience their own trips to the Finger Lakes. If, on the basis of the narration, the hearers were to come to believe that they should take such a vacation, then the effect would be persuasion just as certainly as if the mode were argumentative.

On the other hand, the speaker may wish his audience to believe that enacting an income surtax would be beneficial. Although he could use either argument or exposition, the communicator likely would employ exposition, because he would be under obligation to show how the proposal would produce the benefits he perceives. An alternative to the foregoing would be for the speaker to make exposition subservient to argument, in which case he would select one of the argumentative modes. In other words, if a speaker were attempting to effectuate belief specifically related to causal reasoning, then the best way for him to promote such belief would be to argue that a known cause probably would bring about a given result.

To take another example, the speaker may be preparing a speech to advocate lowering the voting age. Because reasons would be integrally involved in considering this topic, the structure should be in one of the argumentative modes. Such a speech might also include narrative elements, but certainly the structure as a whole should not be narrative. And although there would undoubtedly be expository elements in the speech, there is no reason that even suggests the possibility of an expository controlling structure.

Structuring the Speech

Each mode of communication represents a different mental *configuration,* or *gestalt,*[10] and each constituent of this communicative gestalt derives its meaning from its relationship to the whole configuration. Wolfgang Köhler, perhaps the leading spokesman for Gestalt psychology, says:

> . . . the concept *gestalt* may be applied far beyond the limits of sensory fields. According to the most general definition of *gestalt,* the processes of learning, of reproduction, of striving, of emotional attitude, of thinking, acting, and so forth, may be included as subject matter of *gestalttheorie* insofar as they do not consist of independent elements, but are determined in a situation as a whole.[11]

[10] See Wolfgang Köhler, *Gestalt Psychology* (New York: Horace Liveright, 1929).
[11] Köhler, p. 193.

Because a communication occurs sound-by-sound and second-by-second, the configuration cannot be revealed completely and instantly as can a visual image, such as a painting, photograph, or an object itself. The speaker cannot utter even two words simultaneously, let alone a paragraph. Lacking that ability, the communicator needs to adapt his configuration to his hearers word-by-word.

With reference to verbal behavior and problem solving, Howard H. Kendler points out that proper verbal statement of a problem influences the solution.[12] The order of presentation of the constituents of a communicative gestalt is important. If the communicator can visualize a straight vertical line proceeding from the top, then he has the correct notion of the manner in which he should present his ideas word-by-word. Assertion "1" leads to assertion "2"; "2" leads to "3," etc. If the sequence is perfect, then the speech may be represented by a straight line.

Even as one visualizes a straight line as having a beginning, a middle, and an end, so communicators have realized, at least since the time of Aristotle, that every communication, written and oral, must possess a beginning, a middle, and an end. However, reference to a beginning, middle, and end does not mean a starting, a stopping, and something in between. Rather, the beginning of a communication leads to the middle, and the middle leads to the end. Thus, the relationship between the beginning, middle, and end of a communication is linear. Viewed in another way, the beginning (*introduction*) derives its meaning from the middle (*body*). In like manner, the end (*conclusion*) derives its meaning from the body.[13]

Since the primary integrant of the *body* of the communication is the statement, it is from the statement that all segments of the body derive their meaning. Therefore, if the introduction is properly structured, it ought to lead directly and smoothly into a discussion of the segments of the body of the communication. The introduction has two primary functions: (1) to establish the communicator's *character*,[14] or ethos, with the audience, and (2) to focus the attention of the audience on the point embodied in the statement.

In establishing his character with his hearers, the communicator should formulate each assertion so that he reveals himself to be a man of good sense, goodwill, and good moral character. In addition, the communicator must lead the hearers to feel that the communicator likes and respects them and that the communicator himself is worthy of respect. If the audience should receive the impression that the orator would rather

---

[12] Howard H. Kendler, *Basic Psychology* (New York: Appleton-Century-Crofts, 1963), p. 375.

[13] For specific information regarding the detailed composition of the introduction, body, and conclusion, see Chapters 8–12.

[14] For a discussion of this and related topics, see Chapter 3. One result of properly establishing one's character is to establish rapport.

---

be somewhere else, or that he is untrustworthy, then — to say the least — he has not established his character favorably with his hearers. Thus, the introduction is critical to the process of adaptation.

The speaker not only must establish himself as a person worthy of being believed, he also must focus as quickly as possible on the topic. The alternative is to leave the audience to wander about without a compass. By providing the hearers with a sense of direction, the speaker informs them of the configuration (gestalt) of the course that he intends to follow.

The speaker may provide some idea of the gestalt of his communication by employing a direct plunge. Three kinds of openings facilitate a direct plunge. The first of these is the *strong statement*. For example, the speaker might assert that "Capital punishment should be abolished," or he might state that "As a deterrent to crime, capital punishment is a flat failure."

The second kind of direct plunge is the *strong question*. Because the strong question creates interest and focuses attention, it is an excellent way to introduce a statement. The speaker might lead into a speech in favor of lowering the voting age to 18 years by asking, "Why should the voting age be lowered to age 18?" Strong questions are easily implemented, for any assertion can be formulated as a question.

Finally, the speaker may employ a *strong quotation of authority*. The difficulty with such an opening is finding a quotation that bears directly on the point that the speaker intends to make. Consequently, although this kind of opening is excellent, it lacks flexibility.

In addition to opening with a direct plunge, the speaker may employ the *situation opening*, or case history. Particularly when speaking either to an audience holding views hostile to those of the speaker or to strangers, the speaker should consider opening with a situation. The advantage is that, in addition to attracting and focusing attention to the speaker's statement, it also provides a particularly fine means early in the speech for the speaker to reveal himself as a man of good sense, good moral character, and goodwill. Thus, the situation opening is a particularly excellent way for the speaker to establish rapport with his hearers.

In short, the speaker should under all circumstances select the kind of introduction to the topic that will best allow him to adapt his thought to the listeners. Thus, in his introduction, the speaker simultaneously must reveal his character and focus on the thought that he is predicating.

As important as the introduction is to adaptation, the introduction only initiates the process of adapting the statement to the audience. The essence of the process of adaptation is the body of the speech. The structure of the body involves the *thought analysis*.[15] *Argumentatively*, the body is concerned with *formally proving* the statement by proving the divisions and subdivisions of the statement. *Rhetorically*, the body rep-

---

[15]See Chapter 6 for a discussion of the thought analysis.

resents the primary effort of the speaker to lead the hearers *to believe* the statement by their believing the divisions and subdivisions of the statement. In short, for the speaker to be able to adapt the body of his speech to the hearers, he must have divisions and subdivisions of the statement that are both formally valid and believable.

The conclusion is the final step in the process of adaptation. The form of the conclusion will differ depending upon the mode of public address that the speaker employs. If he employs one of the *argumentative* modes, then inasmuch as the audience's retention of the major points of the body is essential to adaptation, the speaker should employ a brief *summary* as the initial segment of his conclusion. In addition, the speaker may promote adaptation by presenting an appropriate *appeal for agreement*.

On the other hand, if the speaker uses the *narrative* mode, then he would not use a summary and appeal. He probably would conclude his speech either with a *strong statement* epitomizing the essence of the speech or with a *strong quotation* that concisely restates the point of the speech.

Finally, assuming that the speaker uses the *expository* mode, then he has open to him three possibilities for concluding. First, he may employ the *strong statement*. Second, he may conclude with a *strong quotation*. Although the foregoing are acceptable alternatives, perhaps the best conclusion for the expository mode is the *summary*. Inasmuch as the speaker wishes to explain a process, he ordinarily will conclude by summarizing the steps in that process.

Conclusion

By adapting his thought to the hearer through the *meaning* $\longrightarrow$ *identification* $\longrightarrow$ *persuasion* sequence, the speaker attempts to lead the hearer to believe. In making his communication become meaningful, the speaker should complete five phases: (1) select a topic; (2) formulate a statement (complete the assertion "I want my audience to believe that . . ."); (3) test the statement (answer the question "Why do I want this audience to believe this specific point?"); (4) select a mode (answer the question "What mode of communication would best enable me to adapt my specific thought to this group of hearers?"); and (5) structure the speech.

As emphasized throughout this book, the communicator should adapt *his* thinking to the thinking of the *hearer*. Thus, one should regard the modes of public address as flexible, rather than inflexible, paradigms.

In a given speaking situation, the speaker may find it desirable to modify or synthesize modes in order to be of maximum effectiveness.

Finally, the speaker necessarily adapts his speech in minute segments, each one of which must be intelligible in itself. In addition, the thought of a speech must be revealed progressively. Thus, the speaker must adapt his thought in nearly infinitesmal segments that are sequentially related. Further, because speeches are ephemeral, the speaker has but one opportunity to adapt his thought to a particular audience.

Suggested Readings

Aristotle. *Rhetoric*. Book 1, Chaps. 1–4. This section is basic theory dealing with the communicative process.

Eisenson, Jon, J. Jeffery Auer, and John V. Irwin. *The Psychology of Communication*. New York: Appleton-Century-Crofts, 1963. Chap. 1, "The Nature of Speech." This essay provides a brief linguistic look at the communicative process.

Jespersen, Otto. *Mankind, Nation and Individual: From a Linguistic Point of View*. Bloomington, Ind.: Indiana University Press, 1964. Chap. 1, "Speech and Language." This chapter discusses the relationship between the speech of individuals and the language of a community.

Ross, Raymond S. *Speech Communication: Fundamentals and Practice*. Englewood Cliffs, N. J.: Prentice-Hall, 1965. Chap. 1, "Speech and Communication Processes." This chapter represents an interesting and valuable behavioral approach to the process of communication.

Suggested Assignments

1. From a topic of interest, select a point that you would like to make and write it in propositional form. Write your statement after the clause "I want my audience to believe that . . ." Double check your thinking by asking yourself: "Is that *precisely* what I want my hearers to believe?" If the answer is "No"; then keep trying until you have put down what you *really* want your audience to believe.

2. After completing assignment 1 above, write an answer to the following question: "Why do I want this audience to believe this spe-

cific point?" If you cannot arrive at an answer that is precise and important to the hearers, then you should either (1) revise your statement or (2) throw out your statement and select another. Keep trying until you arrive at an answer that is relevant to the audience.

3. State what mode of communication you plan to use to adapt your statement to the audience. Defend your selection of mode as the best one to use in adaptation.

4. Measure your statement by the criteria under "Selecting a Topic," and write an evaluation of your statement according to each criterion.

Proof:
General Processes

The major point in this chapter is that the concept of proof relates directly to whether the hearer believes what the speaker says. As you read this chapter, you should make a conscious attempt to relate each discussion of the various processes of proof to the philosophical concept above. You should ask the question: "How does this particular process of proof relate to the meaning $\longrightarrow$ identification $\longrightarrow$ persuasion *sequence?"*

Every communicator faces the problem of proof.[1] The ultimate question in dealing with this problem is personally expressed: "How can I lead the hearer to believe me?" Arguments and data do not become proof until they are believed. No one has more ably pointed out this concept than Dr. Ashbel C. Williams, president of the American Cancer Society, in this excerpt from his "Annual Meeting Address" in 1967:

> There are multiple complex reasons why we are saving only
> one-third of all those who contract cancer today, and many of these

---

[1]See Chapter 2 on the definition of proof.

doubtless deal with the shadowland of the psyche, and of the ill-defined forces of environment which inhibit personal action in saving one's own life from cancer.

But first among these reasons is disbelief.

The average person doesn't believe that he is going to be the one in four who develops cancer.

He doesn't *believe* there is much point in having an annual check-up to detect cancer early.

The average man doesn't *believe* that cancer of the rectum and colon is usually curable.

And he—and his wife—don't *believe* they should bother the doctor just because a danger signal is present.

And neither of them *believe* their physician has much interest in annual checkups as a safeguard against cancer.

Worst of all, even our own children don't *believe* their wise parents when we tell them that cigarette smoking can give them lung cancer and a dozen other killing diseases.

The most urgent, compelling and timely need is to take a much deeper look at the situation on cigarettes and come up with some answers that will produce positive results.[2]

How, then, does one proceed to prove something to the hearer?

The Directions
of Reasoning

Assuming that men find rationality more meaningful than irrationality, then the communicator should be able to convince the hearers through reason and reasonableness. Reasoning proceeds dynamically. One always reasons to one point from another point; it is analogous to a journey. The speaker departs from one location and travels along a road to his destination, and there are various roads by which he may arrive at his destination.

One of the ways to reach a conclusion is to reason *from categorical premise.* The categorical premise has for its subject, either explicitly or implicitly, a *universal term.*[3] A universal term is one that designates

---

[2]American Cancer Society, "Annual Meeting Address," October 1967, pp. 1–2.

[3]By contrast, a *particular* term refers to an indefinitely designated portion of the total possible individuals, objects, groups, or concepts coming under the definition of the term. A *singular* term refers to *one definitely designated* individual, object, group, or concept coming under the definition of the term. Since there is no exception in the singular term, it is similar to the universal term.

every individual, object, group, or concept coming under the definition of the term. Thus, argument from categorical premise utilizes a general premise from which one reasons to a less general conclusion. For example, in the House of Representatives during debate on proposed legislation to abolish the death penalty in the District of Columbia, one congressman based his attack on the death penalty on two assumed categorical premises that underlay his stated singular premises. He told the House:

> [*Premise 1*] The death sentence is totally inconsistent with modern principles of enlightened penology. [*Premise 2*] It is morally wrong . . .[4]

Expressed more formally, the lines of reasoning might appear thus:

Major Premise: (In hearer's mind) Any law totally inconsistent with the modern principles of enlightened penology should be abolished.

Minor Premise: The death penalty is totally inconsistent with the principles of enlightened modern penology.

Conclusion: The death penalty should be abolished.

His other primary argument would appear as follows:

Major Premise: (In hearer's mind) Any law that is morally wrong ought to be abolished.

Minor Premise: The death penalty is morally wrong.

Conclusion: The death penalty should be abolished.

Because, in both instances above, the speaker's minor premise implied the major (categorical) premise, he concentrated on proving the minor. All the speaker had to do was to prove that the death penalty was "morally wrong," because any course of action that is "morally wrong" is objectionable. If the communicator using the preceding approach properly constructs his line of reasoning, then the categorical premise will be the assumed premise that guarantees the validity of the conclusion once the speaker proves the minor premise. The only way for a person to attack the foregoing argument to abolish capital punishment would be to deny that it is "morally wrong."

There is a variation of the preceding approach. In the following

---

[4]*Congressional Record—House* (June 27, 1960), p. 14585.

statement attributed to Thomas Jefferson, he argued against capital punishment this way:

> Until I shall have been convinced of the infallibility of human judgment, I shall always oppose the penalty of death.[5]

Jefferson established his major premise by referring to common knowledge, with the implicit understanding that the minor premise and the conclusion would be obvious. More formally, his line of reasoning was as follows:

Major Premise: No man having fallibility of judgment should put another man to death.

Minor Premise: (In hearer's mind)   Jurors are fallible.

Conclusion: (In hearer's mind)   Jurors should not put another man to death.

The foregoing examples illustrate that reasoning from categorical premise can lead to a *probable* conclusion as well as to a certain, or necessary, conclusion. For example, any time that one argues that something "ought" to be done (as did the congressman), he can only *urge* an action. Regardless of the quality and quantity of factual material he has, he can hope at most for a probable conclusion. Furthermore, if *either* the major or minor premise is *not absolutely* true, then the conclusion at best can be only probable. On the other hand, Jefferson's argument and the following example can lead to a necessary conclusion:

Major Premise: All men are subject to making mistakes.

Minor Premise: Jurors are men.

Conclusion: Jurors are subject to making mistakes.

In retrospect, then, reasoning from categorical premise involves reasoning from principles either stated or implicit in a given premise. Therefore, if one is reasoning to a conclusion from a principle, he should consider constructing a line of reasoning from categorical premise. Further, reasoning from categorical premise tends to elicit the participation of the hearer in the process of reasoning. For if the hearer supplies one premise or another—which he will do *only if the premise is meaningful* to him—the premise then tends to become a basis for some identification with the reasoning of the speaker and, thus, promotes persuasion.

---

[5]*Congressional Record—House* (June 9, 1966), p. 12303.

A second kind of reasoning to a conclusion is reasoning *from conditional premise*. This kind of reasoning may be characterized by the words, "If-then."[6] The rule governing this form of reasoning is as follows: *If one posits the antecedent in the minor premise, then he must also posit the consequent in the conclusion.* To posit means to affirm or to assert. The *antecedent* in this kind of structure is "that which goes before" — the condition that follows "if." The *consequent* is "that which follows" — the effect that follows "then."

Employing reasoning from conditional premise, one may arrive at either a necessary conclusion or a probable conclusion. The following format illustrates a necessary conclusion:

(antecedent)   (consequent)
Major Premise: If an engine runs out of fuel, then it will stop.

(antecedent)
Minor Premise: The engine is running out of fuel.

(consequent)
Conclusion: The engine will stop.

More informally, many motorists doubtless have followed the same line of reasoning by saying, "I'd better get to a gas station." The major premise in this statement is that "any car about to run out of gas had better get to a gas station." The minor premise (implied) is that "the car in question is running out of gas." The necessary conclusion is, of course, "to get to a gas station."

Although the foregoing illustration reasons to a necessary conclusion, in most public address situations, the communicator will reason only to a probable conclusion. When reasoning to a probable conclusion *from conditional premise*, one should answer the following question: "Is the cause (antecedent) adequate to bring about the alleged effect (consequent)?" One must obtain an affirmative answer to this question. The alternative is to abandon the particular argument involved.

As a practical matter — although not a *logical* one in the strict sense of the word — one should also obtain answers to the following ancillary questions: (1) "Would any force likely prevent the operation of the known cause (antecedent) from bringing about the alleged effect (consequent)?" One must obtain a negative answer to this question. Otherwise, although the cause might be adequate, it would be prevented from working. (2) "Would the known cause (antecedent) bring about harmful side effects sufficient to override the alleged effect (consequent) desired?" One must obtain a negative answer to this question also. The alternative is to advo-

---

[6]Reasoning from conditional premise moves from a known cause to an alleged effect. This kind of reasoning also may be discussed under the heading of "causal reasoning." The correlary of argument from conditional premise is *argument from sign*. Argument from sign reasons from a known effect to an alleged cause. For further information, see the discussion following.

---

cate a course of action that would bring about a net disadvantage. A case in point is the following illustration:

(antecedent)
Major Premise: If city X builds a convention center, then it would
(consequent)
probably benefit city X.
(antecedent)
Minor Premise: City X is building a convention center.
(consequent)
Conclusion: City X will probably benefit.

If one could show that there were a number of organizations that would hold conventions in city X, then it would be likely that building a convention center would be adequate as the cause that would bring benefits to city X. Assuming that there would be no reason for the organizations to change their minds, and assuming that there would be no new obstacle to holding conventions in city X, then one could assume that no force would intervene to keep the cause from bringing about the alleged effect. Finally, presumably the persons behind the drive to build the convention center in city X would have determined that there would be a net advantage, not disadvantage, in effecting their proposal for the city. The conclusion of this line of reasoning from a conditional premise is limited to being probable, since the major premise of the argument is probable.

There is one additional valid form of reasoning from conditional premise: *If one denies* (negates or sublates) *the consequent in the minor premise, then he must also deny the antecedent in the conclusion.* For example, in relation to the car–fuel illustration above, the only valid minor premise and conclusion would be as follows:

Minor Premise: But, the car is not stopping.

Conclusion: Therefore, it is not running out of fuel.

Although the foregoing is valid as formal reasoning, this form of reasoning from conditional negative premise has limited usefulness for the public speaker. The speaker is generally more concerned with what "is" than with what "is not."

A third kind of reasoning to a conclusion is *reasoning from sign.* As is true of reasoning from conditional premise, one may reason from a sign to either a necessary conclusion or a probable conclusion. The first form, called "infallible" by Aristotle, may be illustrated by the premise that "one's having had rheumatic fever is a *sign* that he has had a streptococcus infection."[7] Another illustration of this form is the premise that "laying down an economic blockade is a sign of animosity." The second form—reasoning from sign to a probable conclusion—can be illustrated by the assertion that "admission to college is a sign of graduation from high school." Although there will be the occasional exception, such an exception does not invalidate the probability of this assertion.

The foregoing premises may become major premises from which one reasons to less general conclusions:

Major Premise: One's having rheumatic fever is a sign that he has had a streptococcus infection.

Minor Premise: Joe has rheumatic fever.

Conclusion: Joe has had a streptococcus infection.

Major Premise: Laying down an economic blockade of a foreign country is a sign of animosity.

Minor Premise: Country X has laid down an economic blockade of country Y.

Conclusion: Therefore, country X has animosity toward country Y.

Major Premise: Being admitted to college is usually a sign of having graduated from high school.

Minor Premise: John was admitted to a college.

Conclusion: John probably graduated from high school.

Orators have used argument from sign in one form or another for centuries. Among the outstanding speakers of colonial America, Patrick Henry, in his famous speech on liberty, employed an instructive instance of argument from sign. He reasoned from the sign "fleets and armies" (and "martial array") to the cause—"to force us to submission."

Are fleets and armies necessary to a work of love and reconciliation? Have we shown ourselves so unwilling to be reconciled that force must be called in to win back our love? Let us not deceive ourselves, sir. These are the implements of war and subjugation; the last arguments to which kings resort.

I ask gentlemen, sir, what means this martial array, if its purpose be not to force us to submission? Can gentlemen assign any other possible motive for it? Has Great Britain any enemy in this

---

[7]This is an infallible sign, because the only known cause of rheumatic fever is some form of streptococcus infection.

---

quarter of the world to call for all this accumulation of navies and armies? No, sir, she has none. They are meant for us: they can be meant for no other.[8]

There are three questions governing argument from sign: (1) "Is the alleged cause adequate to produce the effect?" If one receives a negative answer to this question, then he knows that his major premise is incorrect and that he had better drop the line of reasoning. (2) "Are there other possible causes?" One needs a negative answer here. If he obtains an affirmative answer, then he will have to check to see whether the possible causes did in fact operate. (3) "Is there any force operative to prevent the alleged cause from bringing about the effect?" The communicator needs a negative answer. Before one can be assured that he is reasoning correctly, he must receive correct answers to all of these questions.

In retrospect, one discovers that reasoning from categorical premise, reasoning from conditional premise, and reasoning from sign are in essence the same. The difference is largely the degree to which each elicits the participation of the persons involved in any communicative dialog. For instance, it may not be as effective to reason from the categorical premise that "all persons having lung cancer are seriously ill" as it would be to argue from the more personal conditional premise that "if you have lung cancer, then you are seriously ill." A third alternative, about on a par for effectiveness with the categorical premise, is the argument from sign: "having lung cancer is a sign of being seriously ill." The flexibility of choice should aid the speaker in adapting his thought to hearers.

A fourth means of reasoning from a more general assertion to a less general conclusion is reasoning *from disjunctive premise*—a process characterized by "either–or." When one employs this approach, he presumes to know *all alternatives*. Therein lies the major hazard of reasoning from a disjunctive premise: one may miss an alternative. The following paradigm illustrates reasoning from a disjunctive premise:

Major Premise: It is either A, B, or C, or some combination.

Minor Premise: But, it is not A.

Conclusion: Therefore, it is either B or C, or some combination.

Whereas the foregoing argument from disjunctive premise reasons to a necessary conclusion, the following format illustrates reasoning to both a necessary and a probable conclusion:

---

[8]Bryan, William Jennings, ed., *The World's Famous Orations*, Vol. 8 (New York: Funk and Wagnalls Co., 1906), p. 64.

Major Premise: There are three ways to finance new federal government program X: (A) increase income, (B) decrease other expenses, or (C) increase the national debt, or some combination.

Minor Premise: But, (C), increasing the national debt beyond the present limit is illegal.

Conclusion: Therefore, the federal government must either (A) increase income or (B) decrease other expenses, or some combination.

As it stands, assuming that the major premise contains all the alternatives and, further, that the minor premise is correct, then the foregoing format reasons to a necessary conclusion. However, if the minor premise is only probable, then the conclusion can be only probable. For instance, if the minor premise reads "But (C), increasing the national debt is *undesirable*," then, since "undesirable" is a value judgment, the conclusion at most could be probable. "Should" or "ought" would replace "must" in the conclusion to that line of reasoning.

A fifth and very common means of reasoning to a conclusion is reasoning *from similarity*. There are two varieties of this form of reasoning. The first of the two, argument *from analogy*, gains its force from being similar in only one regard to the object with which it is compared. The language of analogy would assert that "she was the apple of her father's eye." Thus, analogical reasoning is connotative rather than denotative, and the truth of the assertion is attitudinal rather than literal. The speaker simply employed the apple, with its desirable qualities, to reflect his value judgment that the daughter was her father's favorite daughter—or at least a highly regarded daughter.

However, if the speaker had said that "His *wife* was the apple of her husband's eye"; then, the apple would have connoted other meanings. One obvious allusion would be to the story of Adam and Eve. Thus, the hearer might conclude that the husband found his wife as desirable as Adam found Eve to be. Another hearer might be reminded that "beauty is in the eye of the beholder."

Certainly, one of the best known examples of the use of analogy is the "Parable of the Sower." However, this example, as well as the "apple of the eye" example, exemplifies a problem associated with using analogy in public speaking: *ambiguity*. Admittedly, most, if not all, linguistic symbols are susceptible to the causes of ambiguity, but analogical reasoning *encourages* ambiguity. For example, ever since the time of Christ, persons have advanced differing interpretations of the "Parable of the Sower."

Hence, since public address requires as much clarity as possible as opposed—say, to poetry—one should argue more from resemblance than from analogy.

Considerably more useful to the public speaker trying to solve problems is the second variety of reasoning from similarity: argument *from resemblance*. It reasons from a *principle* observed in operation in a case history to a similar circumstance in the present. *The point is not the frequency of what happened; it is rather the principle underlying what happened.* In reasoning thus, speakers are following the established procedure of historians, political scientists, and rhetoricians who attempt to understand the present through present thought about the past and who attempt to influence the future based upon their understanding of the past. Patrick Henry, in his "Give Me Liberty or Give Me Death" speech, stated the importance of reasoning from resemblance.

> I have but one lamp by which my feet are guided, and that is the lamp of experience. I know of no way of judging of the future but by the past.[9]

Sir Winston Churchill, whose abilities included that of historian, was adept at analyzing the past so as to bear on the present and the future. In his famous address to a joint session of Congress, December 26, 1941, Churchill said:

> Here we are together, facing a group of mighty foes who seek our ruin. Here we are together, defending all that to freemen is dear. Twice in a single generation the catastrophe of world war has fallen upon us; twice in our lifetimes has the long arm of Fate reached out across the oceans to bring the United States into the forefront of the battle. If we had kept together after the last war; if we had taken common measures for our safety, this renewal of the curse need never have fallen upon us. [Applause.] Do we not owe it to ourselves, to our children, to tormented mankind, to make sure that these catastrophes do not engulf us for the third time?
>
> It has been proved that pestilences may break out in the Old World which carry their destructive ravages into the New World, from which, once they are afoot, the New World cannot by any means escape. Duty and prudence alike command, first, that the germ centers of hatred and revenge should be constantly and vigilantly surveyed and treated in good time; and second, that an adequate organization should be set up to make sure that the pestilence can be controlled at its earliest beginnings before it spreads and rages throughout the entire earth. [Applause.]
>
> Five or six years ago it would have been easy, without shedding a drop of blood, for the United States and Great Britain to have insisted on fulfillment of the disarmament clauses of the treaties which Germany signed after the Great War. That also would have been the opportunity for assuring to Germans those raw materials

[9]Bryan, pp. 63–64.

which we declared in the Atlantic Charter should not be denied to any nation, victor or vanquished.[10]

Churchill, in this segment of his address, drew a resemblance between the relationship Great Britain and the United States shared at the outset of World War II with their relationship during the "Great War." He stated a twofold conclusion: (1) Great Britain and the United States should have "kept together" after World War I, and (2) Great Britain and the United States should ensure that a "Great War" would not happen again. In essence, Churchill's argument from resemblance reasoned from a sign, "this renewal of the curse," to the probable cause: failure of Great Britain and the United States to keep "together." Thus, the nature of reasoning from resemblance should be clear.

A sixth procedure for reasoning from a more general conclusion to a less general conclusion is reasoning *from expert testimony*. An expert is one whose professional attainments and abilities qualify him to draw conclusions from data within the area of his specialization. The conclusions of expert testimony are generalizations that become premises. Then, from these premises one may reason to a less general conclusion.

The speaker should draw a distinction between expert testimony and that of non-experts. It is one thing for a witness to a beating to identify the persons involved and to describe any occurrences. It is another to have a brain specialist testify as to what the probable effect of the beating would be to the brain of the victim. The difference is one of describing as contrasted with drawing conclusions. For reasoning *from expert testimony*, one man's opinion is not as good as another's.

Speakers frequently use expert testimony. It is natural that a speaker who is not an expert in an area would consult the judgment of a person who is. For instance, the congressman who spoke on a proposal to abolish the death penalty in the District of Columbia paraphrased expert opinion to support abolition of capital punishment. He first stated:

Mr. James Bennett, Director of the U.S. Federal System of Prisons, argues for the abolition of the death penalty except in the case of treason and the murder of Federal officers in the line of duty.

After a brief interruption from the floor of the House, the congressman continued by quoting another expert in penology:

Warden Lawes of Sing Sing, in my own State of New York, one of the great wardens, I think, of all time, wrote a book when he retired

---

[10]*Memorial Addresses in The Congress of the United States and Tribute in Eulogy of Sir Winston Churchill*, 89th Congress, 1st Session, House Document No. 209 (Washington: U.S. Government Printing Office, 1965), p. 234.

---

from active life, in which he pointed out that in all his years at Sing Sing, he had arrived at the clear and unequivocal conclusion that the death penalty was totally useless.[11]

The function of expert testimony is to fortify the speaker's position in the minds of the hearers by showing that professional persons agree with him. The fortification occurs when the hearers identify with the meaning of the expert testimony and subsequently identify with the communicator.

Instead of reasoning from conclusions about data as one does in using expert testimony, one may elect to *reason from data,* a seventh and final means of reasoning to a conclusion. Because data in statistical form are much easier to handle than raw data, argument from data frequently employs statistics.

In the history of British public address, perhaps no one managed statistics in relation to audience comprehension better than did Richard Cobden. The following example is from one of Cobden's speeches made during 1841–1846 against the English Corn Laws, laws that kept the price of wheat—and some other grains for human consumption—artificially high by means of protective tariffs. Cobden used statistics to attack the regressive nature of the "bread-tax." By showing the effects of the tax upon various income groups, he explicated his point that the "bread-tax" hit the poorer classes worst.

I have heard them [Corn Laws] called protections; but taxes they are, and taxes they shall be in my mouth, as long as I have the honour of a seat in this House. The bread-tax is a tax primarily levied upon the poorer classes; it is a tax, at the lowest estimate, of 40 percent above the price we should pay if there were a free trade in corn. The report upon the handloom weavers puts down 10s as the estimated weekly earnings of a family, and states that in all parts of the United Kingdom that will be found to be not an unfair estimate of the earnings of every labourer's family. It moreover states, that out of 10s each family expends 5s on bread. The tax of 40 percent is, therefore, a tax of 2s upon every labouring man's family earning 10s a week, or 20 percent upon their earnings. How does it operate as we proceed upwards in society? The man with 40s a week pays an income-tax of 5 percent; the man of 250£ a year pays but 1 percent; and the nobleman or millionaire, with an income of 200,000£ a year, and whose family consumes no more bread than that of the agricultural labourer, pays less than one halfpenny in every 100£.[12]

[11]*Congressional Record—House* (June 27, 1960), p. 14585.

[12]John Bright and James E. Thorold Rogers, eds., *Speeches on Questions of Public Policy by Richard Cobden, M. P.,* Vol. 1 (London: Macmillan and Co., 1870), pp. 3–4.

As one would expect, reasoning from data is rather prominent in technical fields; and with the great explosion in the use of electronic computers, the analysis and use of such data is expanding dramatically. The following example of reasoning from data is from a paper on water pollution delivered in Syracuse, New York, January 14, 1969.

> In a statewide survey the University of Missouri analyzed more than 6,000 water samples in Missouri. Forty-two percent of the water samples contained more than 5 parts per million as nitrogen nitrate. In some counties in northwest Missouri, over 50 percent of the wells sampled contained sufficient nitrogen to be of concern in livestock production. Data obtained indicated animal manure to be one of the major sources of nitrate in water supplies. There was a definite statistical relationship between livestock numbers and shallow wells containing nitrate.[13]

In working with statistics, a communicator must, of course, make certain that he understands the statistics. Then, after stating his point clearly, he should develop the point carefully, paying particular attention to the *order* in which he presents the data.

Aristotle's Modes of Persuasion

With reference to persuasion through the spoken word, Aristotle states that there are three modes or means by which persuasion occurs.[14] Students of communication know these modes as logos, pathos, and ethos. Thus far, this chapter has discussed material classed as logos.

Logos refers to the integrity — the reasoned quality — of the ideas that the speaker asserts. *Pathos* refers to the persuasive effect of the emotional overtones of a speaker's ideas. *Ethos* refers to the persuasive force of the speaker's character, as it is revealed in the particular speech. Logos, pathos, and ethos are interrelated; there is no such thing as a bit of logos here, a little pathos there, and a dash of ethos in between.

[13] John M. Rademacher and Anthony V. Resnik, "Feedlot Pollution Control — A Profile for Action," presented at the Cornell Animal Waste Management Conference, January 14, 1969, in Syracuse, New York. Messrs. Rademacher and Resnik are Director and Sanitary Engineer, respectively, Missouri Basin Region, Federal Water Pollution Control Administration, U.S. Department of the Interior, Kansas City, Missouri.

[14] See *Rhetoric,* 1356a1–20.

Communication always starts with thought. Without reasoned discourse—the substance of communication—one would have nothing. Since the hearer cannot react to nothing, the speaker must use reasoned discourse if he is to get any reaction to his speech and his ideas. If the ideas are meaningful to the hearer, then he reacts to them.

Everything the speaker says has some effect on what the audience thinks of him. If the speaker is logical, then the hearer is more apt to regard him highly than if he should be illogical. If he has dignity, he is likely to be more effective than if he lacks it. If he reveals himself to be sympathetic with the problems of others, then he is more apt to be highly regarded than if he appears to be apathetic to suffering.

To the degree that the hearer has a positive emotional response to the ideas of the speaker, that response fortifies the speaker's logos. Persuasion through pathos occurs, then, only when an idea has meaning for a hearer and he thus identifies with it. An idea or fact is meaningful for the hearer when it relates to his conception of his life's meaning.

Stated negatively, if something in some way threatens to upset the hearer's equilibrium, to destroy him, to cause him pain, or to deny him some expected acquisition or achievement, then it impinges on the fulfillment of his meaning and is very relevant to him. For example, in his paper on the problem of pollution, Rademacher stated:

> There is evidence that animal wastes are a major source of water quality degradation. During the past year, an estimated 12 million fish were killed by pollution in our waters. This terrible toll reflects only the actual kills discovered and reported. Many more thousands of dead fish go unnoticed or unreported each year.[15]

It does not take much imagination to conclude that fishermen or conservationists would identify readily with the factual material presented. For the fisherman and conservationist, the facts would have emotional overtones; they would feel the truth.

On the other hand, a non-fisherman or a non-lover of wildlife—although he probably would acknowledge the truth (logos) of the problem—would likely not have the same emotional reaction that the fisherman and conservationist would have.

Rademacher also pointed out:

> . . . recently, in Kansas, a large dairy herd was decimated after drinking from a well polluted by the runoff from beef cattle waste.[16]

With reference to the foregoing facts, the hearers who would have

---

[15]Rademacher and Resnik, p. 4.
[16]Rademacher and Resnik, pp. 4–5.

Chapter Three

the greatest emotional reaction probably would be dairy farmers — particularly those living near a feedlot. Anyone who might have his life's work blotted out in a few moments could be expected to react emotionally to the facts (logos). On the other hand, although the fishermen and conservationists would certainly acknowledge the truth of this problem and would react emotionally to a certain extent, they probably would not react in the same way or as intensely. They probably would not see themselves — and their life's purpose — threatened with destruction.

The point of the foregoing discussion is that the communicator who wishes his hearers to find meaning in his message will employ reasoning and evidence (logos) with emotional overtones (pathos) *in relation to his specific audience. Pathos tends to fortify logos and thus to promote identification of the hearer with the ideas of the speaker.*

The third mode, the speaker's ethos[17] is, according to Aristotle, perhaps the most important mode of persuasion. Just as there must be a message from the speaker before the hearer can react to it emotionally, so also is a message the basis for revealing the character of the speaker to the audience. Thus, logos is the cornerstone, not only of pathos but also of ethos.

How does one build his ethos? Aristotle stated that "good sense" (using reason and being reasonable) is one of the basic requirements for establishing one's ethos with an audience. The question is, then, whether the hearers in a given situation regard what the speaker says as good sense. In the excerpt below, Rademacher stated:

> Agriculture's effect on nitrate pollution of ground water was also investigated in the South Platte River Valley of Colorado. Most of the 621,000 cattle in Colorado feedlots (February 1, 1967) were located in this valley. Data obtained showed that nitrate under feedlots is moving through the soil and into the ground water supply. Since the feedlots are usually located near the homestead, they may have a pronounced effect on the water quality from domestic wells. The findings that water under feedlots frequently contained ammonium and organic carbon cause further concern about the effect of feedlots on underground water supplies.[18]

To the experts on water pollution at the conference, Rademacher's statement should have made good sense. Everyone at the conference should have been conversant with the general subject and with the technical terminology. Everyone there should have had faith in the scientific studies Rademacher cited.

---

[17]Regarding the Aristotelian conception of ethos, note the remarkable similarity between his (a) "good sense" and I. A. Richards' "sense"; between Aristotle's (b) "goodwill' and I. A. Richards' "tone"; and between Aristotle's (c) "good moral character" and I. A. Richards' "feeling" and "tone." See Richards' *Practical Criticism*, p. 175, and the *Rhetoric*, 1366a23–1368a9 and 1377b21–1378a19.

[18]Rademacher and Resnik, p. 6.

On the other hand, if Rademacher had delivered his paper to non-experts or to non-technically trained persons, then the phrases "nitrate pollution of ground water" and "ammonium and organic carbon" would probably have represented no intelligible threat to them. Thus, that particular scientific reference might not have seemed like good sense to the hearers; they might have dismissed the statements as so much "talk." For them, it would have made better sense to say that "cattle manure in your feedlots is seeping through the ground into your drinking water. If you don't want to become sick, then you must move those feedlots." Clearly, then, good sense is not absolute but is relative to the hearers. Only if statements are good sense to the hearer will he find meaning in them, identify with them, and thus be persuaded by them.

The second requirement of ethos is "goodwill." This requirement, like good sense, is centered about the hearers. In this instance, however, the requirement is attitudinal, in that it concerns the perceived attitude of the speaker toward his hearers.

Because goodwill, as revealed in communication, stems from the perceived attitude of the speaker toward the hearers, the hearers may reject the speaker's message—not because it is irrational—but solely because they do not feel that the speaker likes them. Thus, they would divide from him rather than identify with him.

Perhaps one of the best examples of the development of the ethos of a speaker through his goodwill toward his hearers is the first Inaugural Address of President Franklin D. Roosevelt, March 4, 1933. The nation was in the throes of a depression, and it was essential that Roosevelt speak in such a way that the people would follow his leadership. The initial segment of his address illustrates his technique of showing his goodwill to an audience.

> I am certain that my fellow Americans expect that on my induction into the Presidency I will address them with a candor and a decision which the present situation of our Nation impels. This is preeminently the time to speak the truth, the whole truth, frankly and boldly. Nor need we shrink from honestly facing conditions in our country today. This great Nation will endure as it has endured, will revive and will prosper. So, first of all, let me assert my firm belief that the only thing we have to fear is fear itself—nameless, unreasoning, unjustified terror which paralyzes needed efforts to convert retreat into advance. In every dark hour of our national life a leadership of frankness and vigor has met with that understanding and support of the people themselves which is essential to victory. I am convinced that you will again give that support to leadership in these critical days.[19]

[19] Franklin D. Roosevelt, "Inaugural Address," March 4, 1933, in *Inaugural Addresses of the Presidents of The United States from George Washington 1789 to Lyndon Baines Johnson 1965*, 89th Congress, 1st Session, House Document No. 51 (Washington: U.S. Government Printing Office, 1965), p. 235.

Roosevelt's references to "candor," "the truth, the whole truth, frankly and boldly," "honestly facing conditions," and "frankness and vigor" reflected goodwill toward his hearers.

The third requirement of ethos is "good moral character." The hearers in any given speaking situation must, on the basis of the words of the speech, consider the speaker to have good moral character. A person of good moral character will do things that are intentionally good; that is, based on deliberate moral choice. Thus, as a communicator, such a person would, by word and platform conduct, reflect his good moral character.

What, then, are some of the ways that a speaker communicates his good moral character? First, he does so by advocating principles that are excellent in themselves. For example, one who is loyal to family, friends, club, church, profession, home town, or country projects himself as being responsible and of good moral character. Second, he does so by advocating courageous or selfless actions. As an example, if he advocates programs to assist those who need help but who cannot repay, then he must have done so with no thought of personal gain. Third, he does so by supporting right action. To illustrate, one who identifies with treating all persons alike and with giving an honest day's work for his wages will project good moral character. One who obeys laws and loves justice and urges others to do so portrays good moral character.

In the twentieth century, probably there has been no greater master of ethos than Sir Winston Churchill. In his third address to a joint session of Congress, January 17, 1952, he spoke so as to reaffirm his good moral character. Churchill identified himself with courage when he said:

> During the war we bore our share of the burden and fought from first to last unconquered, and for a while alone, to the utmost limit of our resources. [Applause.][20]

He further established ethos by commenting explicitly about debts that Great Britain had accepted without making counterclaims, thus revealing an altruistic interest in others.

> After the war, unwisely as I contended and certainly contrary to American advice, we accepted as normal debts nearly four thousand million pounds sterling of claims by countries we had protected from invasion or had otherwise aided, instead of making counterclaims which would at least have reduced the bill to reasonable proportions.
> The thousand million loan we borrowed from you in 1946 and which we are now repaying was spent not on ourselves, but mainly in helping others. In all, since the war, as the late government affirmed, we have lent or given to European or Asiatic countries thirty

---

[20]*Memorial Addresses*, p. 237.

Proof: General Processes

hundred million pounds in the form of unrequited exports. This, added to the cost of turning over our industry from war to peace and rebuilding homes shattered by bombardment, was more than we could manage without an undue strain upon our life energies from which we shall require both time and self-discipline to recover.

Why do I say all this? Not to compare our financial resources with yours, for we are but a third of your numbers and have much less than a third of your wealth; not to claim praise or reward but to convince you of our native and enduring strength and that our true position is not to be judged by the present state of the dollar exchange or by sterling area finance.[21]

Churchill further fortified his image of good moral character by supporting right actions in the form of "high causes."

Our complicated society would be deeply injured if we did not practice and develop what is called in the United States the bipartisan habit of mind, which divides, so far as possible, what is done to make a party win and bear in their turn the responsibility of office and what is done to make the Nation live and serve high causes.[22]

Conclusion

Any discussion of reasoning pragmatically derives its significance from the premise that perceived rationality is more apt to be meaningful to a hearer than is perceived irrationality. The forms of reasoning that the communicator employs depend upon a happy blending of two requirements: (1) the logical character of the material and (2) the nature of the audience. The communicator should employ those logical processes that would enable him most effectively to adapt his thesis to his hearers so as to elicit their identification with his ideas and with him.

In addition to the cornerstone of effective communication — its reasoned quality (logos) — effective discourse also pays attention to correlative modes. Without the emotional overtones of a communicator's ideas on his hearers (pathos), and without the persuasive force of the communicator's character as revealed in his speech (ethos), his communication would be antiseptically dull and ineffective.

[21]*Memorial Addresses*, pp. 237–238.
[22]*Memorial Addresses*, pp. 239–240.

Suggested Readings

Ayer, Alfred Jules. *Language, Truth and Logic*. New York: Dover Publications, n.d. Chap. V, "Truth and Probability." This is a challenging philosophical essay on thought.

Ray, Jack, and Harry Zavos. Chap. 4, "Reasoning and Argument: Some Special Problems and Types." *Perspectives on Argumentation*, eds. Gerald R. Miller and Thomas R. Nilsen. Chicago: Scott, Foresman and Co., 1966. This is a solid discussion of some problems in reasoning.

Windes, Russel R., and Arthur Hastings. *Argumentation and Advocacy*. New York: Random House, 1965. Chap. 2, "Problems and Propositions." The student should find this to be interesting and perceptive.

Berlo, David K. *The Process of Communication: An Introduction to Theory and Practice*. New York: Holt, Rinehart and Winston, 1960. Chap. 10, "Inference: The Application of Structural Rigor." This essay provides a valuable perspective that complements the other readings.

Suggested Assignments

1. Discover an example of each of the following kinds of reasoning. Write a concise explanation as to how you conclude that each example is the kind you say it is.
   a. From categorical premise.
   b. From conditional premise.
   c. From sign.
   d. From disjunctive premise.
   e. From similarity (resemblance or analogy).
   f. From expert testimony.
   g. From data.

2. Locate an example of each of the following and defend your conclusion in each case.
   a. An instance of logos.
   b. An instance of pathos.
   c. An instance of ethos.

3. Discuss the relationship between argument and proof.

Illogic

One can discuss illogic only in terms of logic. Therefore, as the most effective approach to this chapter, I suggest that you first make certain that you understand the discussion of correct reasoning in the previous chapter, Chapter 3. To enable you to study Chapter 4 with maximum effectiveness, I have arranged the topics generally to correlate with Chapter 3.

Every communicator needs to know how to detect fallacious reasoning.[1] First of all, he needs to be alert to his own mistakes; second, he needs to know how to detect mistaken processes of reasoning in the communications of others. Obviously, one should avoid committing fallacies simply because they are in error. However, it is equally important that the communicator remember that he is attempting to adapt his message to his hearers and that it is difficult enough to adapt successfully a message without having the handicap of illogic. Hearers in general will not knowingly identify with reasoning that they consider to be unreasoned. Thus,

---

[1] A fallacy refers to an error in the process of reasoning.

hearers in general will tend not to identify with a man that they consider to be irrational.

In the public discussion of issues, if one of the participants is detected in using fallacious reasoning, his image with the audience is adversely affected. By contrast, the public speaker who can detect fallacious reasoning and can expose the fallacy helps to promote the truth as he sees it. Because much communication in a democratic society occurs in an environment permissive of confrontation, the speaker should know how to refute erroneous thinking after detecting it. In a polite but direct and concise manner, the speaker should employ four steps in showing the mistake, and its significance, to the audience: (1) The speaker should state concisely the assertion that he intends to attack. (2) The speaker should state specifically the error in the assertion. (3) The speaker should support with argument and evidence his claim that the error does in fact exist. (4) If applicable, the speaker should show the effect of his attack on the dialog between speaker and hearer.

One major category of fallacy is the *assumed premise fallacy* — proceeding to a conclusion from a dubious premise of one kind or another. This fallacy follows the form of reasoning from categorical premise. The following illustration should point up the nature of this type of error. A public speaker asserts that "The professors of X college disagree among themselves; they are confused." Arranged in a format, that line of reasoning appears below:

Major Premise: (Assumed)   The members of any group who disagree among themselves are confused.

Minor Premise: The professors of X college disagree among themselves.

Conclusion: The professors of X college are confused.

The major premise is the one with the error in it. This is usually the case in the assumed premise fallacy because of two characteristics of reasoning from categorical premise. First, because the major premise is more general than is the minor premise, it is more subject to error. Second, there is a tendency to leave the major premise unstated — particularly in public address situations. The wise communicator or listener should therefore seek out the assumed premises of all lines of reasoning.

A second species of fallacy, *faulty cause-to-effect reasoning*[2] is the counterfeit of argument from conditional premise. An example of this fallacy is the conclusion that "if (cause) the United States unilaterally were to disarm, then (effect) her enemies would do so." This assertion is based upon the assumed major premise that "when any nation disarms

---

[2] See Chapter 3 for a discussion of reasoning from conditional premise.

---

unilaterally, then her enemies will do so." The rest of the line of reasoning goes like this:

Minor Premise: (Assumed)   The United States is a nation.

Conclusion: Therefore, "if the United States were to disarm, then her enemies would do so."

The truth of this conclusion depends upon the integrity of the major premise, and the integrity of the major premise may be determined either intuitively or empirically. Obviously, since the proposal of the major premise would be out of the realm of intuitive abstraction and in the concrete world of governments and men, one would need to establish the major premise empirically. And if one were to look at recent history, he would note that while the United States and Great Britain were all but disarmed during the 1930s, Germany was encroaching on Poland, Czechoslovakia, and Austria; Italy was plundering Ethiopia; and, Japan was attacking China. Eventually, the United States and Great Britain were themselves set upon by the Axis powers. One would have to look somewhere besides history to find a basis for believing the major premise.

A fallacy similar to the foregoing is *faulty argument from sign*. The difference is the direction of the reasoning. It is fallacious to assert that "his having a college degree is an infallible sign that he is educated." The degree *is* an infallible sign only that he has fulfilled the requirements for graduation at a particular institution. At most, graduation from college can be a probable sign that one has obtained an education.

Recently, there was a curious AP story from London[3] that presented the argument that because "children of navy frogmen are nearly always girls," this fact was a sign that the fathers' being navy frogmen was the cause. The British Medical Research council said that it had "no explanation to offer." This story points up the hazard of mistaking a coincidence for a *sign* of an adequate cause.

The fallacy of *faulty disjuncture* results if one fails to consider all alternatives. In the abstract, one might reason as follows:

Major Premise: All N are either X or Y.

Minor Premise: But, no N is an X.

Conclusion: Therefore, all N are Y.

However, when there is *another alternative* (for example, Z), then the conclusion cannot be guaranteed. The following should illustrate the fallacy.

---

[3] The Milwaukee *Journal*, April 14, 1968.

Major Premise: All nations (N) are either friends (X) or enemies (Y).

Minor Premise: But, no nation (N) is a friend (X).

Conclusion: Therefore, all nations (N) are enemies (Y).

In relation to this simplistic conclusion, one encounters the reality that some nations maintain a policy of neutrality. Thus, there should be consideration of a third alternative, the neutrals (Z).

The fallacy of *appeal to misplaced authority* violates the principles underlying the use of expert testimony. The temptation to employ this species of illogic generally occurs when the speaker has read some statements of famous persons about the subject under consideration, but he does not have relevant statements of experts, famous or not. One should cite engineers on building bridges, musicians on playing musical instruments, and brain surgeons on brain surgery.

Another fallacy is the *appeal to tradition.* This fallacy centers about the appeal to tradition *as tradition,* as distinct from appealing to a practice based upon sound principles — but which *coincidentally* is a tradition. The speaker who states that "We have been using collective bargaining for years" appeals not to the principles underlying collective bargaining, but only to the tradition of using collective bargaining. The speaker should have said the equivalent of "Over the X years that we have used collective bargaining, three results have come about: Result A, Result B, and Result C."

A very familiar use of the appeal to tradition fallacy is the frequent reference in argument to George Washington's warning about United States involvement in the affairs of foreign nations. Persons have quoted the nation's first president to justify about every kind of isolation, from pulling out of the SEATO to withdrawing from the UN. First of all, there is no known evidence that Washington envisioned either the SEATO or the UN; therefore, he obviously could not have had these specific organizations in mind. But, if we assume that he *did* have similar organizations in mind, then it would still be fallacious for the speaker to urge that "We ought to honor the tradition that George Washington started many years ago — to avoid becoming involved with other nations." If one is going to urge a course of action, then he should urge it on the basis of reasons apart from the number of years something has been done.

A variation of the fallacy of appeal to tradition is the fallacy of *appeal to party spirit.* The following excerpt is adapted from an appeal made during a political campaign and illustrates appeal to party spirit:

> The fall of 1972 is one time that we should all stand solid for our Party. No one should straddle the fence. Each [party] candidate can be built into the image you desire by advising and counseling what you expect of him. In this way you build party strength; *so vote a straight [party] ticket* [author's italics].

Another relative of the appeal to tradition fallacy is the fallacy of *appeal to newness*. Such statements as "X is outmoded and outdated," "Don't be old-fashioned," or "Our plan is the newest proposal to be presented" are all premised upon the assumption that the newest is the best. The fallacy of appeal to newness seems to be in evidence in the advertising of nearly everything from soap to cars.

Another common fallacy is *appeal to present practice*. The idea is that "We're doing it now, and it's working. What more do you want?" This general position led one speaker to say, "We can't change that. It's basic to our system." He was not only appealing to present practice but also *begging the question,* inasmuch as changing existing practice was the very question under discussion. One cannot argue logically that "We cannot change present practice because it is present practice."

Another fallacy common to public address is *argument by personal attack*. There is a hidden premise here that if the person's personality can be called into question, then the argument that he espouses will be weakened. This fallacy is very simple to avoid: Stick to discussing ideas rather than the personalities of the people associated with the ideas. An example of this fallacy is the comment that "if you don't believe this is the best place to live, why don't you go live some place else?" Every argument should be directed at issues, not people.

One of the most common fallacies is *appeal to the crowd*. The general idea is "Everybody's doing it; so, why not you?" Of course, there is a great deal of pressure in society for conformity. One way to feel accepted and secure is to be as much like one's peers as possible. When Harry's wife says, "But, Harry, everybody in our block has a later model car than ours," she is not concerned about the mechanical condition of the car, nor about its being adequate to the family's needs. She is saying: "Harry, we've got to be acceptable by doing what everyone else does." One should take a specific action, not because "everybody's doing it," but because logical reasons point to that action.

The fallacy designated as an *illicit generalization* occurs unless both of two requirements are met: First, one must take an adequate (quantitative) sample; and, second, one must take a typical sample. In the following story, the sample presumably was adequate; the obvious problem was an atypical sample:

> John Gary, an expert on alcoholism, reports that people whose names begin with the letter "M" are eight times as prone to drink too much as other people. Gary calls his findings the "M hypothesis," and he discovered it in a survey of the files of the council for alcoholism he heads.
> This is rather startling until one reflects that Gary's organization is based in Glasgow, Scotland—where most people's names begin with "Mc" or "Mac." And that makes the theory about as reliable

as one that holds that black horses eat more than white horses—the reason being, of course, that there are more black than white horses.[4]

Another of the common fallacies is popularly known as the *post hoc fallacy,* short for *post hoc ergo propter hoc* (*after* this, *therefore* because of this). The most prominent examples of this kind of fallacy are superstitions: "*After* a man walked under a ladder, he had an accident; *therefore,* because he walked under the ladder, he had the accident." "*After* the bats were crossed during a baseball game, the team did not get a run; *therefore, because* the bats were crossed, the team failed to get a run." Although a number of people are superstitious, one can sort out the illogic in superstitions fairly easily. The difficulty arises in sorting out real causes from spurious ones; for *efficient causes do precede in time* the effects they bring about. If one will take time to test each cause-and-effect relationship according to the appropriate rules for arguing from sign and from known cause to alleged effect, then he will soon differentiate genuine causes and effects from spurious ones.

The *non sequitur fallacy* means simply, "It does not follow." Non sequiturs occur when someone asserts a premise of one kind or another; then, assuming the truth of the premise, he draws a conclusion that does not follow. Non sequiturs are numerous in communicative situations. For example, one person reasoned thus prior to a recent election: "The candidate for that office has opposed his party's boss; therefore, he should be defeated at the polls." Assuming the truth of the charge, *it does not necessarily follow* that the voter should reject the man.

A fallacy that occurs frequently in the public discussion of questions of policy is the *straw-man fallacy.* Some speakers lacking sufficient supporting materials to strengthen their reasoning resort to arguing beside the real issue by setting up a false issue. In January 1845, at a public meeting in the Covent Garden Theatre to discuss repeal of the Corn Laws, William Johnson Fox responded to the straw-man argument of "constitutionality" by saying:

> . . . when persons are annoyed by a proposed measure, if they cannot pronounce it illegal, because it violates no enactment of the laws of the land; or immoral, inasmuch as it implies no breach of the commandments; if they cannot allege that it is dishonourable in principle, and inconsistent with the conventional regulations of life,—why, they fall back upon this word "unconstitutional," which means neither more nor less but that they dislike the thing exceedingly; and, having nothing else which they can assert against it, they say, "Well, at any rate, it is very unconstitutional."[5]

[4] The Milwaukee *Journal,* February 4, 1968, printed by permission.

[5] W. J. Fox, *Memorial Edition of Collected Works of W. J. Fox,* Vol. 4 (London: Charles Fox, 1866), pp. 166–167.

Conclusion

As pointed out, it is important for one to be able to prevent himself from committing fallacies and to be able to detect fallacies made by others. In regard to oral communication, the foregoing knowledge is critical. A speech is transitory, and an audience reaction is possible only after a speech is given. Thus, one has but a very brief period in which to detect fallacies and to react to them.

For every logical process there is at least one counterfeit. The wise speaker will train himself both in correct reasoning and in the quick and accurate detection of illogic. When he encounters illogic in a public dialog, the speaker may refute it by employing the four-step method noted at the beginning of this chapter.

Suggested Readings

Hayakawa, S. I. *Language in Thought and Action.* New York: Harcourt, Brace & World, 1949. Pp. 60–62. This brief segment provides a different dimension to the concept of fallacy.

Windes, Russel R., and Arthur Hastings. *Argumentation and Advocacy.* New York: Random House, 1965. Chap. 6, "Critical Refutation." Students should find this general essay to be both innovative and valuable.

Suggested Assignments

1. Locate a fallacious argument in the text of a speech, and write out a refutation of the argument by employing the four-step method.
2. Discover an example of each of the following fallacies, and show *how* each is an example of that error.
   a. Assumed premise fallacy.
   b. Faulty cause-to-effect reasoning.
   c. Faulty argument from sign.
   d. Faulty disjuncture.
   e. Appeal to misplaced authority.
   f. Appeal to tradition.
   g. Appeal to party spirit.
   h. Appeal to newness.

i. Appeal to present practice.
j. Begging the question.
k. Argument by personal attack.
l. Appeal to the crowd.
m. Illicit generalization.
n. *Post hoc ergo propter hoc* fallacy.
o. Non sequitur fallacy.
p. Straw-man fallacy.

Proof:
Evidence

I have treated the subject of evidence philosophically. I not only define what evidence is but also point out that evidence has quality. As you study this chapter, you should attempt to answer two questions: (1) In terms of the point that the speaker is making, *how adequate is the evidence? (2)* In terms of the specific audience, *how adequate is the evidence? As you prepare to use evidence in your speeches, if you should receive a negative answer to* either *of the foregoing questions, you should employ other evidence.*

Evidence consists of factual materials and information that are provided by testimony (or its equivalent) and used to substantiate assertions. Evidence is always *proof of something.*[1] One may regard evidence from two different but related perspectives: (1) the evidence that is discovered in the course of an investigation and (2) the evidence that is employed by the communicator as he attempts to make his point with his hearers. The concern of the communicator as investigator is "Where does the evidence

[1]See also the discussion of proof in Chapter 3, and the discussion of the evidence triad in Chapter 6.

lead?" The concern of the communicator as speaker is "How can I best select and employ the evidence so as to communicate the conclusions?"

The obvious place for the student to obtain his evidence is in the school library, and the first thing that the student should do is to find out how his particular library is organized. Usually, the library will have a leaflet or brochure describing its services and organization, and the student would save later time and energy by taking his own library tour (or a tour provided by the library) in order to become familiar with library facilities and holdings.

In general, the student speaker looking for evidence will discover it not by *looking* for evidence *per se*, but during the process of investigating the topic he has selected. Research is more a matter of conducting an investigation sufficient to enable the speaker to recognize certain materials as evidence than it is a matter of actually hunting for evidence. The speaker's general understanding of the topic is the essential antecedent to his recognition of materials as useful evidence.

The first step in doing research is a general reading on the topic in news magazines, books, and selected popular periodicals. To initiate this first step, the speaker will find indexes to be of special value. Two indexes that should be particularly useful at the outset are the *New York Times Index* and the *Readers' Guide to Periodical Literature*. The *New York Times* contains complete texts of speeches and of other important documents and is considered by scholars to be a valuable research source. The *Readers' Guide* is the usual place to commence researching a topic that has been discussed widely in periodicals. By reading about a topic in the periodicals indexed in the *Readers' Guide*, one can obtain an adequate overview that will suggest avenues for primary research.

After the student has a general conception about the nature of the topic, then he should begin looking at more specific sources (preferably primary, or original, sources) for the information that he needs. He would be especially well advised to look for original essays and original research reports in the professional journals of the discipline involved in his topic.

If the student discovers that he needs statistical evidence, he should consult the appropriate publications of the United States Government Printing Office. For example, each year the Government Printing Office publishes the *Statistical Abstract of the United States*, which is probably the best single source of general statistics published. If the student's library is a depository for government documents, he could also consult the complete sources of statistics from which the *Abstract* was taken. In addition, other government publications deal with historical statistics going back to colonial times and with annual crime statistics. The student should consult the *Monthly Catalog* listing government publications to discover the items that he could use for information in his speech.

If there should be a lack of government publications in the library, then the student may write to the Superintendent of Documents, United States Government Printing Office, Washington, D.C. 20402, for a selected list of publications in his area of interest. The student may also find it useful to write to his congressman or senator about legislation or legislative proposals pending in Congress. An additional avenue for the student is to write to the appropriate federal department or to consult local or state governmental agencies.

The student may wish also to write for information from various organizations with special interests. The following list of organizations is only suggestive of the host of sources from which the student may be able to obtain information that he can use as evidence:

Organization	Area of Interest
American Academy of Arts and Sciences	Education
American Bar Association	Law
American Cancer Society	Cancer Research
American Council on Education	Education
American Farm Bureau Federation	Agriculture
American Federation of Labor and Congress of Industrial Organizations	Labor
American Institute of Banking	Business
American Legion	Veterans Affairs
American Medical Association	Medicine
American Psychological Association	Psychological Research
American Red Cross	Public Service
Brookings Institution	Public Affairs
Chamber of Commerce of the United States	Business
Foreign Policy Association	Foreign Policy
National Association for the Advancement of Colored People	Civic Affairs
National Association of Manufacturers	Business
National Collegiate Athletic Association	Athletics
National Conference of Christians and Jews	Religion
National Farmers Union	Agriculture
National Federation of State High School Athletic Associations	Athletics
National Planning Association	Public Administration
National Rifle Association of America	Arms
National Right-to-Work Committee	Labor
National Science Foundation	Science Research
United States Catholic Conference	Religion
Urban League	Civic Affairs
Veterans of Foreign Wars of the U.S.A.	Veterans Affairs

The communicator as investigator must measure all evidence against at least two criteria: (1) evidence must be *correct*; (2) evidence must be *consistent* with any conclusions—both explicit and implicit—of the source. With reference to the question of correctness, the issue seems simple enough; but one of the communicator's greatest challenges centers about accuracy.

The following news story illustrates some of the difficulties of determining historical accuracy. In general with regard to written history, the older the information, the greater the difficulty in determining the accuracy of details. The difficulty centers about (1) the lack of records to answer some questions that arise and (2) the uncertainty of the accuracy of some extant manuscripts. The point of the following illustration is that the student researcher/communicator must be aware that there is a difference between a verifiable statement (fact) and an assumption. If he cannot verify alleged facts, then he is limited as to the conclusion he should draw.

The Post Office Department's commemorative postage stamp honoring 17th Century explorer Jacques Marquette was officially unveiled Friday night at Marquette University—without beard and without Indians.

The stamp, depicting Father Marquette and fellow explorer Louis Joliet in a canoe paddled by two bearded voyageurs, marks the 300th anniversary of Marquette's founding on Sault Ste. Marie, Michigan's oldest existing settlement.

The stamp, to be issued Sept. 20, will raise some questions among stamp collectors, Lawrence S. Lewin, assistant to the postmaster general, remarked at the Marquette University ceremonies.

The chief question, he said, will involve the appearance of Marquette as tall and clean-shaven, instead of stocky and bearded.

Most portraits of Marquette show him with a beard, and his statue in the nation's Capitol is bearded. An 1898 commemorative stamp also showed Marquette with a beard.

"Stamp collectors are very sharp-eyed critics of our stamps," Lewin said. "If we deviate one iota from historical accuracy in a stamp design we are told about it in no uncertain terms."

But, Lewin said, there is no historical information that Marquette was bearded when he and Joliet crossed Wisconsin to the Mississippi River in 1673.

Also, he said, it has always been thought Indians accompanied the pair, not French voyageurs—France's fur-trading pioneers in the Great Lakes country.

"We are standing by our guns," Lewin said, "that a beardless Father Marquette was paddled down the river by Europeans, not Indians."

The stamp, selected by a committee, was designed by artist Stanley W. Galli of Kentfield, Calif. The government plans to print 120 million.

Lewin said it was decided to unveil the stamp in Milwaukee because the Jesuit is believed to have been buried here.

That too is debated. Some authorities believe Marquette's bones were buried in 1677 at a mission he founded near St. Ignace, Mich.

Lewin did not remark on a question raised by an observer at the unveiling ceremonies: that Joliet is depicted reading what appears to be a map—in an area relatively unexplored before he and Marquette arrived.[2]

The difficulty of determining accuracy is not limited to events long past—events that make up a part of written history. Persons who write about events that are verifiable and who report them in newspapers also have their problems. Newspapers constitute an invaluable source of material to the researcher, primarily because they may be his primary source of evidence if the event occurred some time before the researcher came along. However, if an event is contemporary with the researcher, he should check any newspaper report with other news media and perhaps with any persons involved. Obviously, any investigator should make every effort to cross-check the accuracy of any newspaper report.

The following two newspaper accounts illustrate how differently newspapers can report the same event. The first account of the accident appeared in the evening paper, October 22, 1960, and the second account appeared in the morning paper on October 23, 1960. If a researcher could not check police records and medical records or could not conduct interviews, he would find it difficult, if not impossible, to determine what actually occurred.

A boy, thought to be about 5 years old, was killed this afternoon when he was struck by a train on the Northern Pacific tracks about $1\frac{1}{2}$ miles west of _____.

His parents, at the scene, were in shock, and sheriff's officers said they were unable to find out immediately the boy's identity, or how the accident occurred.

First word of the accident came shortly before 2:30 P.M. from an unidentified motorist with a mobile telephone who called the sheriff's radio operator.

The coroner was on his way to the scene.

The NP dispatcher's office here reported three trains passed through the area within an hour of the accident, but which of them was involved in the tragedy was unknown. The three included two local freight express.

None reported any incident.[3]

[2]*The Mining Journal*, Marquette, Mich., April 20, 1968, printed by permission of the Associated Press.

[3]Spokane *Daily Chronicle*, Spokane, Wash., October 22, 1960, printed by permission.

The following account appeared in the morning paper.

> An attempt to corral his train-chasing dog claimed the life of 8-year-old _____ _____ of _____, Wash., yesterday, apparently from a heart attack.
> Returning from a picnic with three young friends, the _____ boy took off running down the Northern Pacific tracks near the track crossing one mile west of _____ on the Newman lake highway, after his dog who was chasing a railroad motor cart. The youngsters told Sheriff's officer Ray Guthrie that _____ "just pitched forward." The youngsters hailed a passing motorist. . . .
> Guthrie said the boy apparently suffered a fatal heart attack chasing the dog.[4]

But it is not enough that evidence should be accurate; it also must be consistent with any conclusions of the source. For example, one faces perhaps his greatest difficulty in interpreting statistics—particularly in tables—so that he does not lead to nor imply a conclusion not intended by the source. For instance, in the statistical tables in either the *Statistical Abstract* or the *Uniform Crime Reports*, no conclusions are implicit, and the communicator should not attribute any to such sources. Further, he should be extremely careful in drawing his own conclusions from such tables. The *Uniform Crime Reports—1964* goes so far as to caution those who would draw conclusions from crime statistics:

> Since the factors which cause crime are many and vary from place to place, readers are cautioned against drawing conclusions from direct comparisons of crime figures between individual communities without first considering the factors involved.[5]

Perhaps one of the most fertile areas for the growth of the inconsistent use of evidence is the point at which political science and economics intersect. For example, a speaker would be using evidence inconsistently if he composed a speech blaming "irresponsible labor" for excessive price rises in 1966 and supported his thesis by quoting from the *Economic Report of the President, January 1967*, as follows:

> . . . some of the gain in employee compensation reflected increases in wage rates in excess of the growth of productivity. That part of

---

[4]*Spokesman-Review*, Spokane, Wash., October 23, 1960, printed by permission.
[5]*Uniform Crime Reports—1964* (Washington: U.S. Government Printing Office, 1965), p. xi.

---

the increase in labor compensation served to increase unit labor costs and thereby to push prices up.[6]

The assumption underlying the foregoing use of evidence was that the *Report* blamed labor *entirely* for the price rise, whereas, in reality, the *Report* dealt earlier with the subject of price rises, as follows:

> 2. *Price increases—although less than in many comparable periods—still were greater than we wanted or should long tolerate.*
>   It is tempting to blame the creep of prices on the greed of producers—or the irresponsibility of labor—or Government policies—or bad weather—or economic disturbances abroad. Some of the price rise may have been due to each. But the main causes lay elsewhere . . .[7]

Because of the ease of using words denotatively, and because conclusions involve intention, the speaker should be especially aware of the danger of using evidence in a manner inconsistent with the way it was used in the original source.

During the course of his investigation, a speaker generally discovers that far more evidence exists than he can use in the process of communicating his thoughts to hearers. One reason that the speaker would not use all of the evidence he discovers is, of course, the time factor; a speaker would find it impossible to lead his hearers through the maze of data he uncovered over a substantial period. Furthermore, hearers need know only representative examples of data and testimony that are sufficient to enable them to understand the validity of any conclusion the speaker draws. In addition, hearers are interested in understanding how data and generalizations affect them. Therefore, the speaker must devote a considerable portion of his message to an analysis and summary of his evidence as it affects his thesis and his audience.

Assuming, then, that the communicator has investigated his topic and that he has found his evidence to be correct and consistent, he must now evaluate the evidence in terms of the communicatee. Insofar as public address is concerned, *ultimately the most important dimension of evidence lies in the hearer's reaction to it as he perceives it.* As a means of evaluating evidence in terms of the hearer, the speaker should employ the following criteria: (1) Evidence must be *clear*. (2) Evidence must be *credible*. (3) Evidence must be *appropriate*.

The criterion that evidence must be *clear* centers squarely on the audience. If the evidence is both correct and consistent but not clear,

---

[6]*Economic Report of the President, Transmitted to the Congress January 1967* (Washington: U.S. Government Printing Office, 1967), p. 78.

[7]*Economic Report of the President, January 1967*, p. 5.

Chapter Five

then the evidence is of no avail. Thus, to determine clarity, the speaker should examine each item of evidence in relation to the prior knowledge, sophistication, and interest of the specific audience.

The following excerpt from the *Economic Report of the President, January 1967,* is a clear statement of evidence that should be able to be made safely to any English-speaking adult audience of average intelligence.

> The remaining federal programs are wholly aimed at the disadvantaged. In 1966, the Neighborhood Youth Corps program reached 220,000 needy students, who received an average of $500 of aid from in-school and summer programs which helped them to continue in school, and 100,000 youths no longer in school, who received an average of 7 months of training. Since its inception, the Job Corps has provided training and work experience for 61,500 of the most disadvantaged youths. When first enrolled, more than 50 percent of Job Corps enrollees fail to read at the 5th grade level, and 30 percent cannot read a simple sentence. Despite this handicap, the retention rate for the Job Corps is superior to that of vocational training programs nationally.[8]

Evidence needs to be not only clear but also *credible.* The criterion of credibility refers to believability. Generally, if one's evidence is not credible, someone will likely point that out. Turning the situation around, if one discovers that an opposing speaker's evidence lacks credibility, then he may refute the opponent's argument by employing credible evidence against the argument. In the following example, William Johnson Fox attacked the credibility of the opposing argument that the Anti-Corn Law League had "dwindled into insignificance," by using credible evidence to establish the contrary conclusion that the League had in fact grown.

> If there hangs upon two honourable members of Parliament, who have addressed you this evening, the doom which used to be much more frequently on judge's lips than, happily, it is at the present day, and if they are about to be "taken to the place from whence they came," I trust that, upon reaching their destination, they will report to the assembly collected there that the Anti-Corn Law League is still in existence; for it was announced in that House, no longer ago than last night, that since the declaration of Sir Robert Peel, on the first night of the session, the Anti-Corn Law agitation had "dwindled into insignificance."
>
> Yes, it has indeed dwindled from a revenue of 50,000£ in the year towards one of 100,000£. It has dwindled from small local meet-

---

[8]*Economic Report of the President, January 1967,* p. 109.

---

ings to such gatherings as I now behold around me; and it has dwindled from the humility of petitioning the House of Commons into appealing to the masters of that assembly. What a strange, imperfect, confused, and ignorant notion must any man have of the Anti-Corn Law League, who supposes that the breath of members of the House of Commons, or of ministers of the Crown, can cause it to shrink and shrivel up into insignificance![9]

In evaluating the credibility of his evidence, the speaker should keep in mind that if what he designates in *his* mind as evidence is not credible to the *hearer,* then the speaker's evidence is not really evidence for the hearer. This point is illustrated well, and humorously, by the assertion in the following news story that "we never have had *evidence* [author's italics] that the earth is moving around the sun." The news story appeared in the Kansas City *Star,* December 25, 1968.

> Britain's Flat Earth society acknowledged yesterday after viewing pictures of the earth from Apollo 8 that it must take another look at things.
> The Apollo 8 team's circumnavigation of the moon has somewhat torpedoed the society's idea that the moon as well as the sun are two small objects that go round and round the North Pole.
> Since the moon shot, the Flat Earth society has been more than ordinarily interested, said General Secretary Samuel Shenton.
> "We have hardly had time to get together to form an idea and I wouldn't like to commit myself now at all.
> "They said they could see South Africa and so on. But struggle as much as I could, I couldn't see anything at all.
> "If the earth is a planet, it would have to be traveling around the sun at more than one million miles an hour and we never have had evidence that the earth is moving around the sun.
> "If they show us a very clear picture of the earth from space and the picture does not show all the continents, and the edge of the picture is out of perspective, then that would prove that the earth is round. Until then, we shall continue fighting to prove the earth is flat."[10]

The final criterion for evaluating one's evidence is the *appropriateness* of the evidence. Evidence should be correspondent with the speaking situation in terms of propriety. The criteria for propriety in relation to *topic* (discussed in Chapter 2) also apply to evidence.[11] If the speaker is going to provide a basis upon which the hearer can identify with him,

---

[9]W. J. Fox, *Memorial Edition of Collected Works of W. J. Fox,* Vol. 4 (London: Charles Fox, 1866), p. 68.

[10]The Kansas City *Star*, Kansas City, Mo., December 25, 1968, printed by permission of the Associated Press.

[11]For details of propriety, see "The speaker's topic should be appropriate" in Chapter 2.

the evidence must be appropriate in terms of audience, subject, occasion, and speaker.

Conclusion

Evidence is what makes argument believable. In order for evidence to perform its function, it must be, first of all, correct and, second, consistent with the implicit and explicit conclusions of the source. In addition, if evidence is to be as meaningful as possible to the hearer, it must meet three requirements: (1) It must be clear. (2) It must be credible. (3) It must be appropriate.

Suggested Readings

Beveridge, Albert J. *The Art of Public Speaking.* Boston: Houghton Mifflin Co., 1924. Pp. 25–33. This segment discusses the importance of knowledge in communicating effectively.

Miller, Gerald R. Chap. 2, "Evidence and Argument." *Perspectives on Argumentation,* eds. Gerald R. Miller and Thomas R. Nilsen. Chicago: Scott, Foresman and Co., 1966. This chapter is an excellent treatment of evidence as it relates to argument.

Walter, Otis M., and Robert L. Scott. *Thinking and Speaking: A Guide to Intelligent Oral Communication.* New York: Macmillan Co., 1962. Chap. 3, "Supporting Ideas."

Suggested Assignments

1. Prepare a speech in which a written segment includes statistical evidence. Include enough written material before the evidence to enable your instructor to determine whether you have used the statistical evidence properly.
   a. Do the above for a case history as evidence.
   b. Do the above for authoritative testimony.

2. Prove that the statistics and the case history are accurate.

3. Prove that the three items of evidence above are consistent with the conclusions of the sources.

4. Explain why you think that the statistical evidence above would be clear to your intended audience.

5. Explain why you think that all three items of evidence above would be credible to your intended audience.

Proof:
The Thought Analysis

The first concept that you should watch for in this chapter is the predicative development of the proposition. *As you will discover, this development takes place* throughout *the thought analysis. The second thing that you should consider carefully is the way that the thought analysis aids the speaker in adapting to his hearers. In short, in this chapter you should note how the predicative development of the proposition implements the* meaning $\longrightarrow$ identification $\longrightarrow$ persuasion *sequence.*

The *thought analysis* is a systematic, reasoned sentence outline of the thought (proposition,[1] thesis, or point) that is developed in the body[2] of the communication. Thus, the thought analysis relates — *not* to the conclusion — but to the body. It is the bony structure — the logical skeleton — of the body.

The thought analysis is subordinate to the mode of public address (communicative gestalt) of which it is a part. It varies with the mode of

---

[1] For a discussion of propositions, see Chapter 2.

[2] Each communicative gestalt has a beginning, middle, and an end — the introduction, body, and conclusion, respectively. For further information regarding the meaning of the body in a communicative gestalt, one should consult the preliminary pages of each chapter concerned with the various modes of communication.

communication that the speaker employs. If he employs the expository mode, then the speaker must use the expository thought analysis. If the speaker selects one of the argumentative modes, then he must use an argumentative thought analysis. In other words, one must choose a particular development of thought analysis *only after selecting the mode of communication* (*of which the analysis is a part*). In addition, and most important, *the statement, divisions, and subdivisions of the thought analysis must be meaningful to the hearer;* otherwise, he will not identify with them and, therefore, he will not believe the speaker. Thus, the key to adapting the speaker's thought to the hearer lies in the meaningfulness of the analysis to the hearer.

Every thought analysis has three parts – (1) *statement* (of the proposition), (2) *divisions,* and (3) *subdivisions* – and should be composed in that order. The statement is a proposition consisting of two parts – a subject and a predicate.[3] The statement asserts the thesis that the speaker intends to prove or to explicate. Divisions are propositions that constitute the major reasons supporting the statement. Subdivisions are propositions consisting of either sub-reasons supporting the divisions or evidence or both.

Predicative Development of the Analysis

The first major requirement of the thought analysis is that the speaker must develop the predicate of the statement; for it is in the predicate that the main thrust of any assertion lies. The speaker develops the predicate of the statement in the predicates of the divisions, and he develops the predicate of each division in the predicates of the subdivisions *directly* subordinate to that division. If the thought analysis were to be developed further, then the speaker would develop the predicate of each subdivision in appropriate second-level subdivisions.

The following partial thought analysis illustrates the predicative relationship between the statement and divisions. Later in this chapter, Figure 6-1 shows how the *predicative development* extends through all subdivisions.

subject   predicate

Statement: The emission of air pollutants // should be controlled.

subject   predicate

I. Air pollutants // tend to decompose certain materials.

[3] See Chapter 2.

II. Evidence suggests that air pollutants under certain meteorlogical

conditions // are related to the incidence of asthmatic attacks.

In the foregoing illustration, the predicate of Division I, "tend to decompose certain materials," develops the predicate of the statement, "should be controlled." Similarly, the predicate of Division II, "are related to the incidence of asthmatic attacks," also develops the predicate of the statement.

The speaker may classify what develops in the predicate of any proposition as (1) a *quality,* (2) an *identity,* and/or (3) an *action.* Because the communicator usually advocates the solution to a problem, he generally limits his concern to urging an *action* involving a certain *quality.*[4] For example, one may urge that "the United States should abolish the draft." In this instance, the action or policy lies in the predicate, "should abolish the draft"; and the action is premised upon the value judgment—a quality—that the draft is undesirable. Or, assuming that one were speaking on the statement that "The federal government should require compulsory arbitration of all labor disputes in basic industries," then he again would be urging an action related to a value judgment. The speaker would have to support his proposition by predicating the value judgment that the policy, if adopted, would be advantageous.

On the other hand, rather than to affirm an action, the communicator may posit a value judgment. The basic reason that the speaker may argue a value judgment rather than a policy is subtlety; for arguing a proposition of value is more nondirective than a proposition of policy. The proposition of value may discuss ease or difficulty, good or evil, advantage or disadvantage, the expedient or inexpedient, just to name a few topics; however, it always allows the *hearer* to draw the conclusion as to what action, if any, ought to be taken. For example, in speaking to the statement that "The English parliamentary form of government is preferable to the presidential form of government of the United States," one necessarily would be drawing a value judgment of the quality of both systems. If the communicator could prove the predicate ("preferable to the presidential form of government of the United States") to be probably true, then the desirability of action to adopt the parliamentary system would be implicit. If the opposition to the statement were to prove that probable harms would come about from the parliamentary system, then the implicit action would be for persons to oppose such a system.

One also may assert an identity. For example, the speaker may wish

---

[4] One always urges a proposition of policy (action) upon the assumption that it would be desirable if adopted. If one opposes a proposed action, he does so on the basis of alleged harmfulness. Thus, a proposition of quality is implicit in every proposition of action.

to explain that the United States is a federation. The statement and divisions might be as follows:

subject   predicate

Statement: The United States // is a federation.

subject   predicate

I. The central government // has the power to tax.

subject   predicate

II. The central government // has the power to raise military forces.

Clearly, the predicate of Division I, "has the power to tax," and of Division II, "has the power to raise an army," develop the predicate of the statement, "is a federation."

Whereas the foregoing illustration explains, and thus relates to the expository mode, the following illustration argues, and thus relates to the argumentative modes.

subject   predicate

Statement: Unidentified Flying Objects // are interplanetary spacecraft.

subject   predicate

I. Their flight characteristics // are unknown to earthly aircraft.

subject   predicate

II. They // give evidence of intelligent operation.

The predicates of the divisions do develop the predicate of the statement. Obviously, such craft of necessity would have flight characteristics unknown to earthlings, and such patterns would reflect intelligent operation. Because one would be arguing that something unknown could be known, he would need the strongest possible subdivisions—in this case, empirically verifiable data.

The paradigm of a thought analysis (Figure 6-1) illustrates the relationships between (1) the divisions and the statement, (2) the first-level subdivisions and the divisions, and (3) second-level subdivisions and first-level subdivisions. The communicator should note, in particular, the manner in which the predicates of the second-level subdivisions develop the predicate of the first-level subdivision above them, the manner in which the predicate of the first-level subdivision develops the predicate of the division above it, and the manner in which the division predicate, in turn, develops the predicate of the statement.

The subdivisions that carry the evidence in the paradigm in Figure 6-1 represent three different kinds of evidence: an *evidence triad* of *case history, quantification,* and *expert testimony.*[5] The advantage of using all

---

[5] See Chapters 3 and 5 for a further discussion of the psychological implications of the use of evidence.

Figure 6-1
Paradigm of a Thought Analysis

subject   predicate
Statement: Human beings // should stop smoking cigarettes.

subject   predicate
I. Smoking cigarettes // adversely affects the cardiovascular system.

subject   predicate
A. Smoking cigarettes // adversely affects the heart muscle.

subject   predicate

Case history 1. Smoker A // experienced weakness in the heart muscle.

subject

Quantification 2. X number of smokers compared with non-smokers // have ex-
predicate
perienced weakness of the heart muscle.

subject   predicate

Expert 3. Professor ____ states that smokers // can expect to experience
testimony this problem.

subject   predicate
B. Smoking cigarettes // adversely affects peripheral circulation.

subject   predicate

Case history 1. Smoker B // experienced poor peripheral circulation.

subject

Quantification 2. X number of smokers compared with non-smokers // suffered
predicate
from this problem.

subject   predicate

Expert 3. Dr. ____ states that smokers // frequently experience poor
testimony peripheral circulation.

subject   predicate
II. Smoking cigarettes // adversely affects the respiratory system.

subject   predicate
A. Smoking cigarettes // is a cause of emphysema.

subject   predicate

Case history 1. Smoker C // developed emphysema.

subject

Quantification 2. X number of smokers compared with non-smokers // have
predicate
developed emphysema.

subject   predicate

Expert 3. Dr. ____ states that smokers // are especially susceptible to
testimony emphysema.

subject   predicate
B. Smoking cigarettes // is a cause of lung cancer.

subject   predicate

Case history 1. Smoker D // developed lung cancer.

subject

Quantification 2. X number of smokers compared with non-smokers // have
predicate
developed lung cancer.

subject

Expert 3. The American Cancer Society says that cigarette smoke // is
testimony predicate
a cause of cell changes leading to malignancy.

three kinds where possible is not primarily one of variety—although variety *is* an advantage. Rather, the advantage is that *each triad of evidence reasons the way most men do—from instance to generalization.* Each triad attempts concisely to simulate the process of generalizing from experience. The case history has primarily psychological value; the quantification seeks mainly logical value; the expert testimony attempts to coalesce logical generalization. The communicator also should note that the evidence triads are representative of the general direction of the reasoning, both logically and psychologically, in the modes of communication[6]—the communicative gestalts. Thus, Figure 6-1 reveals structurally and logically the relationship between the evidence triad and the thought analysis.

Organization of the Thought Analysis

After guaranteeing the logical integrity of his thought analysis, the second requirement is that the speaker should consider the organization of the analysis. Assuming that the speaker is working with an argumentative analysis, he may commence his analysis by asking the question "Assuming that my hearers would remember just one argument, which one would I wish them to remember?" The answer to that question indicates the argument that the speaker should place last in the analysis. Next, the speaker should select from among the remaining arguments the one that is the most mind-catching or attractive and place that argument first in the analysis. The idea in doing this is that "One should attract by his initial argument." Any remaining argument, or arguments, obviously would be placed between the others.

Assuming that one follows the predicative development of propositions recommended in this chapter, each division would be autonomously related to the statement; and one can organize the analysis on the basis of the questions, or criteria, mentioned in the paragraph above. However, if the divisions, although mutually exclusive in terms of material or emphasis, are interrelated in such a way that the final division gains force from the truth of the preceding arguments, then the speaker must select an organization based upon cumulative effect. To take an example, a speaker may reason in his analysis of the capital punishment question that there are but three purposes of punishment: (1) rehabilitation, (2) deterrence, and (3) justice. Admittedly, capital punishment eliminates rehabilitation. Therefore, the speaker would need to deal with the ques-

---

[6] See the separate chapters on each mode.

tions of deterrence and justice. From those two questions, the speaker might derive three major arguments based on the rationale (assumed) that if capital punishment did not fulfill any of the purposes of punishment, then it ought to be abolished.

  I. Capital punishment fails as a deterrent.

  II. The act of execution is morally wrong.

  III. An innocent man may be executed.

In organizing these three arguments, or divisions of the analysis, the speaker would undoubtedly decide that arguments II and III would be the most powerful. The speaker would also see that Division III is the more powerful of the two arguments. As the arguments are arranged above, the cumulative effect has two dimensions. First is the dimension of quantity. (The effect of I + II is greater than either one by itself, and the effect of I + II + III is greater than two of the three.) Second is the dimension of intensity. (II is more powerful than I, and III is more powerful than II.) By combining these two dimensions in organizing his analysis, as illustrated above, the speaker constructs a powerful cumulative organization.

On the other hand, if one were to arrange these divisions according to the question approach mentioned above (first, "which is most attractive"; last, "which is most important"), then, he would change Divisions I and II around. Division III, as the most important one, still would be last. Thus, the key question in organizing this analysis of the capital punishment issue is "Would it be more effective (1) to have Division II in the first position because of its greater rhetorical force (and run the risk of destroying continuity) or (2) to leave the less strong division in first position, thus gaining unity, emphasis, and coherence, particularly between Divisions II and III?" The answer appears to be that the movement of thought (the cumulative effect) in the divisions *as they are illustrated* would be the more effective form.

The logical principles regulating predicative development of the statement, divisions, and subdivisions of argumentative analysis apply also to expository thought analysis.[7] However, one organizes the thought analysis differently. Because exposition centers about making a topic clear, it focuses directly on a certain topic and, consequently, upon the topic's natural partitions, or divisions. Thus, the first thing that the communicator should do is to look for the natural divisions of his topic. For example, if one were going to discuss the training of astronauts, he would seek to discover the major steps in the process of the training and then use these steps as the divisions of his analysis. In organizing the divisions,

---

[7] For an example of a complete expository analysis, see Peter Valenti's speech in Chapter 9.

one should attempt to observe some unifying principles. For instance, if one were going to discuss the process by which the Constitution of the United States may be amended, then he would note the ways that amendments can be made. Then, in discussing this topic, he might wish to proceed from the common to the less common ways to amend. He could then illustrate his divisions by beginning with the First Amendment and proceeding to the present time.

The following common topics illustrate the divisions that are typically used in expository analysis. First, one may discuss a topic using some combination of economic, social, or political divisions. For example, the speaker might employ the following statement and divisions:

> Statement: The institution of federal wage and price controls // would affect the nation in two major areas.
>
> I. It // would affect the nation politically.
>
> II. It // would affect the nation economically.

(Note that the predicative development of Divisions I and II relates directly to the predicate of the statement.)

Second, one may discuss a topic using some combination of local, state, national, or international division headings. For example, one might discuss the Arab-Israeli problem using the following statement and divisions:

> Statement: The Arab-Israeli problem // affects the United States.
>
> I. The problem // has national implications.
>
> II. The problem // has international implications.

An alternative to the above topic is the following arrangement:

> Statement: The Arab-Israeli problem // has international implications for the United States.
>
> I. It // affects the United States in the area of international politics.
>
> II. It // affects the United States in the area of international economics.

The other kind of thought analysis is the narrative analysis. The narrative analysis is identical to both the argumentative and the expository analyses as far as the logic of the predicative development is concerned. The narrative speech, because of its first-person quality, sometimes tends toward informality. But however informal the speech may be, the reasoning in the narrative analysis should be just as close as it is

---

Chapter Six

in argumentative analysis. Proper predicative development is essential to a closely reasoned narrative thought analysis, just as it is to argumentative and expository analyses. The only difference is that of focus: Whereas argumentative analysis focuses upon argument (reasons for advocating a course of action) and expository analysis focuses on explaining a process, the narrative focuses upon providing data.[8] However, the organization of the narrative structure is *similar* to the expository in that the best organization derives from the nature of the subject. Inasmuch as most subjects of narrations have a beginning and an ending in time, the most natural — and therefore the most effective — form of organization would be to go from the beginning of an event step-by-step through its major stages to the end.

Not unlike the organization of the expository analysis, the narrative analysis may have a climactic order. That is, one may employ an order that places the most important point last. Inasmuch as (1) the most important point is the one that the speaker most wishes to communicate, and inasmuch as (2) the speaker would find a discussion of another point *after* the most important one to be anticlimactic; therefore, the most important point should be placed last.

To take an example, if a student should like to speak about his trip to Rome, then he might employ the following statement and divisions:

Statement: My trip to Rome // was memorable.

I. I // started my visit by seeing the Coliseum.

II. I // visited one of Rome's most famous restaurants.

III. I // was able to arrange an audience with the Pope the afternoon prior to flying home.

Intentionality and the Analysis

The third major requirement of the thought analysis is that intentionality must be clear. Just as it is true that the predicate of the sentence contains the action or quality constituting the essence of the proposition, so it is also true that the predicate contains the speaker's intention. However, intentionality can present problems in wording. For example, in urging that "The United States should regulate radio and television according to the basic characteristics of the British Broadcasting Corpo-

---

[8] The principles governing narration also govern description.

ration," the intention *as stated* appears to be clear. If the speaker is specifically interested in adopting the basic characteristics of the British Broadcasting Corporation — rather than, say, the Canadian Broadcasting Corporation or the public broadcasting media of France or West Germany, then he should definitely include the BBC in his statement. However, if the speaker's real purpose is to advocate abolishing commercial radio and television in the United States, then he could urge that proposition more effectively by formulating his intention thus: "Commercial radio and television in the United States should be abolished." Similarly, if the speaker's intention is that the federal government should own and operate radio and television; then, he could argue that "The federal government should own and operate all radio and television stations in the United States."

Clearly, intention is explicit. The speaker should make certain that he embodies in his statement those words that reflect his precise intention. In addition, in each division and subdivision, the speaker needs to express his intention just as explicitly as he does in the statement. Thus, *the explicit expression of intention in the statement, divisions, and subdivisions is essential to the clarity of the thought analysis.* Further, because clarity is essential to the forceful effect of the message on the communicatee, a lack of clear and explicit expression in the structure of the thought analysis also results in a loss of force in the entire body of the speech.

In addition to meeting the requirements of predicative development, organization, and intentionality, the speaker's analysis should also (1) reflect the emotional overtones of the truth, and (2) reveal the character of the speaker.[9] The foregoing apply to both the arguments and the evidence of the analysis.

Therefore, the speaker constructs an analysis of psychological value not only through divisions but also — and primarily — through the evidence bearing subdivisions.

For example, in relation to Smoker D, who developed lung cancer, it would likely be very effective to cite Smoker D's case to the audience, if they were members of Smoker D's profession or in his age bracket, and if they also were regular smokers. If the speaker were to use the case history of Smoker Z, who was a derelict picked up in a coma from an alley, and ill with lung cancer, he would need to be addressing an audience of persons like the victim or there would be little likelihood that the case history would be meaningful.

Case histories appropriate to a given audience reflect the character of the speaker. Hearers could hardly regard a speaker who warns about lung cancer as being anything other than a man of "good sense." In addition, the speaker would probably be regarded as a man of "goodwill." Finally, by his implicit interest in eliminating a serious cause of death

---

[9] Chapters 3 and 5 discuss these items in detail.

---

and suffering, he would reflect "good moral character." When selecting a case history for the analysis, the speaker should anticipate predicating (1) reasoning, (2) emotional overtones, and (3) the character of the speaker.

Similarly, in Subdivision 2 under Subdivision B of Division II, the speaker makes the assertion that the frequency of deaths from lung cancer is 10 to 20 times higher among smokers of cigarettes than among non-smokers. Primarily, this evidence is logical—a generalization based on an extensive collection of data. But, in addition—assuming the hearers *believed* the evidence—the generalization would have some emotional impact on them. Quantitative evidence, like the case history, also should reflect good sense, goodwill, and good moral character.

The third major kind of evidence used to support an argument is testimonial evidence. For instance, Subdivision 3, Subdivision B, of Division II, should be acceptable as reasoning. The American Cancer Society, as a scientific body, has done a sufficient quantity of sophisticated research to qualify that organization as a credible source of expert testimony. If, however, the speaker were to prefer, he could use the expert testimony of an individual associated with cancer research, for example, Dr. E. C. Hammond.

Statements by either source would have some emotional impact. In relation to revealing the character of the speaker (in this case, the ACS), the statement appears to reflect good sense, goodwill, and good moral character. Any relevant statement by Hammond also would certainly qualify as evidence on the basis of good sense, goodwill, and good moral character. Whether the speaker would select the ACS or Hammond would depend, not upon the authority of either, but upon which would likely be more effective with a given audience.

Conclusion

The principles of composing the thought analysis are as follows:

1. The communicator should not compose his analysis until he has selected his mode of communication.
2. The communicator should compose the analysis in this order: (a) statement, (b) divisions, and (c) subdivisions.
3. Every analysis must be in sentence form.
4. The predicate of the statement should contain the thought to be proved or explicated.
5. All divisions and subdivisions should employ the principle of predicative development.

6. Each division should be selected and arranged according to the best approach for the particular topic.

7. Every segment of the analysis (statement, divisions, subdivisions) must express a precise intention.

8. Each segment of the analysis (a) should be reasoned, (b) should reflect the emotional overtones of the truth, and (c) should reveal the character of the speaker.

Suggested Readings

Foster, William Trufant. *Argumentation and Debating*, 2nd rev. ed. Boston: Houghton Mifflin Co., 1960. Chap. 3, "Constructing the Brief." This chapter provides a specialized treatment of the argumentative brief.

Hance, Kenneth G., David C. Ralph, and Milton J. Wiksell. *Principles of Speaking*, 2nd ed. Belmont, Calif.: Wadsworth Publishing Co., 1969. Chap. 10, "Outlining for Speaking." The material of the essay represents a clear presentation of the anatomy of an outline.

Wilcox, Roger P. *Oral Reporting in Business and Industry*. Englewood Cliffs, N.J.: Prentice-Hall, 1967. Chap. 7, "Achieving a Clear Pattern of Organization: Outlining." Anyone who needs to make oral reports should find this chapter valuable. It should be of special interest to students in science, engineering, or business.

Suggested Assignments

1. For a narrative analysis, write out the statement and one division with all its subdivisions. Designate all predicates.

2. For an expository analysis, write out the statement and one division with all its subdivisions. Designate all predicates.

3. For an argumentative analysis, write out the statement and one division with all its subdivisions. Designate all predicates.

4. Explain why you selected the particular evidence triad you did in assignment 3 above.

5. Explain the essential difference between a thought analysis in the defects mode and one in the advantages mode.

The Enthymeme

The information in this chapter on the enthymeme can help you to learn how to adapt your thought to the thinking of the hearer; for the enthymeme can make the difference between spoon feeding your audience and communicating with them. Because the enthymeme involves various reasoning processes, you should make sure that you thoroughly understand the material in Chapter 3 before you begin to read this chapter. As you read this chapter, ask the question "How can I use this kind of enthymeme to initiate the meaning $\longrightarrow$ identification $\longrightarrow$ persuasion *sequence?"*

The enthymeme[1] is the master technique for adapting the speaker's thought to the hearer. It reasons from a more general assertion to a less general assertion,[2] or from one assertion to another within the same degree of generality, by means of premises *jointly supplied* by the communi-

---

[1]The literal meaning of enthymeme is "in mind," from the Greek *en* (in), *thymos* (mind).

[2]An alternative to designating the direction of reasoning in this manner would be to classify it as deduction.

cator and the communicatee. Thus, *enthymemes are inherently meaningful to the hearer.*

The communicator initiates the enthymematic process by advancing a premise. But it is the hearer, if he accepts the assertion of the speaker, who completes an enthymeme. However, before the hearer can complete the enthymeme, he must be able and *willing* to supply in *his* mind any missing premise, or premises, essential to the conclusion. If the hearer supplies a missing premise, then, since supplying it would be volitional, he would be identifying with the line of thought initiated by the speaker. By his furnishing such assertions, the hearer joins the speaker in arriving at another assertion: the *conclusion.* Thus, the hearer's participation in the reasoning process is self-persuading.

In terms of implementation, the art of the enthymeme lies squarely with the ability of the speaker to affirm his initial assertion so that it will lead the hearer to provide the logical link to the conclusion. In other words, *the speaker must formulate his initial assertion so that any premises that he wishes the hearer to supply enthymematically will be implicit in the initial assertion.*

On the other hand, in the event that the speaker assumes no premise in his initial assertion—that he spells out all steps in the reasoning process—then no enthymeme is possible. In such a case, the speaker asks the hearer to accept each of his assertions; he does not attempt to elicit the hearer's participation. In this situation, the hearer has but one kind of mental activity: to accept or to reject each assertion of the speaker.

Because enthymemes are applicable to argument, they relate explicitly to the argumentative modes. This is not to say that the narrative and expository modes never contain an enthymeme; it is to say, rather, that because both narration and exposition stress providing complete information, they do not ordinarily elicit audience participation in the reasoning process. It is no accident that Aristotle, at the outset of his *Rhetoric,* called enthymemes the *"substance of rhetorical persuasion"*[3] [author's italics].

Enthymemes are operational in daily life. For instance, two students enter a new classroom building looking for Room 290. One student opens the door to the classroom corridor and observes the number 135 above one classroom entrance. The student promptly says, "We need to go up one more floor." The second student, who also sees the number 135, says only "OK" as he nods his head in assent. By saying "OK," he has joined the first student in creating an enthymeme. How? After the first student made his assertion (*with its implicit assumptions*), the second student had to (1) understand and (2) agree with those premises. Those premises were as follows: (a) all numbers in a certain group are found on one floor; (b) floors are numbered progressively by equal steps from the

---

[3]Aristotle, *Rhetoric,* 1354a15.

bottom floor to the top; and (c) the 200s would be the next level above the 100s.

One might conveniently regard the three foregoing premises as collectively the major premise. However, if one prefers, he may regard all three as a related set of major premises. In either case, the premises were necessary to the following:

Minor Premise: (To be understood by both students)   I am standing before Room 135.

Conclusion: "We need to go up one more floor to find Room 290."

Enthymemes may be classified, and one of these classes is reasoning from premise. The first enthymeme from premise[4] is based upon reasoning *from categorical premise*, which can be illustrated as follows:

Major Premise: All A's are B.

Minor Premise: C is an A.

Conclusion: Therefore, C is B.

or,

Major Premise: No A is B. (All A's are not B).

Minor Premise: C is an A.

Conclusion: Therefore, C is not B.

In more concrete terms, the following format illustrates the applicability of reasoning from categorical premise with a topic that students of public address often consider:

Major Premise: Men are subject to making mistakes.

Minor Premise: Jurors are men.

Conclusion: Jurors are subject to making mistakes.

or

Major Premise: No man is exempt from making mistakes.

Minor Premise: A juror is a man.

Conclusion: Therefore, a juror is not exempt from making mistakes.

In each of the preceding formats, all of the steps are present; nothing has been assumed. However, when a communicator utilizes such for-

---

[4]See Chapter 3.

---

mats, he should initiate the enthymematic process by asserting one or, at the maximum, two parts of each format and depending upon the hearer to supply what is missing. In the second two formats, for example, "Jurors are men" and "A juror is a man" are implicit in the two major premises. Certainly, no hearer would be either unable or unwilling to supply the minor premises for these two formats. In the case of the latter formats, a speaker could also initiate a more sophisticated enthymeme by asserting either "Jurors are subject to making mistakes" or "A juror is not exempt from making mistakes." The hearer should respond quickly by providing the essence of the major and minor premises in each instance.

The speaker of the following line of reasoning leaves only the minor premise implicit when he asserts, "How can we impose a penalty as absolute as death when our knowledge cannot be absolute in imposing it? Juries do make mistakes." Since the minor premise is implicit in the major premise and the conclusion, any hearer should mentally supply the minor. It would have been a much more sophisticated enthymeme for the speaker to assert only, "Juries do make mistakes." The major and minor premises are implicit in the conclusion.

Another speaker arguing on the same subject assumes the major premise when stating, "The possibility of mistakes makes the abolition of the death penalty justifiable under principles of jurisprudence." The hearer should be both able and willing to give a mental nod of approval to the essence of the major premise underlying this sequence of reasoning.

The second of the enthymemes from premise is based upon argument *from conditional premise*. The paradigm of reasoning from conditional premise is as follows:

> Major Premise: If A then B.
> Minor Premise: But, A.
> Conclusion: Therefore, B.

One may express the foregoing more concretely, as follows:

> Major Premise: If one's heart ceases to function, then his life is in jeopardy.
> Minor Premise: Joe College's heart has ceased to function.
> Conclusion: Joe College's life is in jeopardy.

Because of the peculiar makeup of the major premise in reasoning from conditional premise, both the minor premise and the conclusion are contained in the major premise. Therefore, one who wishes to initiate an enthymeme when reasoning from conditional premise may assert either the major premise (containing both the antecedent and the consequent) or the minor premise, but he would be much more effective to affirm the minor. Because of the nature of the minor premise in argument from a conditional premise, hearers should have no difficulty understanding immediately the conclusion and the major premise. For example, if Joe College has been in an automobile crash and someone shouts, "Joe's heart has stopped beating," then every hearer immediately understands that Joe's life is in danger. Thus, the key to this kind of enthymeme lies in affirming the antecedent in the minor premise.

The following excerpt from a speech by Red Jacket, a member of the Seneca Indian nation, is an example of an enthymeme from conditional premise. In the conclusion of his speech "On the Religion of the White Man and the Red"(1805),[5] Red Jacket said:

> Brother, we are told that you have been preaching to the white people in this place. These people are our neighbors. We are acquainted with them. We will wait a little while and see what effect your preaching has upon them. If we find it does them good, makes them honest, and less disposed to cheat Indians, we will then consider again of what you have said.[6]

Red Jacket initiated his enthymeme in his statement, as diagrammed below in Premise 2. If the hearer found Premises 1 and 2 to be meaningful, then he should have been persuaded that Red Jacket's conclusion was reasonable.

Premise 1: (To be understood) Only a religion that does people good is worth having.

Premise 2: "If we find it does them good, makes them honest, and less disposed to cheat Indians, we will then consider again of what you have said."

Premise 3: (To be understood) Time will show whether it does our neighbors good.

Conclusion: Therefore, "we will wait a little while . . ."

A third kind of enthymeme is based upon *argument from sign*. As already observed, argument from sign reasons from a known effect (the sign) to its antecedent, a cause. The classic example of Aristotle in his *Rhetoric* states that a woman's giving milk is a sign that she has recently

[5]William Jennings Bryan, ed., *The World's Famous Orations*, Vol. 8 (New York: Funk and Wagnalls Co., 1906) pp. 9–13.

[6]Bryan, Vol. 8, p. 13.

given birth to a child.[7] Aristotle employed the illustration as an example of an *infallible* sign, because he assumed that there was no other cause of that sign.

An enthymeme is implicit in every argument from an infallible sign. For instance, if someone communicates the sign "Mrs. J. J. is giving milk," then the hearer supplies the conclusion that "Mrs. J. J. has recently given birth to a child." In addition, these two statements are premised upon the underlying statement that any woman giving milk has recently borne a child. In full format, the reasoning appears as follows:

Major Premise: (To be assumed in hearer's mind) Any woman giving milk has recently borne a child.

Minor Premise: Mrs. J. J. is giving milk.

Conclusion: (To be assumed in hearer's mind) Mrs. J. J. has recently borne a child.

Illustrative of reasoning enthymematically *from probable sign* is the argument centered about the nomination of Justice Abe Fortas to be Chief Justice of the Supreme Court of the United States. Both the proponents and the opponents of Justice Fortas employed enthymematic argument from probable sign.

Speaking in favor of Justice Fortas, Senator Jacob Javits stated:

Mr. President, I would like to refer to a few of his decisions in the field of civil rights and civil liberties which reflect his philosophy. This is the basic substantive question which demonstrates his prime fitness to be Chief Justice.

In a significant early case decided very soon after he became a member of the Court, *Brown v. Louisiana* (383 U.S. 131), Justice Fortas, writing for himself, the Chief Justice, and Justice Douglas, reversed the conviction of a group of Negroes who had peacefully participated in a sit-in in the public library of a parish in Louisiana on the grounds that the facts did not support a breach of the peace, and further that the rights of peaceable and orderly protest which the petitioners were exercising were protected by the first and fourteenth amendments.

At that time, the public library system in the affected Louisiana parishes was completely segregated, borrowers' cards were stamped with their name, and even the bookmobiles for whites and Negroes were of different colors. In reversing the conviction, Justice Fortas wrote: "The statute was deliberately and purposefully applied solely to terminate the reasonable, orderly, and limited exercise of the right

---

[7]The author has been told that there are rare cases in which women have given milk without having given birth. If the foregoing is true, then the argument would be from a probable sign rather than from an infallible sign.

to protest the unconstitutional segregation of a public facility. Interference with this right, so exercised, by state action is intolerable under our Constitution," (383 U.S. 142).[8]

Senator Javits argued from the sign that Justice Fortas supported civil rights in the *Brown v. Louisiana* case to the conclusion that this decision along with others "demonstrates his prime fitness to be Chief Justice." This line of reasoning may be placed in the following format:

Major Premise: (To be assumed in hearer's mind)   The Chief Justice of the Supreme Court of the United States must be fit for his office in the area of civil rights and civil liberties.

Minor Premise: Justice Fortas voted with the majority in the *Brown v. Louisiana* decision.

(Premise to be assumed in hearer's mind): The *Brown v. Louisiana* decision was a significant one in terms of civil rights.

Conclusion: Justice Fortas is fit to be Chief Justice.

Inasmuch as the foregoing argument was from probable sign, some persons placed other interpretations on the actions of Justice Fortas in relation to civil rights cases, and opponents drew opposite conclusions as to whether he ought to be confirmed as Chief Justice. One who opposed the nomination of Justice Fortas to be Chief Justice was Senator Spessard Holland. Senator Holland argued from the sign that Justice Fortas had a key role in the support of the *Miranda v. Arizona* decision to the conclusion that Justice Fortas should not be confirmed as Chief Justice of the Supreme Court.

I now plan to deal in my second speech with four or five of the other Fortas decisions which I regard as indefensible. . . .
    The third case, which I plan to discuss later, another 5-to-4 decision in which Justice Fortas was the swingman, is that of *Miranda v. Arizona* (384 U.S. 436) in which the majority opinion was written by Mr. Chief Justice Warren with a strong dissent by Mr. Justice Clark and other strong dissents by Mr. Justice Harlan — joined by Justices Stewart and White — by Mr. Justice White — joined by Justices Harlan and Stewart. This is the case in which, reversing a conviction for kidnapping and rape, the majority of the Court bans a confession found by the jury and the trial court to have been voluntary and affirmed by the State supreme court. The majority opinion sets up new

[8]*Congressional Record*, Vol. 114, No. 158, Washington, D.C., September 26, 1968, pp. S11470–S11471.

rules governing confessions which the four dissenting Judges state, forcibly, will help criminals, discourage law enforcement officers, and weaken the ability of the courts to enforce criminal laws.[9]

Following is a formal representation of the foregoing reasoning:

Premise I: (To be assumed in hearer's mind)   Any judge who helps criminals, discourages law enforcement officers, and weakens the ability of the courts to enforce criminal laws should not be confirmed as Chief Justice of the Supreme Court of the United States.

Premise II: The *Miranda v. Arizona* decision helped criminals, discouraged law enforcement officers, and weakened the ability of the courts to enforce criminal laws.

Minor Premise: Justice Fortas voted with the majority in the *Miranda v. Arizona* decision.

Conclusion: Justice Fortas should not be confirmed as Chief Justice of the Supreme Court of the United States.

A fourth kind of enthymeme is that *from disjunctive premise*. As already pointed out, formal argument from disjunctive premise follows from the premise, "It is either A or B." A classical example of this enthymeme is *St. Mark 9:40:* "For he that is not against us is for us." This assertion constitutes the major premise; nothing else is stated. It would appear that the hearers of Jesus were expected to complete the enthymeme from their contacts with specific persons and that the consummation of this enthymeme might be both delayed and repeated. The minor premise and conclusion might be as follows:

Minor Premise: Mr. X (tomorrow, Mr. Y; the next day, Mr. Z) is not against us.

Conclusion: Therefore, Mr. X (Mr. Y or Mr. Z) must be for us.

A fifth kind of enthymeme, that *from conjunctive premise,* would proceed formally as follows:

Major Premise: One cannot be both A and B.

Minor Premise: But, one is A.

Conclusion: Therefore, one is not B.

One frequently finds examples of the conjunctive enthymeme in criminal trials. Assuming that the prosecution were to allege that the

---

[9]*Congressional Record*, Vol. 114, No. 158, p. S11486.

defendant was in Los Angeles at the time that a certain crime was committed, and assuming that the defendant were to respond, (Minor Premise) "But I can prove that I was in my physician's office in Chicago at the time that you allege that I was in Los Angeles," then the defendant would be initiating a conjunctive enthymeme. The defendant would base his response — beginning with "But I can prove . . ." — on the major premise that he could not be in Los Angeles and in his physician's office in Chicago simultaneously. The defendant would have every reason to believe that any jury and judge would supply the correct major premise in their minds. On the other hand, he would have to prove the minor premise beyond a reasonable doubt if the jury and judge were to come to his conclusion. Formally stated, the line of argument would appear as follows:

> Major Premise: (To be assumed in hearer's mind) The defendant could not be both in his physician's office in Chicago and in Los Angeles at the same time.
>
> Minor Premise: The defendant was in his physician's office in Chicago.
>
> Conclusion: Therefore, the defendant was not in Los Angeles at that time.

Reasoning informally by conjuctive enthymeme is common in human communication, even at a very young age. For example, a parent might tell his unhappy child, who has just spent all his money, that "you can't have your cake and eat it too." The child, thus chastened, is likely to join an appropriate minor premise to the foregoing major premise with the result that he practices some degree of frugality on future occasions.

Another kind of enthymeme is that *from testimony*. In general, regardless of whether it be enthymematic, argument from testimony is argument from generalization and therefore argument from premise. By accepting argument from testimony, the hearer accepts the judgment of a person in lieu of a conclusion established by other means — for example, by experimental studies. Thus, the communicatee who joins in reasoning enthymematically from testimony accepts both (1) the competence and (2) the integrity of the person who has testified.

Enthymemes from testimony appear throughout the historical record of communication. One older example of such an enthymeme occurs in Daniel Webster's speech on Foote's resolution, January 20, 1830.[10] Inasmuch as the meaning of consolidation was important in the debate on the resolution, Webster understandably dealt with that conception. In his

---

[10]Cornelius Beach Bradley, ed., *Orations and Arguments by English and American Statesmen* (Boston: Allyn and Bacon, 1897), p. 185. (At the end of December 1829, Mr. Foote of Connecticut introduced his Senate Resolution regarding the sale of public lands. In his speech on January 20, 1830, Webster upheld the doctrine of a national union and a national policy against the advocates of states rights.)

---

speech, he dealt with consolidation enthymematically by proving the minor premise. The remaining propositions were to be understood by the hearer.

> Major Premise: (To be understood by hearer)   General Washington's consolidation is the one to be used as a standard.
>
> Minor Premise: Foote's Resolution promotes Washington's kind of consolidation.
>
> Conclusion: (To be understood by hearer)   Foote's Resolution should be adopted.

> Consolidation! — that perpetual cry both of terror and delusion — Consolidation! Sir, when gentlemen speak of the effects of a common fund, belonging to all the States, as having a tendency to consolidation, what do they mean? Do they mean, or can they mean, anything more than that the union of the States will be strengthened by whatever continues or furnishes inducements to the people of the States to hold together? If they mean merely this, then, no doubt, the public lands, as well as everything else in which we have a common interest, tend to consolidation; and to this species of consolidation every true American ought to be attached; it is neither more or less than strengthening the Union itself. This is the sense in which the framers of the Constitution use the word *consolidation,* and in this sense I adopt and cherish it. They tell us, in the letter submitting the Consitution to the consideration of the country, that "In all our deliberations on this subject, we kept steadily in our view that which appears to us the greatest interest of every true American, the consolidation of our Union, in which is involved our prosperity, felicity, safety, perhaps our national existence. This important consideration, seriously and deeply impressed on our minds, led each State in the Convention to be less rigid on points of inferior magnitude, than might have been otherwise expected."
> This, sir, is General Washington's consolidation. This is the true, constitutional consolidation. I wish to see no new powers drawn to the general government; but I confess I rejoice in whatever tends to strengthen the bond that unites us, and encourages the hope that our Union may be perpetual.[11]

Another kind of enthymeme, the enthymeme *from maxim,* involves an argument of a general nature regarding some point of practical conduct. Since both a maxim and the major premise of an enthymeme are by nature general statements, the maxim easily serves as the major premise of an enthymeme. However, the enthymeme from maxim has one characteristic that simultaneously makes it both inferior and superior to

---

[11]Callie L. Bonney, ed., *The Wisdom and Eloquence of Daniel Webster* (New York: John B. Alden, 1886), p. 115.

Chapter Seven

other more regular enthymemes—for example, that from categorical premise. The enthymeme from maxim is general—so general that no certain minor premise is implicit in the major. On the other hand, this enthymeme allows the hearer so much latitude in supplying the minor premise that the enthymeme from maxim may have some of the literary subtleties of poetry.

For example, the maxim "A rolling stone gathers no moss" is the major premise of an enthymeme, but no certain minor premise is implicit. If the speaker wishes his hearers to supply a certain minor premise, he had better develop a very closely reasoned context prior to introducing the maxim. If the context were to be laziness, for example, then the hearers of the enthymeme from maxim likely would apply the maxim to themselves within that context.

Other very common examples of enthymemes from maxim are "A penny saved is a penny earned" and "A bird in the hand is worth two in the bush." In each case, provided that the hearer has identified with the context supplied by the speaker, he will supply both the specific minor premise and the conclusion that apply to him. If, for instance, anyone hearing the former of the two maxims says to himself, "Yes, I could add $10.00 per month to my income by walking to school," then he has joined the speaker in forming an enthymeme from maxim.

Related to enthymemes from maxim are those *from stories*. If the story is to be effective, then the communicator must present it at the proper time and in the proper context; otherwise, the hearer may not supply the minor premise and the conclusion. The best enthymemes from story are those that have a moral or lesson that is both obvious (but not spelled out) and applicable, without being overly moralistic. If the enthymeme from story is also humorous, it can make a strong point more palatable and memorable. The following story should illustrate:

> A golfer hit his ball into the rough, and it landed on a large anthill. The golfer was understandably angry about his misfortune, and, after a few moments of meditation, swung hard. He missed the ball completely, smashing into the anthill and killing many ants. Angered further, the golfer backed off a bit and took another vicious cut at the ball—this time hitting the anthill on the *other* side of the ball and killing many more ants. Completely unravelled by this time, the golfer tried to calm himself and bent down to brush away some of the sand. As he bent over, he heard one ant say to the survivors: "For Heaven's sake, men, if you don't want to get killed, get on the ball."

Clearly, one should tell this story only in relation to the proper topic at the proper time. One could tell it to drivers who were accident prone, to students failing school because of laziness, or to workers in an industrial plant in which many workers had been injured because of care-lessness.

The following story is an example of a largely nonhumorous enthy-meme from story.

> The young boy was assisting his father to shingle the roof of the porch. When they were through, the father climbed down the ladder and took it away. Upon discovering that his father had removed the ladder, the boy asked his father to replace it. The father declined with the statement that he was big and strong, that the boy was not heavy, and that the distance was slight; therefore, he would catch the boy if he would jump. After they argued briefly, the boy jumped. The father deliberately stepped back, allowing his son to fall to the ground. The boy was not injured physically, but with tears in his eyes he asked, "Dad, why did you let me fall when you said that you would catch me?" The father replied, "Son, how many times have I told you, 'never trust nobody nohow!'"

Professor Bower Aly of the University of Oregon told this story to his graduate students in connection with his discussion of the need to verify information. It was a very effective enthymeme, in that one of the students, enthymematically applying the story, discovered about 15 errors over several pages of a significant published biography.

Another kind of enthymeme is the enthymeme *from resemblance.* This form involves reasoning from a premise that expresses an explicit similarity in two things, one of which is known, to an implicit conclusion that is supplied by the hearer as a response to the premise. The hearer must also supply the assumed premise that if in one known situation a certain causal relation existed, then in a like situation in which the same or a similar cause would be operative, one could expect the same or a similar effect.

From childhood, human beings learn that some things and events resemble one another and that others differ. It is from the similarities among events that persons begin to reason from resemblance. The more sophisticated the person becomes, the more he looks for the essence of the similarity when attempting to reason enthymematically by resem-blance.

In this kind of argument, the speaker should establish the minor premise; but, in general, both the conclusion and major premise should be sufficiently implicit to enable the hearer to supply them. For instance, one may argue that the Communist tactic of joint occupancy or super-vision of a country with the Western powers (as in a divided Germany or Korea) resembles the tactic of Bismarck in relation to his joint occupation of Schleswig-Holstein with Austria. This argument would be intelligible if the hearers are able to supply the information that Bismarck knew when he persuaded Austria to join him in taking Schleswig-Holstein that he would annex Schleswig-Holstein for Prussia when he felt that the time was right. The hearers would also have to know that Schleswig-Holstein was a convenient source of conflict between Prussia and Austria which Bismarck exploited whenever it would suit his purposes to do so. If the hearers are able to supply the foregoing, then they ought to be able also to supply the conclusion that the Communists deliberately arranged to divide countries so as to create crises (as in Germany and Korea) whenever doing so would serve their purpose.

However, in arguing enthymematically from resemblance, one must question not only whether the hearers are able to supply a missing premise and conclusion but also whether they are *willing*. Inasmuch as the enthymeme from resemblance commonly involves interpretation of historical events, the speaker must be very careful to make certain that the basic interpretations of events *are not open to serious question*; otherwise, the hearers may not be *willing* to supply the speaker's interpretation, with the result that the enthymeme from resemblance will fail.

Within the general enthymematic configurations described in this chapter, there may also be *enthymematic implications in individual words*. As a case in point, the simple assertion that "he ran the mile in under 4 minutes" is enthymematic. First, the main clause, "he ran the mile," is in itself an enthymeme; for who "runs the mile" unless he is a participant in track? This enthymeme might be stated formally as follows:

Major Premise: (To be assumed in hearer's mind)   A person running the mile is a participant in track.

Minor Premise: "He (Joe X) ran the mile."

Conclusion: (To be assumed in hearer's mind)   Joe X is a participant in track.

To analyze this enthymeme even further, one can discover, first, that the noun phrase, "the mile," could be a singular term referring explicitly to the track-and-field event, the mile. Second, the employment of the verb, "ran," explicitly suggests a race. Thus, in the main clause of the assertion, the major parts that are enthymematic are a noun phrase and a verb that, taken together, point enthymematically to a track-and-field event.

Now, taking the complete assertion—"he ran the mile in under 4 minutes"—one can see that the prepositional phrase, "in under 4 minutes," when it is combined with the main clause, initiates the primary enthymeme. The point of the assertion as a whole is bound up in the words "under 4 minutes," since a knowledgeable hearer will supply the major premise and the conclusion illustrated on the following page:

Major Premise: (To be assumed in hearer's mind)   Anyone running the mile in under 4 minutes is a champion miler.

Minor Premise: He (Joe X) ran the mile in under 4 minutes.

Conclusion: (To be assumed in hearer's mind)   He is a champion miler.

Several more assertions should be sufficient to illustrate the enthymematic quality of words and phrases. In the assertion "Eat your spinach," for example, the enthymematic word is the noun, "spinach." The assertion represents the conclusion in the following format:

Major Premise: (To be assumed in hearer's mind)   You should eat what is good for you.

Minor Premise: (To be assumed in hearer's mind)   Spinach is good for you.

Conclusion: "Eat your spinach."

One variation of the foregoing would be for the speaker to say that "Spinach is good for you." The enthymematic word in this instance is the adjective, "good." This assertion would appear as the minor premise in a format identical to the foregoing. The only difference is that the major premise and the conclusion, *not* the major and the minor premises, must be assumed by the hearer.

Epithets are good examples of the enthymematic quality of words and phrases. Indeed, the strength of epithetical language lies primarily in its enthymematic quality. Here are two examples:

1. Suzy Q. is a golddigger.
2. That quisling deserves to be deported.

In the first illustration, the only word with enthymematic characteristics is the epithet, "golddigger." Stated in a full format, the reasoning would be as follows:

Major Premise: (To be assumed in hearer's mind)   All girls who are golddiggers are after a man's money.

Minor Premise: Suzy Q. is a golddigger.

Conclusion: (To be assumed in hearer's mind)   Suzy Q. is after a man's money.

This enthymeme would be completed almost instantaneously by the hearer after he heard the word "golddigger" used to describe Suzy Q. Perhaps the hearer would not consciously fill in the major premise, but he would certainly be aware of having filled in the conclusion.

In the second example, the entire enthymematic process centers about the epithet "quisling." Of course, the speaker should make certain that the hearer knows that the word "quisling," which became a part of the language when a Norwegian named Quisling collaborated with the Nazis, is the term used in describing a particular type of traitor. A hearer not understanding the word could not complete the enthymeme. The chain of reasoning in this enthymeme would approximate the following:

Premise I: (To be assumed in hearer's mind)   All traitors should be deported.

Premise II: (To be assumed in hearer's mind)   A quisling is a traitor.

Minor Premise: (Implicit in the assertion)   That person is a quisling.

Conclusion: "That quisling should be deported."

Conclusion

The enthymeme appears to be the dominant pattern in the fabric of human communication. Perhaps it is so because of the innate desire of all persons to be believed, which in turn, leads to man's attempt — regardless of how clumsy — to adapt his notions to those of other human beings. The speaker's aim in adapting through the enthymeme is to affirm an assertion with which the hearer will identify, so that the hearer will subsequently participate in the speaker's reasoning process and thereby persuade himself. By studying the enthymeme systematically, and by practicing its formulation, the effective speaker will become sophisticated in initiating enthymematic communication.

Suggested Readings

Bitzer, Lloyd F. "Aristotle's Enthymeme Revisited." *Quarterly Journal of Speech,* Vol. 45 (December 1959). Pp. 399ff. This essay embodies a definitive statement on the nature of the enthymeme.

Weaver, Richard M. *The Ethics of Rhetoric*. Chicago: Henry Regnery Co., 1953. Pp. 173–174. This concise definition of the enthymeme makes a subtle point as to what is "in mind."

Suggested Assignments

1. Obtain three different kinds of enthymeme and do the following things:
   a. Designate the reasoning process in each case.
   b. Designate the way in which the speaker initiated the enthymeme.
   c. Designate what the speaker attempted to lead the hearers to supply.
   d. Evaluate the likelihood that the hearers would have supplied the missing premise(s), thus completing the enthymeme with the speaker.

2. Construct an enthymeme in relation to one argument of a speech you are to give. Designate the following:
   a. How you plan to initiate the enthymeme.
   b. What premise you expect the hearers to supply "in mind."

The Narrative
Mode

In Chapter 8, I point out that narration not only occurs as a distinct mode, but that it also occurs in the other modes as well. When I refer to the narrative mode by itself, I refer to the controlling structure as being narrative.

In particular, I should like you to observe how narration is effective in leading the audience to believe the speaker's statement. In addition to other examples, I have provided for your study an excellent narrative speech illustrating adaptation to the hearer through the meaning ⟶ identification ⟶ persuasion *sequence.*

If the oldest extant literature is any indication, then man developed the theory and practice of narration very early in his history. Although pre-literate culture must remain largely unknown, certain early literary works hint at the state of learning in pre-literate times. For instance, the epics of Homer are *prima facie* evidence that by Homer's time men had developed at least some theoretical principles in the areas of poetry and rhetoric; for the ability of Homer's characters to make critical distinctions among the tellers of tales presumes the existence of criteria by which to judge narrations. In addition, the widespread presence of the tale in the earliest literature of cultures throughout the world suggests that narration is a mode of communication indigenous to mankind.

The most plausible explanation for the prominence of the narrative mode in ancient literature is that those early tales were a meaningful mode of communication for the hearers. Such tales preserved the history and mythology associated with tribes, gods, heroes, cities, and states; and inasmuch as persons in antiquity commonly found their meanings in such history and mythology, they could be expected to find meaning in narrations that perpetuated or created such meanings. Persons hearing tales of tribe and nation that strengthened the conception that "our nation is the most blessed and glorious" could enthymematically supply the equivalent of "It's worth fighting for" and then follow that premise by marching off to war.

Although men no longer depend entirely upon the narrative tradition to preserve tribal and national history, they still employ narration in two primary ways: First, the communicator will occasionally employ the narrative mode as the basic structure of his communication. Second, he will employ the narrative mode as a segment of a communication in another mode. With regard to the first of these functions, inasmuch as the basic purpose of the narrative mode is to provide information, the first obvious requirement in employing this mode is that the communicator know precisely the point that he wishes to assert. The second requirement is that the communicator know why he is taking the trouble to communicate that point. Regarding this second requirement, the communicator should remember that his point should be worthy of the specific audience with whom he is discussing it. In addition, the communicator should be willing and able to go beyond this minimum of worthiness and discuss his point in terms of those qualities of the point that transcend the specific audience. In particular, the speaker should take care to discuss the universal qualities which the readers of the text of the speech might find to be meaningful and, therefore, with which they might identify.

Narration in general centers about the questions: Who? What? When? Where? Inasmuch as every event is time-bound, the most natural means of selecting and arranging the segments of a narration is to present them as they occurred in relation to each other in sequence. Therefore, the following is the most natural narrative mode:

Step 1: State the point. (Introduction)

Step 2: Narrate the segments in sequence. (Body)

Step 3: Close the narration. (Conclusion)

One may also employ narration in communicating in either the expository or argumentative modes. Extant literature provides many examples of the various ways that narrative segments are used to explicate the body of a speech in the expository or argumentative modes. One of the earliest examples of such use of the narrative form comes from Pericles' "On Those Who Died in the War." In the following narrative segment, Pericles supported his argumentation by stating the causes of the greatness of Athens in relation to the dead who had fallen in the first Peloponnesian War.

> For we enjoy a form of government which does not copy the laws of our neighbors; but we are ourselves rather a pattern to others than imitators of them. In name, from its not being administered for the benefit of the few but of the many, it is called a democracy; but with regard to its laws, all enjoy equality, as concerns their private differences; while with regard to public rank, according as each man has reputation for anything, he is preferred for public honors, not so much from consideration of party as of merit; nor, again, on the ground of poverty, while he is able to do the state any good service, is he prevented by the obscurity of his position. We are liberal then in our public administration; and with regard to mutual jealousy of our daily pursuits, we are not angry with our neighbor if he does anything to please himself; nor wear on our countenance offensive looks, which, tho harmless, are yet unpleasant. While, however, in private matters we live together agreeably, in public matters, under the influence of fear, we most carefully abstain from transgression, through our obedience to those who are from time to time in office, and to the laws; especially such of them as are enacted for the benefit of the injured, and such as, tho unwritten, bring acknowledged disgrace [on those who break them].[1]

In his concise historical narrative, Pericles stated that the government did not "copy" the laws of neighbors but, rather, that it was the "pattern" for others. Pericles thus provided a basis upon which his hearers could find meaning in their government and thus could identify with it and with Pericles, a symbol of the government. In providing meaningful conceptions as a basis for identification, Pericles also included the idea that the government was administered for the benefit of "the many" and the conception that government existed so that "all enjoy equality." By thus reminding his hearers of some of the history of Athens, Pericles provided a basis for identification and subsequent persuasion.

In the following excerpt from Sir Winston Churchill's speech to the Congress in 1952, the modern master of all communicative modes wove together a bit of beautiful narrative fabric to portray to Congress the pattern of bipartisanship that characterized British foreign policy. To create the effect he desired, Churchill combined his uncommon ability to write cogent narration with just the right touch of humor.

---

[1]William Jennings Bryan, *The World's Famous Orations*, Vol. 1 (New York: Funk and Wagnalls Co., 1906), pp. 17–18.

In our island we indulge from time to time in having elections. I believe you sometimes have them over here. [Laughter.] We have had a couple in 20 months, which is quite a lot and quite enough for the time being. [Laughter.] We now look forward to a steady period of administration in accordance with the mandate we have received. Like you we tend to work on the two-party system. The differences between parties on our side of the Atlantic, and perhaps elsewhere between British parties, are often less than they appear to outsiders. In modern Britain the dispute is between a form of socialism which has hitherto respected political liberty on the one hand, and, on the other, free enterprise regulated by law and custom. These two systems of thought, whose differences, I assure you, give plenty of room for argument between political opponents, fortunately overlap quite a lot in practice.

Our complicated society would be deeply injured if we did not practice and develop what is called in the United States the bipartisan habit of mind, which divides, so far as possible, what is done to make a party win and bear in their turn the responsibility of office and what is done to make the Nation live and serve high causes.

I hope here, Members of Congress, you will allow me to pay a tribute to the late Senator Vandenberg. [Applause.] I had the honor to meet him on several occasions. His final message in these anxious years gave the feeling that in this period of United States leadership and responsibility all great Americans should work together for all the things that matter most. That, at least, is the spirit which we shall try to maintain among British leaders in our own country and that was the spirit which alone enabled us to survive the perils of the late war.[2]

Churchill's statement, or thesis, was that the United States and Great Britain should work together for the common good. He knew that if both countries were to work together on a long-term basis, both would need continuity in foreign policy. He believed, further, that this continuity would necessitate a bipartisan approach to foreign policy. Churchill's approach to his topic was, first of all, to laugh at differences arising from political considerations. The obvious enthymematic premise underlying Churchill's humorous narrative about elections (to be supplied "in mind" by his audience) was equivalent to "If he can joke thus about his own recent experiences with elections, then he must not regard them as a threat to British-American relations." Inasmuch as Churchill was addressing the Congress of the United States in joint session, every hearer — also being an elected official — could find meaning in Churchill's joking about elections. In addition, Churchill's joking about his own recent election experiences was based upon the widely held enthy-

[2]*Memorial Addresses in The Congress of the United States and Tributes in Eulogy of Sir Winston Churchill*, 89th Congress, 1st Session, House Document No. 209 (Washington: U.S. Government Printing Office, 1965), pp. 239–240.

mematic premise that "If one can laugh at himself, he must be a pretty good fellow." Thus, Churchill's joking should have initiated a double enthymeme.

Following this humorous introduction, Churchill then positively identified with bipartisan foreign policy in a straightforward way and narratively reinforced that identification by linking his conceptions with those of the late Senator Arthur Vandenburg, a strong advocate of bipartisan foreign policy. Since the Congress also identified with Senator Vandenburg, Churchill's tribute to Vandenburg should have strengthened his identification with them. Thus, Churchill—by the simple expedients of reminding and informing his hearers—provided a meaningful basis for identification.

Two recent examples should be sufficient to illustrate some of the common forms of the narrative mode that communicators employ in relation to the expository mode. The following excerpt is a brief narrative segment leading into an explanation of the procedures by which Texas had been attempting to guarantee an adequate source and supply of water. The function of the examples narrated by the speaker was to lead the hearers to be willing to accept the generalization that "Texas is making progress in its efforts to assure water for present and future use." Thus, the speaker's narration of data became an integral part of the speaker's exposition. As to audience reaction to the generalization, it seems fair to say that some hearers would supply enthymematically the equivalent of "If Texas can do it, so can we." To the extent that hearers would respond enthymematically, the narrative segments and the exposition as a whole would result in persuasion.

Almost 300 years ago those who occupied the land now known as Texas were involved in the development of the land's water resources for their beneficial use. Their schemes, naturally, were not the grandiose plans of present-day planners nor were they inhibited by the constraints and restrictions which confront us today.

In 1680, more than one hundred years before the Thirteen States realized their need for unity and bound themselves together, the Spaniards near El Paso began the first irrigation by non-Indians. Today some of those works remain as testimony to their expertise and dedication to provide water for an arid land and its people. In the early and mid-1700s, stock raising began along the Lower Rio Grande. As migration to Texas increased, small communities were formed at locations having available water supplies.

From these modest beginnings there evolved the innumerable laws which govern the development and uses of water with the State. The gradual but growing realization that this is not an unlimited resource has made Texas a jealous guardian of her water.

I do not intend to review today the history of the development of Texas' water resources, although I can say in all sincerity and with a deep sense of pride we are making progress in our efforts to assure water for all present and future legitimate uses in Texas. The number of major reservoirs — those having a capacity of 5,000 or more acre-feet — has increased in the past 30 years from 34 to 147. Twelve more reservoirs are under construction. The Soil Conservation Service has authorized and constructed 1,261 of the 4,000 flood retardation structures planned for the State. The Texas Water Development Board is nearing completion of the Texas Water Plan, a program designed to meet the State's water requirements to the year 2020, when Texas will have an estimated population of 30.5 million. The cost of this water program has been estimated from \$5–\$7 billion, with State or local interest providing at least \$2 billion of that cost.[3]

To take another case, Congressman Henry S. Reuss asserted in the House of Representatives that "the needs of state and local governments continue to grow" because "Americans are demanding more and better public services." The data that he provided through narration supported his basic expository structure. Congressman Reuss' line of reasoning was that (1) the demand by Americans for more and better public services leads to (2) greater needs of state and local governments; therefore, he was presenting a bill to provide for sharing federal income tax revenues with state and local governments. Since the members of the House are elected every two years, and since they are closer to the people [because they represent only their specific districts], Congressman Reuss' hearers should have been able to find meaning in the narrative segments of his exposition.

> . . . Americans are demanding more and better public services. More children study longer in better schools. More police services are needed for a population which is restlessly mobile and is crowded into cities. Cars have outgrown two-lane country roads for expensive city throughways. Public health services cost more because of population growth, city living, and advances in medical knowledge. People seeking new jobs move from region to region, from State to State, and country to city, and from central city to suburbs. Public facilities in old communities are abandoned, but new facilities in new communities are needed. Hence, State and local government has been the country's largest growth industry.[4]

From the foregoing illustrations, one should be able to glimpse the uses for the narrative mode as segments of both the expository and argumentative modes. However, the following speech, reproduced *in toto*, will provide a more complete illustration of a sophisticated approach to

---

[3]Remarks of Joe G. Moore, Jr., Executive Director, Texas Water Development Board, and Chairman, Texas Water Quality Board. National Reclamation Association Annual Meeting, Honolulu, Hawaii, November 16, 1967, p. 1.

[4]*Congressional Record* — House, January 8, 1969, p. H 159.

---

the use of the narrative mode to produce persuasion. The speaker was Clarence K. Streit, editor of the periodical *Freedom & Union* and author of *Union Now*. The title of his speech was "The Rise of Man."

Streit's speech illustrates well the foregoing conception. First of all, the title itself is attractive and promising. Where is the man who could not find some meaning for himself in the idea of the progress of his species? From the outset of the narration, Streit's audience should have been able to identify philosophically with the conception that man is rising and to find meaning for their lives in identifying with the upward progress of man. Secondly, by narrating the story of man's rise, Streit established his statement that "Man is rising." Specifically, through pointing out that primitive man lacked freedom until he joined with other men who wished to be free, Streit established his premise that man is rising from "Cave Man to World Man" by pursuing freedom through a union of the free, corresponding roughly to the NATO nations.

The foregoing premise—if accepted by the hearer—should have been expected to evoke enthymematically a conclusion the equivalent of "If I wish to continue to rise, then I should support freedom through union." This line of reasoning may be diagrammed as follows:

> Premise 1: Man is rising from Cave Man to World Man by pursuing freedom through the union of the free.
>
> Premise 2: (To be understood by hearer) I am a man.
>
> Premise 3: (To be understood by hearer) I am rising toward becoming a World Man.
>
> Conclusion: (To be understood by hearer) Therefore, if I wish to continue to rise toward World Man, then I should support freedom through union.

The Rise of Man*

Step 1
State the point.

In a tiny buried seed the sequoia starts on its giant journey to the sky. The light seems hidden from it. It has no roots, no leaves, no trunk. It has only a power to create these, a sense of direction, a will

---

*Clarence K. Streit, "The Rise of Man," *Freedom & Union* (April 1947), pp. 26–28. Reprinted by permission of Mr. Streit. The author gave this speech a number of times to many different kinds of audience. Thus, its universal applicability—along with its other qualities—suggests that it deserves the accolade "rhetorical literature."

to grow. A power, a sense, a will so feeble that a chipmunk can destroy them—and yet so strong that the sequoia, once beyond the sapling stage, can live for thousands of years, towering above the earth, secure from nearly all the dangers that cut short the life of others.

The sequoia begins with the odds a myriad to one that it will never reach the light. It rises from danger to danger. The odds long remain against it. But they lessen as it rises. At last they turn in its favor when it stands firm, deep below and high above the ground.

Step 2
Narrate the segments
in sequence.

As the sequoia starts, so Man started long ago on his much vaster human venture. He set out, with a sense of direction, a power, a will no less mysterious, to free himself from everything that hemmed him in and held him down, to govern himself and all his world.

Mankind then was in the condition in which all the other species, from the whale to the microbe, still remain—without government and without law, save the law of Nature.

Man was then free only in the sense that the wolf is now.

Something—I call it the soul—told Man that this sense of freedom was false, that it left him in subjection to powers outside him, beyond his control, left him at the mercy of accidents of heat and cold, storm and drought, land and water. Something began to make Man see that this "freedom" left him a prey to leviathan and the wolf, to the viper and the hunger-spreading grasshopper . . . and to other men.

Dimly, in one and another of his myriad embodiments, Man began to feel that to be truly free he must free himself in every way, control the forces that were controlling him. He found, gropingly, that he must begin to govern himself before he could begin to govern others. He had to tame the wolf inside himself before he could tame the sheep . . . or dog. He began then and there his great evolution from *human* to *humane*.

Early, he began to learn that he could not free himself without the help of other men. His freedom depended on their friendship, just as their freedom depended on his friendship. We know that he sensed this connection long ago—back when he was beginning to govern his tongue and ear so as to free the thoughts within him and befriend those of others. For it was then that he formed his words for both *friend* and *freedom* from the selfsame root—the Sanskrit word, *priyon,* which means *beloved.*

He had discovered the great truth that escaped the other species: To free oneself, one must free others. He had begun to see the vast implications in the combined words, *man kind,* that stand for our species. He had begun to understand that to govern his world, he must govern himself, both individually and in society, must have both *freedom* and *union.*

Chapter Eight

Many difficulties that once made this enterprise heroic are child's play now.

Here was Man, one species among countless cut-throat competitors, and one that was handicapped a hundred times over. He was weaker physically than some other creature in almost every way. He did not have the gorilla's powerful arms, the antelope's speed, the tiger's spring. He did not have the armor of the rhinoceros, the mass of the elephant, the crocodile's jaws, the sheep's warm coat, the rabbit's ear, the eagle's eye.

He lacked the fish's power to swim under water; he lacked the duck's webbed foot. In flying, the grasshopper could outdo him. Nature made the spider a more gifted engineer than primitive Man, the bee more industrious, the ant more social. The camel surpassed him in endurance, the turtle in years of experience, the squirrel in forethought.

"Man is the only one that knows nothing, that can learn nothing without being taught," Pliny the Elder observed nearly 2,000 years ago. "At the prompting of Nature only, he can not speak, walk, eat, or, in short, do anything, but weep."

Pliny forgot that man could also laugh, and began with four other assets. He had a pair of hands, though they were not so clever then as now. He had a mind, not so filled as now with knowledge, nor so skilled in thinking, or in expressing thought and in understanding others. He had a heart, not so warm as now, or so capable of loving others, or of binding to him for so long so many others.

Above all, Man had a soul. It gained greater power to govern him as his hands and head and heart developed. Yet I think the soul of Man has served him best. As wise Alexis de Tocqueville said in his *Democracy in America:*

"The thing that makes us superior to the beasts is that we use our soul to find the material wellbeing to which instinct alone leads them . . . It is because man is capable of rising above bodily welfare and disdaining life itself—a thing of which the beasts have no idea— that he also knows how to multiply material goods to a degree they cannot conceive of, either."

Because Man is capable of rising above bodily welfare and disdaining life itself . . . How many, many inventions and discoveries of Man, how many of his liberties and rights, have depended on his willingness to risk his life!

Favored only with hands and heart, mind and soul—and a gift of laughter—Man set out on his vast adventure. Long ago he made the bee and the elephant, and many animals in between help him overcome his handicaps.

"Canst thou draw out Leviathan with a hook?" the Lord asked Job. It has become a minor matter that Man should master leviathan, and be the only living force that can quickly fell the secular sequoia. For Man has extended his puny powers fantastically, far beyond the best that Life could do before.

He has extended the power of his eye until he can see the microbe in his blood, gaze through his own body, dissect fast motion, sift out the chemical elements in the hidden heavens. He has extended tongue and ear until he can speak to millions all around the earth, or hear above the clamor of battle a voice coming from afar. He can know the thoughts of men who died thousands of years ago; he can make the dead sing to him in their living voice.

Man has made himself jaws that grind rocks and trees into powder and pulp; he measures his bites in tons. His hands spin silky web out of grimy coal; at the touch of his finger mountains are sundered. He stops missiles in mid-flight, and hurls them faster than sound can travel. He crosses continents and oceans; he circles the earth; he defies the jungles, the deserts, and the Poles of his planet. He is at home now on, and under, and above the land and the sea. In the heavens he outflies the wind. He, too, makes lightning, and he makes it serve the weakest of men. And now he has harnessed the power of the atom.

How can we help but be proud of our species when we survey its achievements, despite the odds against it? Who can not glory in this creature who made his name stand for *virtue* — and such virtues as the *manly, womanly, humane?*

The Rise of Man has not been the work of any individual, tribe, nation, race or color of men. All have contributed to it. Some men have gained ground here, others there, and many have held these gains. Few important innovations and discoveries have been lost. The conservatives have been no less important than the rebels.

The races and nations of Man who seem to have contributed the least, so far, may well contribute the most in centuries to come. Perhaps Providence is holding them now in reserve, as the American continents were held in reserve for so long. Who knows?

The marvelous thing about Man is not simply that so many, many men must be created before one of them discovers such simple, obvious things as zero, ABC, the straight line, axis, wheel. It is perhaps even more marvelous that it takes only one of us to see such truths, and demonstrate them clearly, for each of us to see them, too, and for all of us to cling to them forever. It is a marvel, too, that nothing can stop the man who finds a truth from doing all he can to make it known to us. He will do without comfort, spend all his money, borrow all he can, slave through day and night, wear himself out, risk his life; he will do anything he needs to do in order to force us by our common sense to see that he is right — that we *can* free ourselves from malaria by killing a certain kind of mosquito, that we *can* free ourselves from earth and fly. We can not contrive to discourage the men who have found some way to free us further.

These marvelous powers in Man are, paradoxically, both freed and harnessed by the principle of freedom and union — of free union of the free for the sake of greater individual freedom. What men achieved before this principle began to make innovation easier and safer, suggests . . . feebly . . . the wonders Man will know when a World Republic gives an equal chance to every individual in our species, frees all its vast and varied talents.

When we survey the Rise of Man we feel more respect for the

Cave Man, and more kinship with him. When Man 10,000 years from now considers us, do you not hope that we ourselves shall seem to him as backward, and as brave as early Man seems now? In the year 12,000 the Sky Man, the Cosmic Man may smile indulgently at what we now call science, civilization, freedom, love, and say:

"When you consider how little they knew and how barbarously they lived, those men showed astonishing insight, ingenuity, courage, faith. Without the people of the twentieth century, we could not be where we are now. They were the first to fly and to split the atom.

"And it was back in their time that our species at long last ceased cutting its own throat, ended those savage nationalistic wars, created the nucleus of the first World Republic. That was quite a little thing to do in those benighted days. Of course, it was easy compared to the problems of interplanetary government that we face now. But they did their part; they kept the faith. Is it not awe-inspiring, this ancient, stubborn, invincible faith of Man in Man? They even had it back in the twentieth century!"

The Rise of Man is already sublime.

Because the spirit that has carried on this human venture resides in the individual, its most fruitful achievement has been the freeing of the individual, its most marvelous achievement the union of the free for greater freedom.

True no man is yet fully free. Hardly 300,000,000 individuals of the 2,100,000,000 of our species have enjoyed even 30 years of fair political freedom, unbroken save by war. This small fraction is not yet united; it is divided into more than a dozen different sovereign nations. That is all true — but the great and varied flowering of human genius since the first union of the free was created in the United States 160 years ago shows the possibilities that lie in greater freedom for the individual, and a broader union embracing all the free.

It is also true that the freeing of the individual has led to greater development materially than morally, mechanically than politically, scientifically than spiritually. Therein lies the basic actual danger to our species.

Men have proved much more capable of learning how to make and operate the most complicated, devastating engines of destruction than of learning how to govern themselves in freedom and peace. We have learned how to divide the atom, but not how to unite humanity, or even federate the dozen freest peoples in the nucleus of a World Republic. And so we have magnified war's danger.

Cave Man and Tribal Man have done their part, and passed on. Their progeny, National Man, remains . . . over-long. He has not yet produced World Man, even in the nuclear form with which Nature invariably begins all her greatest living creations, even as the Citizen of some Union freely formed by a few historic nations.

And so World Man waits . . . to be born . . . and grow gradually to manhood and produce, in his turn . . . Man.

Will the human venture never reach this climax? Will Man come to an untimely end, as have so many other species? Whenever he fails to adapt himself to change he will surely perish from the earth. This can happen in our time. But I do not think it will. Despite our atomic bombs and all our highly publicized end-of-worlders, I believe that, all things considered, our species was, if anything, in more danger 10,000 years ago than now.

There is something splendid in the human spirit that makes it rise superbly in the face of danger. The prophets of doom overlook this happy fact.

Fear, of course, far more frequently characterizes it, so much so that it is often regarded as the chief human motive force, for good as well as ill. Just as the old time preachers counted on fear of Hell to drive man to Heaven, the modern prophets depend on the terrors of atomic war to bring Man to world government. So much good indeed is expected from sheer cowardice that one would think the unmanly were Man's finest virtue.

Enough of these appeals to cowardice. If there is no man who is not afraid of many things, there is also no danger, however great, that frightens all men always, that does not come as a challenge, as a tonic, to some men and women.

In all its thousands of years, and in all its perils, our species has never known a single danger that did not cause some men to rise up against it, rise above themselves and their fellows, rise superior to their species . . . and so Man has risen.

Step 3
Close the narration.

Not to the timid in us but to the brave, not to the vacillating but to the steadfast, not to the flesh but to the soul, do we owe our presence here. Not to those who frighten us shall we owe our future, but to those who give us courage, who appeal to the best in Man.

Are you not weary of the people who bemoan the times we live in? We live in momentous years. Would you expect them to be easy? Have you not been told enough that the French are finished, the British bankrupt, the Americans apathetically riding for a fall — that the freest of our species are the feeblest? It is not vitality they lack but merely union.

I can agree that conditions will grow worse than they are now. But I also expect to see those greater dangers awake the bolder spirit needed to bring us safely through them. I believe the end of this period of travail will not be the death of the free civilization that our species has developed round the North Atlantic, but the end of its cramped stage in the dark womb of nationalism, an infant Union of the Free, the beginning of World Man.

Like the secular sequoia Man may be felled in his gallant rise. Forces outside him, beyond his powers, may bring him crashing down. His Creator can destroy him . . . without atomic bombs . . . or preserve him in spite of them.

I have faith. I do not see the Creator of the soul of Man bringing to a senseless doom the human venture he inspired. I believe this generation will not fail our species. And I believe this, too: So long as there are men who rise above the body and disdain life itself, God will not fail us, will not cut short the Rise of Man.

Conclusion

When the communicator elects to talk about a statement, or thesis, concerned primarily with Who? What? When? Where?, then he should employ the narrative mode. In terms of implementation, one should follow three basic steps:

Step 1: State the point.

Step 2: Narrate the segments in sequence.

Step 3: Close the narration.

A primary use of the narrative mode relates to other modes. Indeed, that may be the dominant use. It is a practical impossibility to use the expository and the argumentative modes without employing one or more narrative segments.

Perhaps in relation to the narrative mode more than in other modes, the communicator experiences the temptation to tell a story for its own sake. He should be aware of the temptation and should resist it. If the communicator is to be effective, he must provide speeches in the narrative mode that enable the hearer to discover or to enhance his life's meaning. Specifically, the speaker should present information that the hearer would find meaningful. Thus, the speaker should carefully select his divisions and, in particular, his illustrations so that they provide a meaningful basis for identification.

Suggested Readings

The narrative mode has been largely neglected in publications concerned with oral communication. However, the following readings, although briefly or only indirectly related to narration, should assist the student in understanding the narrative mode.

Ross, Raymond S. *Speech Communication: Fundamentals and Practice*. Englewood Cliffs, N.J.: Prentice-Hall, 1965. Chap. 8, "Presenting Information." Although this chapter focuses as much on exposition as it does on narration, it should be useful in promoting the understanding of the narrative mode.

Smith, Donald K. *Man Speaking: A Rhetoric of Public Speech*. New York: Dodd, Mead & Co., 1969. Pp. 197–198. These pages contain a segment of a speech by a journalist on the subject of censorship. There are important implications for the narrative mode in this speech.

Suggested Assignments

1. Select a topic in the narrative mode and do the following:
   a. Complete the statement: "I want my audience to believe that . . ."
   b. Give a satisfactory answer to the question: "Why do I want this audience to believe this specific point?"
   c. Give a satisfactory answer to the question: "Why would the narrative mode of communication best enable me to adapt my specific thought to this group of hearers?"
2. Construct a narrative thought analysis for your speech in that mode.
3. Write out the introduction and the conclusion for your narrative speech.
4. Write out a segment of your speech centered about any one division with its subdivisions.
5. Present a speech in the narrative mode.

9

The Expository
Mode

As you read Chapter 9, observe carefully the two primary uses of the expository mode: (1) as the controlling structure of a speech and (2) as one or more segments of an argumentative mode. In both instances, explanation is the means by which the speaker causes his conceptions to become meaningful, thus initiating the meaning $\longrightarrow$ identification $\longrightarrow$ persuasion *sequence. You should, of course, take note of the three primary qualities of effective exposition: (1) precision, (2) clarity, and (3) force.*

Note in particular the examples of the two complete speeches in this mode. The outlines accompanying the texts of the speeches should assist you to see the relationship of the mode to the finished speech.

An exposition[1] involves the unfolding of the speaker's idea to his hearers. The underlying assumption of the expository mode is that an idea precisely perceived by the speaker, and properly explicated, will create a strong impact on the minds of hearers. Thus, when the speaker

[1] Although there may be some duplication, the following distinctions are essentially valid. Narration and description answer the question "What?" Exposition answers the question "How?" Argument answers the question, "Why?"

selects the expository mode, he does so because he judges that exposition, rather than another mode, would be the most effective means for adapting his thought to the hearers.

Clarity (in terms of the perception of the hearers) must be the prime quality of the expository mode; for clarity is the key to the hearers' understanding of the speaker's thought. If the speaker should fail to symbolize his ideas so that his hearers understand, then obviously he will fail to create his intended impact[2] in their minds.

The prime means of acquiring clarity is precision. This quality of precision is subordinate to clarity, but it is also essential to it. That is, although one may be precise without being clear, he must be precise in order to be clear. For example, if the speaker is to explain the workings of an atomic reactor, he would treat the topic differently when speaking, on the one hand, to a group of majors in nuclear physics and, on the other hand, to a group of sixth-graders. He must be precise in both instances, but he must relate (adapt) his precise notions to his specific audience if he is to achieve clarity and, consequently, maximum impact. In short, the three primary qualities of the expository mode are *precision, clarity,* and *force,* in that order.

The communicator commonly employs the expository mode in two ways: First, because most deliberative discourse centers about solving a problem, he uses exposition to explain the origin and nature of the problem. Second, he employs exposition to explain how a proposed plan of action would function to bring about the alleged benefits. For example, in relation to the first common function of exposition—explaining the origin and nature of a problem—one might establish how large cattle-feed lots cause water pollution. If the speaker's explanation has been precise, clear, and forceful, a number of the hearers should respond to the premise that cattle-feed lots are a serious cause of water pollution. The responses probably would be similar to "Something's got to be done about that," "That's pretty bad," or "That must stop." Each hearer who responds with such a mental affirmation will have joined with the speaker to create an enthymeme and, therefore, will have helped to persuade himself. The following formal structure illustrates the nature of this process of reasoning:

> Major Premise: (In hearer's mind) Serious causes of pollution must stop.
>
> Minor Premise (Exposition): Feed lots are a serious cause of pollution.
>
> Conclusion: (In hearer's mind) Feed lots must stop polluting water supplies.

Assuming that the speaker and hearer were jointly to construct the

---

[2] Rhetorically known as "force." See Chapter 13 on style.

---

foregoing enthymeme, the speaker should then propose his plan for re-solving the problem — the second common function of the expository mode. The theme of explaining a plan is "This is how it works." If the speaker is successful in showing that the plan probably would work, then the hearer is likely to join him in forming another enthymeme: "If it will do that, then I am in favor of it." More formally, the enthymeme might look like this:

> Major Premise: (In hearer's mind) If it will do that, then I am in favor of it.
>
> Minor Premise (Exposition): The plan will work.
>
> Conclusion: (In hearer's mind) I am in favor of it.

In summary, it should be clear at this point (1) that the expository mode relates to persuasion and (2) that the expository mode regularly involves a subtle use of the enthymeme.

After the speaker has selected his topic and decided on the expository mode,[3] he then should proceed to compose his speech. If the speaker uses the following format for the expository mode, he will be able to explain his idea accurately, quickly, easily, and unobtrusively.

> Step 1: Designate the topic.
> Step 2: Narrate background material. } (Introduction)
>
> Step 3: Affirm the point of the speech.
> Step 4: Partition the point of the speech. } (Body)
> Step 5: Explicate the point of the speech.
>
> Step 6: Conclude the explication. (Conclusion)

Although some speakers prefer to omit Steps 1 and 2 of the exposi-tory mode, they commonly provide sufficient background material in their speeches to supplant these introductory steps. In any case, *Step 1* provides the communicator with the opportunity to announce his topic in generic terms that will lead into Step 2. For example, President Robert F. Goheen of Princeton University, in discussing the role of the univer-sity in the community, plunged directly into his topic as follows:

> I want to talk with you about Princeton University in her role as early settler, citizen, neighbor, and taxpayer in the community of Princeton.[4]

---

[3] For details, see Chapter 2.

[4] This address was given by Princeton University President Robert F. Goheen before the Princeton Bar Association, October 19, 1965. This excerpt is from page 1 of the text as printed by the Greater Princeton Chamber of Commerce and Civic Council, Princeton, New Jersey.

Although not all members of his audience could be expected to find Princeton's role as "early settler" entirely meaningful, it is a safe assumption that all members of the audience could find the university president's discussion of Princeton's role as a "citizen, neighbor, and taxpayer" to be meaningful. The audience, therefore, could have been expected to identify with at least three divisions of the speech as forecast in the opening statement.

In addition to his announcing his topic in Step 1, President Goheen elected to partition the topic into its major divisions. Although it is the more common practice to partition the topic immediately prior to the discussion of each separate division, the foregoing method is equally acceptable. The choice of location for the partitioning depends upon the topic, the occasion, the audience, and the personal style of the speaker.

Step 2 consists of background material presented in a narrative fashion and leading into the point of the exposition. President Goheen handled the narration this way:

> One might suppose that when an institution and a community have lived together for over two centuries, the relationship could be called a great success and no questions asked. The truth is, though, that both the community and the university have changed greatly in those 200 years and are changing at an even faster rate today. Occasional reexaminations of the relationship are therefore in order.
>
> Perhaps it goes without saying that the community and university still love each other, but it never hurts to count the ways! And this I propose to do this evening as the guest of the Princeton Bar Association.
>
> President James Perkins of Cornell—a former member of our faculty and former prominent resident of your township—has said that a medium-large university such as Cornell in a rather small city such as Ithaca, N.Y., "is like a fat boy in a canoe. Every move has to be made very carefully."
>
> The comparison, though not very flattering, is probably applicable in some degree to our situation, and I accept it.[5]

As illustrated in Step 2 of President Goheen's address, the introduction not only points to the topic and prepares the listener for the discussion to follow but also reveals the attitudes of the speaker—his attitude toward the hearer, his attitude toward himself, and his attitude toward the topic. These attitudes cannot help but be revealed in a speech, and the wise speaker will make certain that he has adopted the appropriate attitudes from the beginning. Appropriate attitudes do as much as any factor in a speech to reveal the speaker's character to the hearers and to affirm for the hearers that "He (the speaker) is a good man."[6]

[5] *Ibid.*
[6] See Chapter 3.

President Goheen's narration presented him to be sincere and humorous. It should have been meaningful to his audience that the president of one of the great universities of the world exhibited these qualities and, by doing so, demonstrated his "goodwill" toward the hearers. The hearers should enthymematically have decided the equivalent of "the president of a university who can joke about the relationship between his school and the community can't be all bad," and they should have identified with him to some extent. At the moment of this identification, the president could be said to have established some ethos in the minds of the audience.

Step 3 is equivalent to the statement of the thought analysis.[7] Inasmuch as the statement embodies what the communicator wants the hearer to believe, the speaker must be precise and clear in formulating the statement. If the statement is imprecise, then the development cannot be precise. If the statement is not clear to the hearer, then there is little point in talking about the divisions. Therefore, if the speaker fails at this point, he fails at all the subsequent points.

In 1968, George A. Spater, president of American Airlines, Inc., told the American Society of Travel Agents:

> I want to say something about machines, but more about men and, particularly, the relationship of men and their aspirations to machines.[8]

Next, Spater partitioned his subject. *Step 4* provides a preview of the divisions of the exposition to help the hearers to comprehend the divisions and the supporting subdivisions as the speaker later introduces them individually. Thus, partitioning aids both in following the ideas and meanings of a speech as it is delivered and in retaining the ideas after it has been delivered. Spater then continued as follows:

> Scientific progress seems to fall into three stages:
> First, there is a desire for something — a demand or requirement — sometimes only a dream.
> Second, the scientists find a way of meeting the desire, frequently only in the crudest sort of way.
> Third, somebody, or a group of somebodies, makes a practical application of the scientists' discovery and the dream comes true.[9]

Note that the partitioning of Spater's speech revealed divisions that were clear in themselves; but more than that, they revealed a clear, smooth

---

[7] See Chapter 6 on the thought analysis.

[8] This address was given by George A. Spater, president of American Airlines, Inc., before the American Society of Travel Agents, San Juan, Puerto Rico, September 16, 1968. It was recorded in the *Congressional Record—Senate,* October 4, 1968, p. S12069.

[9] *Ibid.*

progression in thought. The thought moved in sequence from the first point to the second, and from the second to the third.

Step 5 represents the substance of the body; it is here that the case is proved or lost. This step of the expository mode is the speaker's most ambitious bid for the minds of his hearers. In the preceding speech, Spater used Divisions I and II of his partitioning of the speech to lead to the substance of what he wanted to say in Division III. In other words, he placed his most important point last, dealt with it in more depth than he did the first two, and — most important — made his greatest effort to adapt to his specific audience during his discussion of the final point.

In the following segment (Division III), Spater explicated in an interesting and relevant fashion, man's desire and dream for something new and better — in this case, flying. But, most important, the speaker claimed that it was the non-scientist who did the dreaming and made dreams come true. His audience, being non-scientists, could be expected to find Spater's point agreeable to their thinking. If the travel agents did indeed find their own meaning in dreaming and in making these dreams come true, then it would be reasonable to assume that they would identify with the speaker; for both the hearers and the speaker were practical men in the real world whose activity could be anthropocentric — making dreams come true for others.

This, then, is Spater's explication of the major part of the body of his speech:

Lindbergh made his flight in May 1927. The *Atlantic Monthly,* for November 1927, six months later, carried an article by Lt. Commander Bruce G. Leighton, member of the U.S. Bureau of Aeronautics, entitled "The Limits of Aviation." This carefully explained that an airplane's power plant and fuel were so heavy that it was impossible to build an airplane to provide transportation over long distances. He added, "The future of the airplane, both in peace and in war, lies in pursuits other than transoceanic transportation or other independent long-range operations."

Within less than 20 years after that statement it became apparent that not only was this assessment wrong, but in fact that the *greatest* advantage of the airplane was in the field that scientists thought impossible — that is, in transportation over long distances. This, then, became the third stage in the development of the industry: the practical application of the scientists' raw discovery of a way to move a man through the air. . . .

We have not run out of ideas. We have a full-time squad of experts working on a system of fully automated ticketing and fare computation. We have recently designed, and turned over to the other airlines for development and installation, a system of automated baggage delivery. This is way beyond the fanciful stage. There is today, in operation, a working model of this system. It has the ability to read the passenger's baggage check and deliver his baggage to him, anywhere in the airport—at the taxi stand or in the lot where his car is parked—within 3 minutes. The same system will automatically transmit baggage between carriers for connecting passengers. It will result in fewer misconnections, less lost baggage, less damage to baggage and shorter waiting time for baggage. The new regional airport between Dallas and Fort Worth is being designed for the use of the system.

These past improvements and those we are working on are for the purpose of making air transportation safer, more comfortable and easier to sell. They create demand and, in turn, satisfy the demand they create. But, as has always been true, the machines themselves are not much without people.

The large new aircraft are going to require much greater volume to fill them. Automated ticketing and automated baggage delivery systems, likewise, can be paid for only by very substantial increases in volume.

Where is this volume going to come from? A recent forecast by the Hudson Institute provides a partial answer. They predict that by the year 2000—

The U.S. population will be about 300 million—50 percent more than the present population.

The average family income will be almost $21,000 as compared with less than $9,000 today.

People will work an average of 147 days a year, with 218 days off including 13 weeks of vacation.

Fortunately you and I will not have to wait until the year 2000 to get some of the benefit of this trend. Every year we see an increasing population, a rising family income, and a growing tendency toward longer vacations and more of them.

You ladies and gentlemen have always been an essential part of the process of making air transportation economically feasible by working with us to create the demand that could justify the introduction of mechanical improvements. And we again need your help to convert this rising population, this increasing income and these lengthening vacations into millions of more airline passengers. The new air transport machines, as great as they are, could not exist unless men and women like yourselves can find the revenues to pay for them.

No matter how many new computers we buy, we will still need people. People will still answer telephones at reservations offices. People will still assist passengers aboard airplanes. People will still serve martinis aloft. In your offices people will still advise prospective travelers about how and where to go and what to see and how much it will cost. And this is what we must rely on to fill our airplanes.[10]

---

[10] *Congressional Record—Senate*, pp. S12069–S12070.

The Expository Mode

Step 6 consists of drawing the communication to an appropriate conclusion. The form may be a summary of the major points of the body, or it may be a capsule of the thought of the body. The variations in structure are many, and the speaker should select the one that is most appropriate in adapting the topic to his particular audience.

Exposition permeates man's activities, and the following is an illustration. John Quincy Adams, Professor of Rhetoric and Oratory at Harvard (1806–1809), author of *Lectures on Rhetoric and Oratory*, and sixth President of the United States, considered his inaugural address, March 4, 1825, to be expository. He concluded the exposition by saying:

> Fellow-citizens, you are acquainted with the peculiar circumstances of the recent election, which have resulted in affording me the opportunity of addressing you at this time. You have heard the exposition of the principles which will direct me in the fulfillment of the high and solemn trust imposed upon me in this station. Less possessed of your confidence in advance than any of my predecessors, I am deeply conscious of the prospect that I shall stand more and oftener in need of your indulgence. Intentions upright and pure, a heart devoted to the welfare of our country, and the unceasing application of all the faculties alloted to me to her service are all the pledges that I can give for the faithful performance of the arduous duties I am to undertake. To the guidance of the legislative councils, to the assistance of the executive and subordinate departments, to the friendly cooperation of the respective State governments, to the candid and liberal support of the people so far as it may be deserved by honest industry and zeal, I shall look for whatever success may attend my public service; and knowing that "except the Lord keep the city the watchman waketh but in vain," with fervent supplications for His favor, to His overruling providence I commit with humble but fearless confidence my own fate and the future destinies of my country.[11]

In the conclusion of his explication, President Adams related his exposition to what his new office expected of him: "fulfillment of the high and solemn trust imposed upon me in this station." The focus, then, of his search for meaning centered about, not himself or his party, but the "high and solemn trust imposed upon me." The implication of his closing remarks was that his was a fate imposed from the throne of God. In saying to his fellow-citizens that he would stand "more and oftener in need of your indulgence," he seemed to be asking not for sympathy but rather for the citizenry's identification with the principles with which

---

[11] *Inaugural Addresses of the Presidents of the United States from George Washington 1789 to Lyndon Baines Johnson 1965*, 89th Congress, 1st Session, House Document No. 51 (Washington: U.S. Government Printing Office, 1965), pp. 52–53.

he ran for the presidency and their understanding as he sought to implement those principles.

The following speech texts represent two variations of the expository mode. In both instances, the relationship between the nature of the topic and the audience seems to have determined the variation. Peter Valenti, the author of the first speech, presented his address to fellow students in a class in public address. Therefore, Mr. Valenti emphasized his major lines of thought. The second speech, by Dr. J. I. Bregman, was given before a professional audience concerned with a highly technical and specialized interest. Thus, Dr. Bregman presented appropriate technical data.

The Dollar Drain*

Step 1
Designate the topic.

International confidence in the U.S. Dollar is going down the drain — and it's easy to see why.

Step 2
Narrate background material.

Two weeks ago the United States had about $11 billion in gold to pay off dollar claims of over $30 billion against this gold. People around the world seriously began to doubt our ability to pay and started demanding gold for their dollars. Others joined them, fearing we would raise the price of gold to make our supply cover all our debts. Then hordes of outright speculators rushed into the market to buy gold — many of them with dollars. They were hoping we would have to raise our price; they would simply resell it for a tidy profit. The net result of all this: we lost a lot of gold, and the rest of the world lost confidence in our ability to stand behind our dollars.

A two price system for gold was established as a short-run solution. Under this plan, the principal noncommunist trading nations of the world agreed to buy and sell gold only among

*This speech was composed and delivered by Peter Valenti as a student in the basic public address course at Northern Michigan University, Marquette, Michigan, during the spring of 1968.

themselves and at a fixed price. They also agreed to allow speculators and anyone else interested in gold to buy it anywhere at any price.

This amounts to another chance for the United States to get behind its dollar. It enables foreign nations already holding dollars to continue to keep them—there is no immediate fear that we will raise the price of gold to pay off our debts. But foreign nations are still free to demand gold for their dollar holdings, and may do so if there is fear that our dollars will cheapen in other ways.

Failure to do something now could easily lead to a collapse of confidence. This would wipe out our gold supply and make the dollar unacceptable in world trade.

Step 3
Affirm the point of the speech.

One solution which would get to the heart of the problem would be to adopt a strong deflationary policy right now. Essentially this means higher taxes, reduced government spending, and tight money. You are probably wondering how I can stand here and advocate raising taxes and interest rates and cutting government spending. There would be two main effects of following a deflationary policy now.

Statement: The adoption of a strong deflationary policy by the United States would bring about two major effects.

Step 4
Partition the point of the speech.

First, it would help to reduce excess payments to foreign countries and, second, it would tend to make foreign nations more willing to hold dollars they receive.

Step 5
Explicate the point of the speech.

I. It would reduce the outflow of dollars into foreign hands.

I should now like to explain these advantages individually. First, a deflationary policy would help reduce our excess payments to foreign countries—dollar claims against our gold. It does this in several ways.

A. Deflationary taxes limit the spending of dollars abroad.

First, higher taxes, essentially on consumers, would reduce the amount of money available for spending purposes, and in turn the amount of money which can be spent on foreign goods. We would buy less from foreign nations simply because we would have less money to spend.

Another aspect of deflationary policy, tight money, is a second way of reducing our excess payments to foreign countries. Tight money means basically that high interest rates would make borrowing money expensive. It would make American businessmen less willing and less able to invest or lend money abroad because available capital would be expensive and difficult to get.

B. Deflationary policy reduces investment and lending abroad.

A third way deflationary policy would help reduce our excess payments to foreign countries is by reducing government spending. This is because government spending cuts quickly affect marginal programs. Direct monetary gifts to foreign countries are the most probable items to be cut. Again, fewer dollars would wind up in foreign hands.

C. Deflationary budget policy reduces monetary gifts to foreign nations.

Thus deflationary policy acts to reduce the outflow of dollars into foreign hands — dollars that are claims against our gold. This is the first important advantage of following a deflationary policy now.

The second main advantage of a deflationary program now is that it would tend to make foreign nations more willing to hold our dollars. There are two principal reasons for this.

II. It would tend to make foreign nations more willing to hold dollars they do get.

First, we would be solving our problems at our own expense — not at the expense of the rest of the world. Tax increases mean less money for you and me. Tight money would make borrowing more difficult and more expensive for consumers as well as businessmen. And, since foreign investment would be reduced, returns from foreign investments would be reduced — causing domestic business profits to fall off. These are sacrifices, but they are necessary if we're going to solve our real dollar problems.

A. A deflationary policy would show the world we are solving our problems at our own expense.

The second reason foreign nations would be willing to hold our dollars is that deflationary policy helps protect our dollars from inflation. This is because it directly attacks the basic causes of inflation in our country — excessive consumer demand, loose money, and unnecessary government spending. By showing foreign nations that our dollars would hold their value and not be eaten up by price rises, we would make it easier for them to keep the dollars they receive in international transactions.

B. Deflationary policy would prevent our dollars from cheapening quickly.

The Expository Mode

In short, a deflationary policy would reduce the number of dollars which find their way into foreign hands and can be exchanged for gold, and by fighting domestic inflation it would make foreign countries more willing to hold the dollars they do get.

Detection and Control of Water Pollution*

Step 1
Designate the topic.

Once upon a time the detection and control of water pollution was relatively simple. A serious epidemic due to water pollution could be traced to its source and corrected. The other effects of water pollution that plague us so badly today were minimal because of the relatively small population and the lack of industrialization.

As an example of this, when a sudden outbreak of cholera occurred in London in 1853, a bright London physician by the name of Dr. John Snow postulated that water might be the carrier. He mapped the occurrences of the cholera cases and found that they seemed to have one thing in common. All were in households which drew the water from one well located on Broad Street in the Soho District. Since Dr. Snow did not have a multimillion dollar research and development program going which would allow him to determine how to remove the infectious agent from the water, he had to choose a much simpler solution. That simple solution was to remove the pump handle from the well. It worked. The epidemic quickly came under control and the removal of the pump handle probably saved hundreds if not thousands of lives.

Things aren't so simple today. We can't cure water pollution by removing pump handles. It's true that drinking water doesn't transmit bacteriological diseases such as cholera, dysentery, diphtheria, and typhoid any more. However, we've ruined just

---

*Remarks by J. I. Bregman, Deputy Assistant Secretary of the Interior for Water Quality and Research, before the University of Illinois Colloquium on Man's Health and Environment, Champaign, Illinois, December 5, 1968. In June 1969, Dr. Bregman became president of Water Pollution Research & Applications, Inc., Baltimore, Maryland.

about every river system in this country today for the recreational, fishing, and even esthetic values that we prize so much. Practically no water in this country is fit for human consumption without continual addition of chlorine.

Step 2
Narrate background
material.

We are a nation of paradoxes. Today, in the midst of the greatest prosperity that any nation has ever enjoyed and with more creature comforts than were deemed possible in the wildest dreams of the mightiest emperors of the past, we literally wallow in luxury inside our homes. When we step outside, we literally wallow in filth. The air is dirty, our waters are contaminated and garbage and junked automobiles line our streets and highways.

Just as we are a nation of paradoxes, so are we a nation of crises. We let things go until a solution becomes urgent, and then, we want an answer right now. This is what has happened in the case of the pollution of our environment. We've awakened to the fact that it has reached crisis proportions and we are demanding an overnight answer to it. But there is no overnight answer to it. The days when we could call on Dr. John Snow to remove a pump handle from the well are gone. The solution to our environmental contamination problems today must be found in a lengthy and expensive sequence of steps involving legislation, development of technology, the imposition of adequate controls, and most important of all, the development of a new attitude towards our resources. We must wake up to the fact that America is no longer a land of plenty. We can no longer use up our resources indiscriminately because "there are always more where they came from." We now have to learn that there is not an endless supply of water or even air. We have to learn how to clean up our water so that we can use it again.

Step 3
Affirm the point
of the speech.

Even more important, we have to learn to practice preventative medicine in connection with all of our natural resources and particularly water. We have to learn that it is much cheaper not to pollute our waters in the first place. We have to learn that the waterways of this country resemble a giant human body that is already quite sick and has to be nursed back to health in a time-consuming and expensive process. Above all, just as we wouldn't continue to feed a sick man the things that made him sick in the first place, we must also greatly reduce the level of contaminants that we are pouring into our waters. Every dollar that we save by putting a contaminant into our rivers and lakes results in many many dollars that must be spent to take it out.

Step 4
Partition the point
of the speech.

Let's take a look at water pollution in this country. Specifically, let's look at the following questions:
Where does the pollution come from?
Why did we let it happen?
How much will the cleanup cost?

Step 5
Explicate the point
of the speech.

Where Does Pollution Come From?

Pollution comes from many sources. It is metal, mineral, chemical, organic, and radioactive matter. Some pollutants decompose, others do not. Some pollutants float, others sink, and others remain in suspension. Some pollutants you can smell and not see, others you can see and not smell. And there are pollutants which you can neither see nor smell, but which can kill you.

There is almost an infinite variety in pollution from as many sources.

Pollution is the run-off from huge animal feedlots. It is the seepage of acids from mines. It is mineral-laden return flow from irrigation systems. It is oil and phenol and cyanide. It is seepage from septic tanks and the waste-laden effluents from municipal and some federal sewage treatment plants so poorly designed or so poorly operated that they are barely worthy of the name. It is completely raw sewage from over 2000 U.S. communities.

Pollution is the surface run-off from city streets, and the mud that was once the topsoil of improperly managed fields. It is phosphates from detergents. It is wastes of all sorts from boats and ships. It is the used motor oils from service stations. It is the huge outpourings of wastes of all kinds and descriptions from industry.

Why Did We Let Pollution Happen?

Why did we let such pollution happen? Perhaps the simplest answer is that it just crept up on us. Years ago, before the population explosion and industrial expansion began, the supply of good quality water was taken for granted. Because we were clean-water rich, we developed bad habits and poor attitudes of waste and degrading quality of our natural resources. These habits and attitudes have not changed to keep pace with our growth. The result is we are now clean-water poor.

The main factors responsible for the pollution crisis are:

Population growth: The population of the United States began to grow at an annual rate of almost 2 percent after World War II. The 200 million people of today are expected to double in the next 50 to 60 years, placing staggering demands on our resources and, at the same time, increasing the production of wastes that threaten the cleanliness of the environment.

Urbanization and suburbanization: The move to the cities concentrates wastes and increases the level of pollution to hazardous proportions. Towns sprawl out and together in a megalopolis, eradicating open spaces and reducing the clean environment that could absorb and render harmless the increasing wastes. Today, everyone lives in someone else's backyard; everyone lives downwind or downstream from someone else. We can no longer throw our wastes carelessly away and expect them to harm no one.

Industrial expansion: The rapid growth of industry has in turn increased the per capita production of wastes. The production of goods requires energy and our production of electricity, a serious source of air and water pollution, has doubled every ten years since World War II. This rate is still increasing; today some estimate the the doubling time for future production will be only five years. The same industrial expansion not only puts out more wastes, but demands more clean available resources for the production cycle.

Higher individual incomes and expectations: When more consumer goods are used or consumed, wastes increase.

While more affluent Americans produce more wastes, they also demand more clean beaches and unpolluted waters for swimming, boating, and fishing.

New and increased use of technology: As fast as new technology is devised, it is thrust on the environment, often without the required research and precautions necessary to protect our living space. We must learn to control that technology and to require that new products and techniques must have built into them protection against their effects on the environment.

Until the last few years, these physical facts of pollution have been compounded by an attitude problem and an institutional failing.

The attitude problem is this: Most Americans and most American industrialists have considered our waters and, indeed, all of our environment as a free dump for their wastes. The American system thoughtfully and imaginatively considers and pays for acquiring raw materials, transforming them into goods, getting those goods to the markets and consuming them. There the cycle has ended — or so most Americans thought. You can just throw the remains of what we use and consume "away." But that's the rub. There is no more "away" in a populous, urban, technological society. One person's trash basket is another's living space. We all live downstream, or downwind from someone else.

Our lack of concern for the environment has, in part, resulted from our lack of understanding of how the environment works. Now, the science of ecology — the interrelatedness of things — is just becoming fashionable and commonly understood. For it is fact that as our waters have become polluted, the natural cleansing process has been stifled and the pollution increased rapidly.

What are we doing at federal, state and local levels about cleaning up our polluted waters?

In 1965 and 1966, Congress passed two major water pollution control bills unanimously. This legislation set the strategy for a cooperative nationwide attack on the problem.

The backbone of the national cleanup program is administered by the Department of the Interior in three segments: (1) the water quality standards; (2) substantial federal aid for comprehensive planning, research and development and for grants to municipalities to construct waste treatment works; and (3) legal enforcement for those times when positive incentives fail.

Before I discuss the water pollution control program of Interior, I would like to point out its relationship to the public health program administered by the Public Health Service in the Department of Health, Education, and Welfare.

The Public Health Service program—Water Supply and Sea Resources concerns water quality in two ways: (1) drinking water standards and (2) shellfish sanitation.

The drinking water standards were revised in 1962. The Public Health Service is presently revising these standards. They are now at the guideline stage. These standards apply to finished water; that is, water that comes out of your faucet after treatment. The water quality standards administered by Interior apply, by contrast, to raw water, or water in the stream, before water treatment is applied to make it drinkable. The water quality standards, however, incorporate the drinking water standards by reference.

The Public Health Service also directs the program of shellfish sanitation. Among its other functions in this area, the Service sets standards for shellfish waters—strict bacteriological standards and the like—and the water quality standards program of Interior sets identical or more strict standards for waters that produce shellfish.

Water Quality Standards

The 1965 Act provides that each state adopt water quality standards for all interstate and coastal waters and formulate a plan to implement and enforce those standards.

To set standards, the states were required to decide three important questions:

What are our goals? Specifically, what uses can and should be served by a particular stream or body of water?

A scientific decision as to the water characteristics that will permit these uses—dissolved oxygen, temperature, acidity, and so on, and

A schedule for remedial measures needed to achieve water of this quality defined city by city and industry by industry, as well as plans to legally enforce standards.

The states' role in the process, as drawn by the Act, is substantial. The states were given the first opportunity to adopt and submit to the Secretary of the Interior water quality standards for their interstate (including coastal) waters.

All fifty states, Puerto Rico, the Virgin Islands, and the District of Columbia exercised the initiative and chose to adopt and submit their own standards to the Secretary of the Interior by June 30 last year.

While the states made the initial decisions, the federal role in the standards setting process is also substantial.

The Secretary of the Interior is charged to review the states' submissions to assure that they are consistent with the requirements of the Clean Water Act. If the Secretary determines that the water quality criteria and plan of implementation and enforcement meet the intent of the Act, the standards become federal standards as well and are enforceable by the Federal Government.

Forty-two of the 50 states' standards have now been approved by the Secretary of the Interior as federal standards.

In reviewing states' submissions, the Department of the Interior follows these policies:

(1) *No degradation of existing water quality*: In order to "enhance the quality of the water," as required in the 1965 Act, standards shall include a provision to assure that present water quality will not be degraded except when the social and economic factors involved are compelling. This requires a careful study of each case and a conscious public decision by the state to make a specific exception.

(2) *No waters shall be used solely or principally as a waste carrier.*

(3) *All wastes must receive the best practicable treatment or control prior to discharge into any interstate water, unless it can be demonstrated that a lesser degree of treatment or control will provide for water quality enhancement commensurate with proposed present and future water uses.* In practice, we are seeking, and for the most part the states are making, a commitment in standards' implementation plans to secondary treatment for all municipal wastes within the next five years. A reasonably high degree of treatment or control is also being outlined by states for industry.

(4) *General acceptable range of values for key indicators of water quality,* such as temperature changes and levels of dissolved oxygen.

There are gaps in our information on the present quality of some waters and the natural requirements of aquatic life and the environment. The Secretary has determined that standards which he approves shall be set within safe limits, rather than at the extreme limit of what we believe aquatic life can tolerate. In this way, if new information proves us wrong, any error is on the side of protection, rather than destruction of an assigned use.

(5) *There must be consistency among standards of adjacent and downstream states:* We recognize that standards will vary to some extent in different parts of the country and in states with differing water use desires and financial and technical capabilities.

However, for common waters or adjoining sections of waterways, the standards must be consistent.

(6) To meet the goals established by the Act, *water quality standards must be adequate to protect and upgrade water quality in the face of population and industrial growth, urbanization and technological change.*

(7) *There shall be no exemptions from the standards* for a particular industry, or for a particular area.

(8) *Standards must be feasible and achievable:* Through all the standards setting process runs the important consideration of reasonableness. We do not seek clean water for its own sake, but for man's benefit. In balance, our clean water efforts must therefore be reasonable.

Federal Clean Water Aids

The states and local governments made a giant commitment when they — with the federal government — set water quality standards, a commitment to future action in terms of money, time, and technical knowhow.

We have in the Department of the Interior substantial financial and technical aids to help the states, communities and industries meet this commitment.

Here they are in summary:

(1) *Construction grants to communities* for waste treatment plants authorized at a level of $3.5 billion over a four-year period ending June 30, 1971. We have not yet seen this authorization translated into actual appropriated dollars to any substantial degree, but we are hopeful that it will happen in the coming session of Congress.

(2) A program of $20 million authorized per year to assist states and municipalities in the *development and demonstration of advanced waste treatment projects,* water purification methods, and new or improved methods of joint treatment of municipal and industrial wastes. The maximum federal share is 75 percent of project costs.

(3) A grants program authorizing $20 million a year for states and municipalities *to demonstrate new or improved methods of controlling discharges from combined sanitary and storm sewers.* The federal government can pay up to 75 percent of the costs.

(4) Grants to recruit cooperation and *participation of industry* against pollution, totaling $20 million a year, made directly to industry or private persons to aid in finding improved ways to treat industrial wastes. The maximum federal share is 70 percent of project costs.

(5) *Research funds* to develop more efficient and economic technology, through direct, contract and grant research, and field evaluations of promising solutions.

(6) *Comprehensive planning grants to state or interstate agencies* which represent all affected levels of government to develop

and implement comprehensive programs for water pollution control in each of the major river basins.

(7) *Grants to states or interstate pollution control agencies* to help develop sound programs.

(8) Technical assistance from the Federal Water Pollution Control Administration.

In summary, we have substantial federal funds and efforts committed to the cleanup. But it's important to remember we are asking the states, industry and communities for an even greater commitment.

How Much Will the Cleanup Cost?

Estimates for the five-year period 1969 through 1973 were developed by the Federal Water Pollution Control Administration and submitted to the Congress in a January 1968 report. They indicate:

(1) Costs of constructing needed municipal waste treatment plants and interceptor sewers are about $8.0 billion during this five-year period. This assumes a level of secondary treatment in most cases.

(2) Construction of sanitary collection sewers will require an additional estimated $6.2 billion.

(3) Facilities to treat industrial wastes to a reasonably high degree of treatment is estimated to be in the range of $2.6 to $4.6 billion.

Step 6
Conclude the explication.

Conclusion

In closing, let me say that I think this nation has what it takes for clean water.

We have the technical know-how for effective pollution control and even better information is coming forth every day.

We have a positive strategy for clean water in the water quality standards. These will soon be set for the entire nation. They will be enforced and, if changes are made, standards are likely to become stronger, not weaker.

The President has ordered clean water in the strongest directive on the subject in our nation's history.

The Congress backs clean water. Both major water pollution control bills passed unanimously in 1965 and 1966.

But most important the vast majority of the American people are militantly anti-pollution. More perceive and oppose pollution today. A recent poll indicates nearly 90 percent of Americans support a vigorous clean water program.

With these ingredients the conclusion is clear. We will have clean water.

Conclusion

Clearly, the expository process is integrally related to effective adaptation of ideas to hearers. Exposition may be either the controlling mode or a subordinate segment used to initiate the *meaning* ⟶ *identification* ⟶ *persuasion* sequence. The communicator should be particularly alert to the potential for initiating enthymematic reasoning in the expository mode.

An unintelligible exposition is no exposition. Therefore, in constructing his exposition the speaker must make certain that he is (1) precise and (2) clear. In addition, he should be forceful.

In presenting his exposition, the communicator should follow six steps:

Step 1: Designate the topic.

Step 2: Narrate background material.

Step 3: Affirm the point of the speech.

Step 4: Partition the point of the speech.

Step 5: Explicate the point of the speech.

Step 6: Conclude the explication.

Suggested Readings

Ray, Jack, and Harry Zavos. Chap. 4, "Reasoning and Argument: Some Special Problems and Types." *Perspectives on Argumentation,* eds. Gerald R. Miller and Thomas R. Nilsen. Chicago: Scott, Foresman and Co., 1966. Pp. 103–106. This excellent reading contains information about the relation between explanation and argument.

Wilcox, Roger P. *Oral Reporting in Business and Industry.* Englewood Cliffs, N.J.: Prentice-Hall, 1967. Pp. 24–28. This segment is outstanding for its clarity and for its relevance to exposition.

Winans, James Albert. *Public Speaking: Principles and Practice.* Ithaca, N.Y.: Sewell Publishing Co., 1915. Chap. XI, "The Expository Speech." This chapter further explicates the expository mode.

Suggested Assignments

1. Select a topic in the expository mode and do the following:
   a. Complete the statement: "I want my audience to believe that . . ."
   b. Give a satisfactory answer to the question: "Why do I want this audience to believe this specific point?"
   c. Give a satisfactory answer to the question: "Why would the expository mode of communication best enable me to adapt my thought to this group of hearers?"

2. Construct an expository thought analysis for your speech in that mode.

3. Write out your introduction and your conclusion.

4. Write out a segment of your speech centered about any one division with its subdivisions.

5. Present a speech in the expository mode.

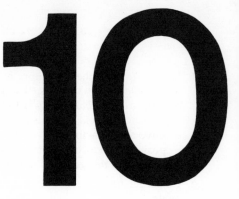

The Defects
Mode

In this chapter, I discuss the defects mode in terms of adapting the speaker's thought to the thinking of hearers. As you read this chapter, you should remember that the defects mode symbolizes an approach. *Thus, the format or paradigm — although typical — must be considered flexible and therefore subject to modification as determined by the relationship of the speaker's thought to the audience.*

You should take special note of the two examples of speeches. The student example is in the typical defects mode and was well suited to the speaker's audience. On the other hand, the professional example is atypical, but it too was well suited to the speaker's audience. If you had been either speaker, would you have handled the material any differently?

The thesis underlying the defects mode of communication[1] asserts that one can solve certain problems best by eliminating rather than altering the defects. In the economic, social, and political areas, for example, one might argue that capital punishment should be abolished or that the electoral college should be abolished. Wherever a structural defect exists, one might argue that capital punishment should be abolished or that the

[1] For the leading alternative to this mode see Chapter 11, The Advantages Mode.

relationship between the speaker's thought and his hearers suggests that discussing defects would be more effective than emphasizing advantages, then the speaker should employ the defects mode.

A format for the defects mode follows:

Step 1: Employ a case history. } (Introduction)
Step 2: Show the extent of the problem.

Step 3: Present the solution.
    A. Affirm the solution in one sentence. } (Body)
    B. Present any machinery.
    C. Show arguments for the solution in terms of defects.

Step 4: *Urge* the adoption of the solution and *summarize* the reasons. (Conclusion)

Step 1 of the defects mode (the case history) promotes the two-fold purpose of an introduction by (1) revealing the speaker's character and (2) focusing the audience's attention. The case history points explicitly to the *nature* of the problem; and in focusing the attention of hearers on the nature of the problem, the speaker also reveals his character to his hearers. By his selection and portrayal of the case history, the speaker either identifies with good causes or divides from bad causes and thus reveals his character to his hearers.[2]

In order to make Step 1 as effective as possible, the case history should involve persons who are sufficiently like the hearers in character and in circumstances. In addition, the speaker should, through the case history, point out to his hearers that persons like themselves are even then suffering from the problem under discussion and that others who are stronger—or in a less vulnerable position—have experienced the problem. Further, the speaker should show, where possible, that others suffered those evils (1) at the hands of unexpected persons, (2) in an unexpected form, or (3) at an unexpected time.[3] In these ways the speaker can lead the hearers to find meaning in the case history and, therefore, to identify with the implicit need to solve the problem. Thus, Step 1 relates inherently to adapting the thought of the speaker to the mind of the hearer.

For example, in arguing for the abolition of capital punishment, the speaker should select an instance of the execution of an innocent man. Such a case history would attract great attention, and nothing would be more apt to focus the attention of hearers on the problem. In particular, the speaker would be identifying himself with the principle of protecting the lives of the innocent. By such identification, he would project the image of a "good man" and aid his efforts to adapt his thesis to his audience. Thus, Step 1 should initiate the process of adaptation, with its ultimate goal of persuasion.

---

[2] See Aristotle, *Rhetoric*, 1356al-20, also 1367b28-1368a9.
[3] See *Rhetoric*, 1383a8-12.

Step 2 reveals that the case history, far from being an isolated happenstance, is representative of a condition of sufficient significance to society to warrant concern and action. Ordinarily, the speaker shows the extent of the problem in statistical form. However, he also may show the extent by illustrating the pervasiveness of the problem. For example, with regard to arguing for the abolition of capital punishment, the speaker would be much less concerned with the number of executions of innocent men than he would be with the occurrence of *any* cases and with the *potententiality* for the occurrence of other such cases. Most of all, the speaker likely would emphasize the pervasiveness of the problem by pointing out that, so long as capital punishment exists, an innocent man *could be* executed. By his showing extent through pervasiveness, the speaker can promote adaptation to the hearer; for, after all, any hearer *could be* that innocent man.

Step 3A is a simple, declarative sentence setting forth the speaker's thesis or proposition. This step is the statement of the thought analysis — the answer to the question "What do I want my audience to believe?" For instance, with regard to the previous example, one might argue simply that "Capital punishment should be abolished." By thus stating his point concisely and precisely, the communicator would promote adaptation to the hearers by sharpening the focus on the solution to the problem.

In *Step 3B,* the communicator presents any machinery necessary to implement the solution. The nature of the problem and of the proposed solution determines the structure of the machinery. For instance, in urging the abolition of capital punishment, one would need only to propose legislation to abolish capital punishment. On the other hand, if one were to propose to abolish the electoral college, he would be obligated to tell his hearers how he would go about electing a president. Although the speaker obviously could not give every minute detail, he would be expected to provide the essential features of his system to replace the electoral college.

The sole reason that the speaker presents the machinery for implementing his proposal is to enable his hearers to perceive how the plan would facilitate the elimination of the defects of the existing structure. Thus, the presentation of the plan in Step 3B is an integral part of the total process that the speaker employs to adapt his thought to the hearer.

Step 3C represents the heart of the body of the speech — the thought analysis.[4] Inasmuch as the thought analysis represents the greatest effort of the speaker to establish his thesis, it represents also his greatest effort to adapt. The speaker should select and arrange his best arguments at this point so as to facilitate maximum adaptation. The speaker, first of all, should examine the analysis as a whole to determine whether it would stand by itself. Next, the speaker should examine each argument to determine whether, by itself, it is rational and plausible. Finally, the speaker

[4] For further information regarding the thought analysis, see Chapter 6, Proof: The Thought Analysis.

should examine each item of evidence to determine both whether it supports the argument to which it structurally relates and whether it is plausible. Both rationality and plausibility are requisite characteristics for adaptation, but plausibility is critical. If either the argument or evidence is implausible *to the hearer,* then the hearer certainly will not find that it relates to his quest for meaning.

Each argument in the defects mode represents a defect, and the items of evidence must support the argument appropriately and should follow the evidence triad.[5] For example, if one argues that "capital punishment is exacted predominantly from the poor," then, in order to adapt the argument to the hearers, he needs to provide evidence that would show the argument, first of all, to be true and, second, to be plausible to the hearers. The speaker then should provide a case history of a poor person who was executed. The speaker should quantify the illustration in terms of statistics or other form of pervasiveness, and he should finish adapting the argument by employing appropriate testimonial evidence. The speaker should follow this same procedure for all other arguments.

Step 4 (the conclusion) brings the communication smoothly to an effective close. Inasmuch as the conclusion presumably contains the last words that the communicator utters to his audience, he should be very certain that he leaves the clearest impression of the arguments supporting his thesis. The communicator's conclusion is his final attempt to adapt his statement to the audience.

The following speeches—the first by a student, the second by a professional person—illustrate two approaches to implementation of the defects mode. These variations reinforce the critical notion that *one always adjusts the mode of communication to the thought and never adjusts the topic to the mode.*

---

[5] For information on the evidence triad, see Chapter 6, Proof: The Thought Analysis.

Abolition of Final Examinations*

Step 1
Give a case history
illustrating the problem.

Last semester a nineteen-year-old friend of mine came home from East Carolina University with the sad news that he had been dropped from school for low grades.

---

*This speech was composed and delivered by G. H. Conner while a student in the basic public address course at Park College, Kansas City, Missouri.

The Defects Mode   143

Jim was but one of over 100,000 students who were dropped from our nation's colleges last year for that reason. Although many can trace their low grades to lack of effort or aptitude, others were like my friend who did better than average daily work but could not pass his semester exams. Actually, final exams do little more than allow students to be ranked — and this I believe can be better done with grades based on quizzes and papers.

Step 3
Present the solution to
the problem.

Statement: Semester exams
should be abolished.

Therefore, I believe that semester finals should be abolished. I believe this for two major reasons. One, final exams are an inadequate measure of knowledge gained; and second, final exams on occasion are a health hazard.

I. Semester finals are an
inadequate measure of
knowledge gained.

Let me talk first about the reasons that I believe that the semester exam is an inadequate measure of knowledge gained. Have you ever taken an exam and have left the room only to remember an answer that you could not recall because of the stress of exam taking? I'm sure you all have. How many of you have flunked an exam when the knowledge was there but could not be recalled? None, I hope. However, many have. The percentage is probably higher than generally believed. A recent study at a military installation showed that a student's recall ability improved by 13 percent when the stress of a final exam was removed from the testing situation. W. Lee Garner, a leading proponent of programmed instruction, believes in continuous testing rather than on special occasions such as during term finals. According to Dr. Garner, "Testing should be an integral continuous part of the learning process."

A. Emotional stresses
generated at exam
time inhibit recall
ability.

B. A menstrual period
adversely affects the
recall ability of coeds.

A second reason why semester exams are not an adequate measure of knowledge gained was documented by psychologist Katharina Dalton. She had long suspected that a woman's menstrual period affected her recall ability, so while teaching at a girls' school set out to test her hypothesis. In her study of 180 teenage girls, she found that a woman's recall ability could be reduced by as much as 35 percent if she were tested

Chapter Ten

during either her menstrual period or in the four days preceding her menstrual period. Although Dr. Dalton's recommendation is not so extreme as mine, it certainly lends weight to any argument to abolish final exams. She recommends that "The obvious handicap of the menstruating woman *vis-á-vis* men and her non-menstruating classmates should be rectified by giving two exams eight days apart." It seems to me, however, that abolition is the *best* solution.

II. Semester finals are a health hazard.

I'm sure you have been wondering just what health hazard could possibly be associated with semester exam taking, so let's look now at that reason for abolishing final exams. Bob C. recently graduated *summa cum laude* from one of the nation's major universities. "A real honor," you say. I would agree if it were not for the price Bob has paid and is paying. In cramming for his first set of final exams, Bob used pep pills. It worked so well that Bob continued to use them, not only for semester exams, but for all tests. And when he left college he took the habit with him. He now uses a pep pill to turn on with in the morning and a sleeping pill to turn off with at night. I'm sure you will all agree that Bob is headed for serious health problems. Bob is not an isolated case. A recent press study showed that 23 percent of college students who habitually use stimulant type drugs can trace their first use to all-night cramming sessions.

A. The first use of pep pills by college students can often be traced to all-night cramming sessions.

Stephen Minot in his article "Examining the Examination" raises the question as to whether the final exam is really serving any useful purpose. I quote: "Most instructors know before the final examination is given what grade he will give each student. In all but the largest lecture courses, he has been forming opinions about each student throughout the term. Further, most instructors consciously or unconsciously doctor final examinations to fill those preconceived evaluations."

B. The stress of taking final exams can cause nervous breakdowns.

And finally we come to Susan A., who when confronted with her first set of term finals suffered a nervous breakdown. I am happy to report Susan eventually recovered and did graduate from college. However, her doctor believes that if it hadn't been for the semester finals, Susan probably would not have had a nervous breakdown.

The extent of this problem, although not documented in numbers, is pointed up by John C.

Abbott of Arizona State University who, in a recent discussion on grading, stated: "The students have a variety of problems concerning tests that play on the emotional side of their lives. There are those students who actually get physically ill at the very thought of a final exam."

Even though John C. Abbott does not go the full route and advocate the abolition of the final exam, he certainly raises a question as to its usefulness.

Step 4
Conclusion and appeal for the adoption of the solution.

To conclude, I urge that semester exams be abolished because they are an inadequate measure of knowledge gained, and they can create health problems. Further, a professor who has not been remiss in his duties in conducting an intellectual interchange with his students is able to assign valid grades based upon the student's accomplishments, including quizzes, throughout the semester.

Oil Pollution and the Law*

Oil is the life blood of our modern industrial society. It fuels the machines and lubricates the wheels of the world's production.

Step 1
Present a case history.

But when that vital resource is out of control, it can destroy marine life and devastate the environment and economy of an entire region. The costs of the *Torrey Canyon* disaster, for example, are still being counted. 100,000 birds and millions of fish were killed. Over 100 miles of Cornish coast were soaked in an oily slime that further washed across the Channel to ruin French beaches. Vacation seasons and tourist economies were decimated. The cleanup costs to the British Government alone were about $8 million in addition to the expenditures incurred by local government and private business.

*Remarks by Max N. Edwards, Assistant Secretary for Water Pollution Control, U.S. Department of the Interior, Washington, D.C., before the International Conference on Oil Pollution of the Sea, Rome, Italy, October 8, 1968.

Chapter Ten

Step 2
Present a quantification.

The plain facts are that the technology of oil—its extraction, its transport, its refinery and use—has outpaced laws to control that technology and prevent oil from polluting the environment. In short, oil is largely out of legal control. It is out of legal control in the United States and around the world.

Step 3
Present the solution.

I recommend new laws be passed in the United States to close the serious gap between oil technology and the law. I recommend, too, that we close the gap in our international controls of oil pollution. We have an international convention on oil pollution, but it is so inadequate—it is so seriously out of date—so unable to cope with present pollution potential, that we in the United States believe it must be replaced. We must close the gap between the sources of oil pollution and the law and put oil—the threat of spills and cleanup—under legal control. The survival of our crucial marine environment is at stake.

Step 4
Present the basic defect.

Oil pollution of the seas is both a national problem for all coastal countries and an international problem.

Pollution respects no national boundaries. Oil dumped onto the high seas can slosh into the internal waters of any coastal nation and onto its beaches. Vessels constructed in one country, registered in another, and owned in still another move in and out of ports around the globe. Some of these tankers are safe and carefully run, yet seldom controlled by law. Others are obsolete and negligently operated by crews of questionable skill and experience.

Step 5
Prove the defect.

Let us focus on the *Torrey Canyon* again as the classic example of the international complexities of oil pollution. Five nations are involved. The Barracuda Tanker Company of Bermuda, a subsidiary of Union Oil Company of Los Angeles, California, owned the vessel. For tax purposes, the ship was leased by the subsidiary to the parent company, and it was registered in Monrovia and flew the Liberian flag. The crew was Greek and she was on a charter to the British Petroleum Company.

The legal complications are legion. The vessel was not British and crashed outside British territorial waters, beyond the area in which that government has clear authority to act. But escaping oil threatened the British realm. To complicate matters, the vessel was not abandoned, in the sense of maritime law, for some time, so the British government could not legally take charge of the situation.

By the time it was decided who had legal authority to deal in an effective way with the *Torrey Canyon,* two thirds of the oil had escaped.

Responsibility for the damages caused by the tanker presented a unique number of legal questions concerning venue, jurisdiction, recourse and the extent of damages.

When the British government sought to recover from the tanker owners it was not clear where liability rested or where suit should be filed. An action could be brought in the United States (where Union Oil was based), in Bermuda (where the Barracuda Tanker Company was registered), in Liberia (where the ship was registered), or even in the British courts. Since there is little uniformity in maritime law throughout the world, the amount of recovery sought would depend upon the country in which the action was filed.

The legal ripples from the hulk on Cornwall's Seven Stones Reef will be felt around the world for years. And it is clear today that the legal inadequacies of oil pollution control turned a spill into a disaster, with unnecessary delays, damage, and loss of money to governments and citizens.

After the *Torrey Canyon,* the world was alerted to the need for accelerated oil pollution controls. Of course, there are countless chances for oil to pollute from stationary sites — at terminals, water-side industrial plants, pipelines, refineries, docks, and off-shore oil drilling sites, sunken tankers, and natural oil seeps.

But the greatest threat to the marine environment comes during oil's transport — when oil moves across the seas and is loaded, unloaded, transferred, and cleaned up. It is here we must tighten our legal controls.

Huge tanker disasters, as dramatic as they are, are not the major source of oil pollution. The most serious pollution comes from the thousands of insidious incidents — small ones, but preventable — incidents of countless, minor dumpings and spills from thousands of tanker operations — from emptying salt water ballast, pumping bilge waters, cleaning oil tanks, transferring and handling oil cargos.

In 1966, only 6 tankers were actually sunk at sea. This amounts to less than 0.1 percent of the tankers in operation. But of course when such a major tanker mishap occurs, the results are devastating because of the great volumes of oil that escape and persist in the entire marine environment.

Think of the pollution potential — about 1 out of every 5 vessels transports oil — oil amounting to 700 million tons in 1966 — about half of all goods transported at sea from the standpoint of cargo weight. And these tankers are busy. There were about 10,000 tanker visits to the United States' ports alone in 1966.

Tankers are getting bigger, too, so there are greater volumes of oil to spill. The average tanker size in 1955 was 16,000 tons. The tankers turned out lately average 76,000 tons, and some tankers being delivered now exceed 300,000 tons. Remember the *Torrey Canyon* carried 119,000 tons. Tankers are so big now that the two officers of the new 1,010 foot British tanker *Esso Mercia* were recently given bicycles to make it easier to patrol the 166,820-ton vessel's decks.

Step 6
Existing law is
inadequate.

State of the Law

Let's look at the legal capability — nationally and internationally — to prevent and clean up these major and minor spills and recover damages which they create.

The International Convention for the Prevention of Pollution of the Seas by Oil, 1954, as amended by the Conference of Contracting Governments, is a direct approach toward international control of oil pollution from vessels. Thirty-eight contracting governments are members of this — the only international agreement on oil. This Convention is implemented in the United States by the *Oil Pollution Act of 1961,*[1] as amended. This Convention:

Defines prohibited zones (offshore bands, 50 or 100 miles wide) in which discharges of oil are regulated.

Requires logging of oil discharges and losses.

Obliges signatory governments to promote the installation of oil-receiving facilities in their ports.

Sets procedures for apprehension and prosecution of vessels which violate the provisions of the Convention.

The U.S. Coast Guard enforces these provisions in the United States waters. The International Maritime Consultative Organization, a body of the United Nations, has study and recommending power in the area of oil pollution, but has no enforcement authority.

We in the United States are vitally concerned with the problems of oil pollution. One million tons of petroleum products move up and down our coasts and inland waters each day, past valuable estuaries, fish spawning grounds, resorts and vacation beaches. An estimated 2,000 oil spills occurred in our waters in 1966 alone. We have enacted several laws to control oil pollution in our nation, in addition to those provisions of the International Convention. It is clear, though, in the United States, just as it is clear in the international arena, that these laws are not sufficiently effective.

The Federal Water Pollution Control Act,[2] as amended, is an important U.S. tool in the prevention of water pollution from shore facilities. The Act requires the states to establish enforceable water quality standards applicable to interstate waters. Development of these standards is underway. These standards must be approved by the Secretary of the Interior and must protect public health and wel-

[1] 33 U.S.C. 1001 *et seq.*
[2] 33 U.S.C. 466 *et seq.*

fare and enhance the quality of the water. If a state fails to establish acceptable standards, the Secretary of the Interior is empowered to adopt such standards.

The water quality standards and their enforcement is one of the most effective methods of preventing pollution of a continuing nature. However, the time period between notice of a violation and its abatement is unreasonably long in the case of sudden, nonrecurring pollution incidents.

The Oil Pollution Act, 1924,[3] as amended, now makes unlawful, with some exceptions, the "grossly negligent" or "willful" discharge of oil from a vessel into U.S. navigable waters and adjoining shorelines. The Act applies to foreign and domestic vessels within our territorial sea and navigable inland waters. The Act establishes both civil and criminal sanctions for violations. Excepted from liability are cases related to emergencies imperiling life or property, and unavoidable accidents, collisions, or stranding, and those cases where discharges are permitted by regulations established by the U.S. government.

The Convention on the Territorial Sea and the Contiguous Zone, 1958, permits the United States to exercise within a 9-mile zone contiguous to its 3-mile territorial sea the control necessary to prevent the infringement of its "sanitary regulations within its territory or territorial sea."

There is debate within the United States whether the U.S. can enforce within the 12-mile band the measures now available to us in the 3-mile territorial waters under the Oil Pollution Act, 1924, as amended.

Some contend the Convention, by its ratification by Congress, becomes enforceable; others say that specific enforcing statutes must be enacted to implement the Convention. This question has not been resolved, but the President has recommended to the Congress legislation to specially implement the 1958 Convention and extend control of oil pollution to the contiguous zone.

The U.S. government has mobilized all its existing authority to cope with spills of oil and other hazardous substances. We have developed a set of contingency plans, tailored to various parts of our nation, involving all talent and equipment available to the U.S. government under existing laws. The president ordered the most effective system devised to discover and report a pollution incident, stop the spread of oil, clean up and dispose of the pollutants, and institute available legal action to recover cleanup costs and enforce other federal statutes. The plans will operate in our inland, coastal and territorial waters, the contiguous zone and the high seas beyond this zone, where there exists a threat to United States waters, shores or continental shelf.

Closing the Gap

We in the United States have done a great deal under existing authority to control oil pollution. The Intergovernmental Maritime

---

[3]33 U.S.C. 431 et seq.

Consultative Organization (IMCO), a specialized agency of the United Nations, has proceeded under the limited authority of the oil pollution Convention.

But clearly this is not enough. Massive oil pollution continues and will surely worsen if steps are not taken to close the gap between our growing technology and outdated laws.

Even if our laws are updated, we still face the question of whether we can stop pollution by oil. Probably not entirely. But I firmly believe it will be significantly reduced. Most oil pollution, after all, is from intentional cleanings and dumpings and human negligence. The major pollution of the sea from oil can be prevented. We must convince the producers, the shippers and dealers of oil that pollution prevention makes good sense. Several major oil companies in America, for example, have initiated effective pollution controls on their own vessels and operations. They advertise this, for they are sensitive to growing public demands for clean water.

What are the specific changes needed to close the gap and put oil under legal control both in the United States and the international arena?

Step 7
Present the machinery
to solve the problem.

Deterrent: In the first place, dumping oil at sea—either intentionally or through a preventable accident—must be made too costly to continue. Penalties must be tough and enforcement vigorous.

Under present U.S. law, an oil discharge must be "grossly negligent or willful" to be illegal. Proof of gross negligence is a difficult task in any court. Legislation recommended by my department would delete this criterion to make enforcement more effective. We asked that all oil discharges be made unlawful, except unavoidable accidents, collision, or stranding. These amendments, which the Senate has passed, would apply criminal penalties to willful discharges. Civil penalties would apply in all but those excepted cases I just mentioned. The criminal penalty is a fine not to exceed $2500 and/or by 1 year imprisonment. The civil penalty is limited to a $10,000 fine. In addition, any oil discharger would be responsible for all costs of oil pollution cleanup, except when the discharge was due to an act of God.

Another controversy with which we in the United States must ultimately deal is whether liability should attach to shore installations and off-shore drilling operations. In this matter it is significant to know that in 1966, 40 percent of the oil spills in our nation were caused by discharges from shore installations.

In international waters we have no effective oil pollution deterrent either. Enforcement of the requirements set forth by the International Convention on Oil Pollution is not credible. There are no teeth in the prohibition against dumping in certain zones because the reporting of violations is on the honor system. Unfortunately, the pangs of a sea captain's conscience are not an adequate deterrent to oil pollution. IMCO has no enforcement authority and the high seas are unpatrolled.

Any Convention to prevent pollution needs enforcement authority and more funds to hire enforcement personnel. IMCO today operates at a funding level of about $1 million per year, making it one of the most poorly financed organizations of the United Nations.

Financial responsibility: The best deterrent to oil pollution is making those who could cause pollution financially responsible for the damages.

Amendments to U.S. law proposed by our executive branch and passed by the Senate would require vessel and shore installation owners to remove the discharged oil from U.S. waters or pay cleanup costs, in all cases, except where the spill was due to an act of God. The amendments would also authorize our Secretary of the Interior to clean up the oil from waters and shorelines when the discharger failed to act and to send the bill to the pollutor.

We believe that payment to those who suffer should not be paid out of general revenues of governments or by levies against the product. This simply does not provide the incentive needed to prevent oil pollution. Furthermore, it is clearly not equitable to make the public pay for the mistakes or accidents of a few.

On the international front—on the high seas—the cleanup of spilled oil, not removed by the discharger, is another question. In this case, it would seem most appropriate to extend the legal rights of a coastal state to act—a coastal state which may have no direct interest in a ship or its cargo, but which is threatened by spilled oil.

I would like to examine the elements of financial responsibility that should be covered by a new international Convention. These are the elements: Who should be financially responsible for oil pollution damages? When should he be responsible? For what damages and to what extent? Where should the Convention prevail? How do we assure financial responsibility? Who should be financially responsible in a new Convention?

Who: Who should be financially responsible for the costs of cleanup and damages under the provisions of a new Convention?

Internationally, the carrier may now secure insurance for various risks and he usually does. It would be logical, then, for the carrier to assume the same responsibility for any risks added by a new Convention. By a carrier, I mean the ship owner or person who has the charter, depending on the terms of the charter. Some provision should be made, too, for the carrier to recover from a negligent owner or operator of another vessel in collision situations.

Specifically, the innocent carrier should be able to recover the full extent of his pollution costs from the negligent carrier.

When: When should the party be financially responsible—be liable—for pollution damages under a new Convention? In fixing liability, it should be recognized that there are some advocates who strongly believe in invoking the "doctrine of absolute liability," which fixes the blame regardless of the degree of care used or negligence involved. These proponents insist that because of the nature of the industry and the inherent quality of oil, that liability without fault or absolute liability is necessary to adequately protect against pollution from oil. They feel that assuming the risk of accidental oil pollution must be assumed as a regular cost of doing business.

Others contend that the degree of proof should be limited to "ordinary negligence" because absolute liability would impose too harsh a judgment of conduct on the oil producer, carriers, and dealers.

What: For what should a carrier be financially responsible? Pollution—in all its forms of discharges. The next Convention should not cover just the damages from oil pollution. We are now aroused—and properly so—by the disaster of the *Torrey Canyon*. But it would be false logic to design a Convention just to prevent another *Torrey Canyon*, only to have the next pollution disaster be sulfuric acid or methane gas or concentrated insecticide. We need not be one Convention behind the next major pollution disaster. The Convention should cover pollution damage from any cargo. Perhaps we could simply define pollution as a kind of specified damage to third parties from any source. The damage covered should only be limited by a requirement of proximate cause and proof of loss, not by type of damage or by class of persons or property affected.

The damage from all kinds of pollution, then, should be covered, but for how much of that damage should a carrier be liable? In other words, should there be a limitation of liability, considering the magnitude of damages we have experienced in some of the major disasters?

Today, and since 1851, U.S. law, much like British law, permits a shipowner to limit his liability to the value of the ship after the casualty, plus the value of the cargo. After the *Morro-Castle* disaster, the so-called Sirovich Amendment was added. This makes the shipowner also liable for $60 per gross ton for both property and personal injuries. But the damages done in a major oil pollution incident—or sometimes even a minor one—far exceed the salvage value of the ship and cargo, even with that $60 a ton limitation.

The question should be answered quite simply whether any limitation would be in the best interests of protecting the public. The industry quite frankly contends that it is financially unable to operate under the terms of a law or policy invoking unlimited liability. They contend that it would be impossible to insure against such a risk and insist upon fixing a reasonable limit to any liability that might be incurred in oil spill damage. In judging both questions of absolute and unlimited liability, many scholars have said that the most proper and equitable compromise is to invoke liability without fault but with a reasonable limit on the recovery of damages.

In any event, the limit on liability, however, should be large enough and flexible enough to realistically cover the costs of pollution damage. Several limits have been suggested—an absolute amount of $30 million per incident, or perhaps a set sum per ton, such as $250. One limit would be appropriate for one cargo, another more appropriate for another product.

Where: The new Convention should certainly govern pollution control of the high seas. If the Convention could effectively protect the interests of the coastal nations, then the territorial and inland waters could be covered as well. There is a practical problem, here, though. Two or more sets of standards might prevail, depending upon the exact location of an oil pollution incident. This is particularly true because some nations claim as much as 200 miles or more for their territorial sea, others claim only 3.

As to jurisdiction in an injury suit, the U.S. government believes that a jurisdictional provision is essential for an effective Convention. The provision should permit private parties injured by pollution to bring suit in their own state for any part of damages which occurred in that state.

Enforcing judgments—that's a difficult problem. Perhaps, where more than one country's nationals have claims, the limitation fund should be deposited in one country where most or at least a large part of the damage took place. Provision should then be made for satisfaction of foreign judgments against that fund on the same basis as domestic judgments.

In addition, jurisdiction should not be based upon seizure of a person.

How: How under the terms of a new Convention do we assure financial responsibility? This is such an important element of oil pollution control that some proof of responsibility should be required. Insurance is the obvious method. Some companies, however, may be capable of self insurance, and these should only be required to post a bond.

Proof might well be demonstrated by a certificate, that a sea captain would have to show upon entering a nation's waters, as well as keep on the high seas.

Ship construction and operations: A new Convention should also provide the means to set worldwide standards for the construction and operation of vessels carrying hazardous materials.

We must support proposals along these lines which the International Marine Consultative Organization is now studying.

Traffic lanes at sea are needed, too. The International Marine Consultative Organization should set up such sealanes. IMCO is now considering such action.

Step 8
Present the
conclusion.

Summary

These controls—legally imposed—will deter oil pollution, clean up spills and recover costs from oil incidents. These will close the gap between oil technology and the law.

The principle the United States observes in closing this gap is that we should establish, immediately, within our nation, the necessary controls to protect our own shores and waters. But, in addition, and simultaneously, we are seeking effective controls worldwide. It necessarily takes many nations longer to act than it takes one nation to act unilaterally. We know this, and also know know that we in the United States must do everything we can to protect our shores and waters now. We know, too, however, that the final solution will come only when all the maritime nations of the world adopt suitable pollution controls.

The United States endorses universal maritime action, supports it, and is working for international action.

Conclusion

The communicator should consider selecting the defects mode whenever the evil or harm involved represents a significant obstacle to the hearer's being able to realize his own meaning. Obviously, under such conditions, the hearer should find meaning in a proposal to eliminate the obstacle or threat. For example, if a student in Mr. Conner's audience had ever felt his future as a student (part of his life's meaning) to have been threatened, then that student would have found as meaningful Mr. Conner's arguments to get rid of the threat. Or again, since Mr. Edwards' hearers were professionally interested in solving the specific problem of oil pollution on the seas, particularly as related to the beaches of nations, each hearer should have had no difficulty finding meaning in the speech.

If one desires to emphasize elimination of an evil, then he should follow the defects mode format:

Step 1: Employ a case history.

Step 2: Show the extent of the problem.

Step 3: Present the solution.
    A. Affirm the solution in one sentence.
    B. Present any machinery.
    C. Show arguments for the solution in terms of defects.

Step 4: *Urge* the adoption of the solution and *summarize* the reasons.

Suggested Readings

Walter, Otis M., and Robert L. Scott. *Thinking and Speaking: A Guide to Intelligent Oral Communication.* New York: Macmillan Co., 1962. Pp. 127–133. This is a valuable section focusing on presenting a problem to an audience.

Wilcox, Roger P. *Oral Reporting in Business and Industry.* Englewood Cliffs, N.J.: Prentice-Hall, 1967. Pp. 48–55. This section is a particularly lucid statement of one way to employ the defects mode.

For additional references useful to this topic, see the suggested readings for Chapter 11.

Suggested Assignments

1. Select a topic in the defects mode and do the following:
    a. Complete the statement "I want my audience to believe that . . ."
    b. Give a satisfactory answer to the question "Why do I want this audience to believe this specific point?"
    c. Give a satisfactory answer to the question "Why would the defects mode of communication best enable me to adapt my specific thought to this group of hearers?"
2. Construct a defects thought analysis for your speech in that mode.
3. Write your introduction and your conclusion.
4. Write a segment of your speech centered about any one division with its subdivisions.
5. Provide a written defense of your selection of the defects mode over the advantages mode.
6. Present a speech in the defects mode.

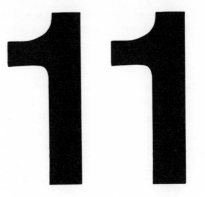

The Advantages
Mode

You will note that the advantages mode format and the defects mode format are identical except for different emphases. As you study this chapter, you should arrive at a careful understanding of the philosophical and psychological implications of the advantages mode. The alternative is to select haphazardly between the defects and advantages modes.

The second major thing that you should carefully consider is the residues variation of the advantages mode. In this case, there is no change in the advantages mode; there is one step added to it.

Communication in the advantages mode involves arguing for the acceptance of a policy for its alleged benefits. Although Aristotle was not the first to use the advantages mode, he was the first writer to discuss it in a treatise on the theory of rhetoric:

> The political orator aims at establishing the expediency or the harm-fulness of a proposed course of action; if he urges its acceptance, he does so on the ground that it will do good; if he urges its rejection, he

does so on the ground that it will do harm; and all other points, such as whether the proposal is just or unjust, honourable or dishonourable, he brings in as subsidiary and relative to this main consideration.[1]

In short, then, the communicator selects the advantages mode when he wishes to show that the net effect of his proposal would be beneficial.

Because man's inherent interest in his survival leads him to determine the courses of action that are the most expedient, his speeches throughout the ages frequently emphasize advantages. Before Aristotle, one of the earliest speakers to use the advantages mode was Hermocrates, who argued the proposition that Sicily should unite against the Athenians:

> And now, on account of our indefinite fear of this unknown future, and our immediate dread of the Athenians' presence, being alarmed on both these grounds, and thinking, with regard to any failure in our ideas of what we severally thought to achieve, that these obstacles are a sufficient bar to their fulfilment, let us send away from the country the enemy that is among us, and ourselves make peace forever, if possible; but if not that, let us make a treaty for the longest term we can, and put off our private differences to a future period. In a word, let us be convinced that by following my advice we shall each have a free city, from which we shall, as our own masters, make an equally good return to him who treats us either well or ill; but if, through not following it, we are subject to others, then, not speak of avenging ourselves on any one, we necessarily become, even if most fortunate, friends to our greatest enemies, and at variance with those with whom we ought not to be so.[2]

Hermocrates argued that if the Sicilians would unite, they would have two "blessings": (1) ridding Sicily of the Athenians and (2) ridding Sicily of civil war. Hermocrates argued, in effect, that Sicilians would have more to gain than to lose by uniting. Presumably, Sicilians could find meaning in ridding Sicily of Athenians [enemies] and in no longer enduring the hardships of civil war. If so, then Sicilians should have identified (1) with those arguments, (2) with the conclusion of Hermocrates, and (3) with Hermocrates.

One of the more significant speech writers of the fourth century, B.C., was the famous teacher of rhetoric Isocrates. From his practice, one may glimpse his theory. For example, in his oration "On the Peace," Isocrates revealed his conception of the proper relation of orators, hearers, and advantages. His comments suggested that the responsible orator should point out policies that, when followed, would be genuinely ad-

---

[1]Aristotle, *Rhetoric*, 1358b21–25.

[2]William Jennings Bryan, ed. *The World's Famous Orations,* Vol. 1 (New York: Funk and Wagnalls Co., 1906), pp. 58–59.

Chapter Eleven

vantageous to his hearers. His introduction presented his basic philosophical stance with regard to speaking on questions of public policy.

All those who come before you on this platform are accustomed to assert that the subjects upon which they are themselves about to advise you are most important and most worthy of serious consideration by the state. Nevertheless, if it was ever appropriate to preface the discussion of any other subject with such words, it seems to me fitting also to begin with them in speaking upon the subject now before us. For we are assembled here to deliberate about War and Peace, which exercise the greatest power over the life of man, and regarding which those who are correctly advised must of necessity fare better than the rest of the world. Such, then, is the magnitude of the question which we have come together to decide.

I observe, however, that you do not hear with equal favour the speakers who address you, but that, while you give your attention to some, in the case of others you do not even suffer their voice to be heard. And it is not surprising that you do this; for in the past you have formed the habit of driving all the orators from the platform except those who support your desires. Wherefore one may justly take you to task because, while you know well that many great houses have been ruined by flatterers and while in your private affairs you abhor those who practise this art, in your public affairs you are not so minded towards them; on the contrary, while you denounce those who welcome and enjoy the society of such men, you yourselves make it manifest that you place greater confidence in them than in the rest of your fellow-citizens.

Indeed, you have caused the orators to practise and study, not what will be advantageous to the state, but how they may discourse in a manner pleasing to you. And it is to this kind of discourse that the majority of them have resorted also at the present time, since it has become plain to all that you will be better pleased with those who summon you to war than with those who counsel peace; for the former put into our minds the expectation both of regaining our possessions in the several states and of recovering the power which we formerly enjoyed, while the latter hold forth no such hope, insisting rather that we must have peace and not crave great possessions contrary to justice, but be content with those we have—and that for the great majority of mankind is of all things the most difficult. For we are so dependent on our hopes and so insatiate in seizing what seems to be our advantage that not even those who possess the greatest fortunes are willing to rest satisfied with them but are always grasping after more and so risking the loss of what they have. Wherefore we may well be anxious lest on the present occasion also we may be subject to this madness. For some of us appear to me to be overzealously bent on war, as though having heard, not from haphazard counsellors, but from the gods, that we are destined to succeed in all our campaigns and to prevail easily over our foes. . . .

You, however, do neither the one thing nor the other, but are in the utmost confusion of mind. For you have come together as if it were your business to select the best course from all that are proposed; nevertheless, as though you had clear knowledge of what must be done, you are not willing to listen to any except those who speak for your pleasure. And yet, if you really desired to find out what is advantageous to the state, you ought to give your attention more to those who oppose your views than to those who seek to gratify you, knowing well that of the orators who come before you here, those who say what you desire are able to delude you easily — since what is spoken to win favour clouds your vision of what is best — whereas those who advise you without regard to your pleasure can affect you in no such way, since they could not convert you to their way of thinking until they have first made clear what is for your advantage. But, apart from these considerations, how can men wisely pass judgement on the past or take counsel for the future unless they examine and compare the arguments of opposing speakers, themselves giving an unbiased hearing to both sides?[3]

The premise undergirding Isocrates' speech was that Athenians should do what would be advantageous to the state. In structured form, his reasoning would appear as follows:

Major Premise: (Assumed) Athenians should do what would be advantageous to the state.

Minor Premise: Peace would be better than war for the state.

Conclusion: Athenians should seek peace.

Isocrates could expect that Athenians would find meaning in the assumed premise and would thus identify with it and supply it enthymematically. Then, if Isocrates should be successful in meeting his challenge to lead Athenians to find meaning in the minor premise, they presumably would be able to find meaning in his conclusion.

Clearly, man has been concerned over the years with what would benefit him. One of the more interesting examples of such oratory is found in Anglo-American history. In the eighteenth century, Edmund Burke urged Parliament to effect a reconciliation with the colonies on the North American continent.[4] Burke asserted that the "proposition is peace." He argued that from peace would flow two advantages: (1) permanent satisfaction of the people and (2) reconciliation of the people. Burke's line of argument was reminiscent of both Hermocrates' and

[3]George Norlin, trans., *Isocrates*, Vol. 2, in *The Loeb Classical Library* (New York: G. P. Putnam's Sons, 1929), pp. 7–13.

[4]Cornelius B. Bradley, ed., *Orations and Arguments by English and American Statesmen* (Boston: Allyn and Bacon, 1897), pp. 1–74.

Chapter Eleven

Isocrates' arguments for peace among their own people. Presumably, orators have historically regarded peace as a conception in which men in general find their meaning and with which they identify.

Regardless of any variations in the advantages mode, the communicator must attempt to lead each hearer to believe that adopting the course of action that he recommends would be beneficial. The communicator can prove that a claimed net advantage probably would become a gain to the hearer *only* if the claimed advantage is meaningful to the hearer and if the hearer thus identifies with it. In proving that a proposal would have a net gain for the hearer, the speaker should employ the following format or some appropriate variation of it:

Step 1: Employ a case history.
Step 2: Show the extent of the problem. } (Introduction)

Step 3: Present the solution.
    A. Affirm the solution in one sentence.
    B. Present any machinery. } (Body)
    C. Show arguments for the solution in
       terms of advantages.

Step 4: *Urge* the adoption of the solution and *summarize* the reasons. (Conclusion)

The essential difference between the advantages mode and the defects mode lies in Step 3C. In presenting a given advantage, the communicator first should state the advantage, then he should point briefly to existing conditions that would be improved by the advantage. After dealing with existing conditions, the speaker should deal with projected future conditions under the advantage.

The following student examples illustrate the way that two students handled claimed advantages. In the first example, the speaker argued the statement that it would be advantageous to establish a nationwide system of civilian review boards. The following excerpt illustrates the way that she handled a segment of her argument.

I. Civilian review boards
   would promote justice.*
   A. Employ a case history.

Hector C. was found guilty of murder in the first degree. He confessed to this crime after more than ten hours of police questioning. Hector's mother asked the police chief to review the case. The chief of police was rather annoyed at the accusation of police abuse and would not help this woman. The boy was sentenced to life imprisonment on the grounds of his confession.

---

*This is a segment of a speech composed and delivered by Sophia Vali while a student in the basic public address course at Park College, Kansas City, Missouri.

If it had been in existence, the civilian review board would have been able to conduct an independent investigation to determine the facts.

In the following excerpt, the speaker supported her statement that team teaching provides the student with the best education possible.

I. Team teaching provides the opportunity for self-improvement.*
A. Self-improvement is attained through small-group learning.
1. Provide a case history.

At Marshall High School in Portland, Oregon, there was a 9th grade small-group composed of slow learners. Tired of "childish" literature, they wanted to read *The Adventures of Huckleberry Finn,* which was reserved for the 9th grade college-bound students. The group was given the book to read, and the students succeeded. Motivation came from a desire for equal intellectual status with better students, and they wanted to prove to the teacher that they could meet the challenge to succeed.

In the following speech by another student, the arguments (divisions) regarding strengthening state governments, equalizing the disparity between the poor and the rich states, and strengthening state fiscal planning all initiated three enthymemes, the major premise of which would need to be supplied by the hearer. For example, the first division might be diagrammed as follows:

Major Premise: (To be supplied by the hearer) A proposal that would strengthen state governments would be beneficial.

Minor Premise: The proposal would strengthen state governments.

Conclusion: Therefore, the proposal should be adopted.

One may arrange the other divisions in a similar way. Collectively, the enthymemes should have resulted in persuasion. Of course, whether each division initiated an enthymeme would depend upon whether it were meaningful to the hearers involved. To a taxpayer in a poor state, the proposal might well elicit a favorable response. However, to a taxpayer in a rich state, the same argument likely would elicit an unfavorable response. Thus, the meaningfulness of a given division would not be abso-

---

*This is a segment of a speech composed and delivered by Blanche Sapede while a student in the basic public address course at Park College, Kansas City, Missouri.

lute but would have different meanings depending upon the differences in the hearers.

Federal Revenue Sharing*

Step 1
Give a case history illustrating the problem.

The states are in financial trouble. One way to discover the seriousness of the gap between income and outgo is to look at state debt. Let us take as an example one of the two richest states in the Union, the State of New York. According to the *Statistical Abstract of the United States* for 1969, at the end of the fiscal year 1966 the debt for New York stood at better than $17.7 billion—largest overall in the nation, and third largest on a per capita basis.

Step 2
Show the extent of the problem.

But, New York is not an isolated case. According to the *Statistical Abstract,* no state is without debt.

However, most distressing of all, the situation is becoming worse. A leading economist who has studied fiscal policy is Dr. Joseph A. Pechman, executive director of studies of government finance at the Brookings Institution, and author of *Federal Tax Policy.* According to Dr. Pechman, the overall gap between state revenues and expenditures in 1970 will be $15 billion.

The question, then, is not whether the federal government will continue to aid the states financially, but rather the means by which it will do so.

Step 3
Present the solution.

Statement: The federal government should grant annually a specific percentage of its income tax revenue to the state governments.

Because revenue sharing is the best way to solve the problem, I should like to urge that the federal government grant annually a specific percentage of its income tax revenue to the state governments.

---

*This speech was composed and delivered by Carol Sowards while a student in the basic public address course at Park College, Kansas City, Missouri.

The Advantages Mode

In order to implement my proposal I am recommending the adoption of the basic features of Dr. Walter Heller's plan of revenue sharing. Dr. Heller is Professor of Economics at the University of Minnesota and author of *New Dimensions of Political Economy.*

1. The federal government will each year set aside and distribute to the states 1 to 2 percent of the federal individual income tax base.
2. The sum collected for the states will be placed in a trust fund from which periodic distributions will be made.
3. The states will share the income tax proceeds on the basis of population.
4. Between 10 and 20 percent of the funds could be set aside for states with low per capita incomes. In order to receive funds, states would need to do but two things: (a) abide by Title VI of the Civil Rights Act; and (b) meet the usual public auditing, accounting, and reporting requirements on public funds.

Ultimately, the question that must be answered is: Why should this proposal be adopted? The answer lies in three reasons. First, it would strengthen state governments; second, it would tend to equalize the disparity between the poor and the rich states; and third, it would strengthen state fiscal planning.

I. The proposal would strengthen state governments.

For the next few moments, I should like to discuss the reasons that my proposal would strengthen state governments.

A. Quantification of the problem.

From 1934 to 1964, federal grants increased from $126 million to $10,060 million. According to Mr. William H. Robinson in *Revenue Sharing and Its Alternatives: What Future for Fiscal Federalism?,* nearly three fifths of the total number of grants involve project grants. Those grants are provided on the basis of applications received from prospective recipients.

On the other hand, under my proposal, the state governments will be given decision-making power in the use of the funds.

B. Statement of authority.

Professor H. F. McClelland, a political scientist and contributing author of *Essays in Federalism,* states that "The centralization of government functions which has already occurred arises from an imbalance between revenue sources and expenditures needs at both the state and local levels. The solution to date has been national support of 'state and local functions' by grants-in-aid. The current program necessarily tends toward some degree of national control. Any such control, however, weakens state and local autonomy, makes the concept of federalism less clear, and becomes cumulative with the passage of time and the increase in grants."

In contrast to the situation described by Professor McClelland, my proposal would give control to the states, thus strengthening them.

A second reason for the adoption of my proposal is that it would tend to equalize the disparity between the poor and the rich states. Let me illustrate the problem: In 1964, expenditures for public education ranged from $201 in Utah to $91 in South Carolina, a ratio of more than 2 to 1.

But, all the states were caught up in a similar situation. Overall total state-local expenditures per capita in 1964 ranged from a high of $576 in Nevada to a low of $217 in South Carolina.

A number of persons and groups have become aware of this problem. One such group is the Advisory Commission on Intergovernmental Relations. This commission was established by Congress to coordinate activities between levels of government. According to the Commission, "Regrettably, expenditure levels tend to be least adequate in the very areas where needs are greatest — where the economically underprivileged predominate."

On the other hand, under my proposal, the needy states would be provided with equalizing funds.

Third, if the federal government granted annually a specific percentage of its income tax revenue to the state governments, it would strengthen state fiscal planning. I can well illustrate the problem by referring to the state of Missouri.

At present, Missouri offers an excellent analogy illustrating the advantages of being able to engage in long-range fiscal planning. Governor Hearnes has stated that he does not know what will happen to various state programs until he knows what will be the result of the state income tax referendum. Ladies and gentlemen, this illustrates the point that only by knowing how much money will be available can government engage in adequate planning.

Under my proposal, states would gain one such source. According to Dr. Walter Heller, the revenue sharing funds would "be available automatically year to year and would not be contingent on the realization of a federal budgetary surplus. In this way, the states would have a continuing and a dependable source of income and could plan their programs without fear that this revenue source might suddenly be withdrawn."

Step 4
Conclusion and appeal
for the adoption of
the solution.

To conclude, because first of all, my proposal would strengthen state governments, because, second, it would tend to equalize the disparity between the poor and the rich states, and, third, because it would strengthen state fiscal planning, the net effect of its adoption would be advantageous. Therefore, I should like to urge you to work with me to promote the adoption of my proposal of revenue sharing.

The following speech is by Senator Mark O. Hatfield of Oregon upon the occasion of his introducing S. 503 – Voluntary Manpower Procurement Act of 1969. Senator Hatfield's speech to the Senate is an excellent example of the flexible applicability of the advantages mode. Following his first statements and the phrase "In the past two years," Senator Hatfield proceeded to use the equivalent of a case history. In showing the extent of the problem, Senator Hatfield emphasized its pervasiveness in relation to procuring military manpower. Then following his discussion of the problem *per se,* Senator Hatfield affirmed his solution (statement). Shortly thereafter, in his explication, the senator stated the one advantage that he would argue: The volunteer service system would provide efficiency and quality. He employed contrast to argue that the existing structure was inherently incapable of bringing about what was really needed. He argued that although the present system had quantity, what was needed was quality. He argued, further, that a voluntary procurement policy would provide the needed quality. Certainly, the advantage of quality should have been meaningful to legislators. Thus, instead of presenting the machinery of his bill before the advantage, Senator Hatfield waited until after he had pointed out the virtues of the advantage. Then, he said in effect that "This is how the machinery will bring about the advantage."

Because one of the important aspects of proposed legislation would be its viability, Hatfield spent considerable time arguing that the proposed legislation, if adopted, would function effectively. Hatfield's concern with viability was the corollary of the *confutatio* step of the classical mode.[5]

[5]See Chapter 12.

The "viability" step of Hatfield's speech appeared to be designed to prove feasibility, thus perhaps forestalling some attacks.

S.503 — Introduction of Bill — Voluntary Military Manpower Procurement Act of 1969*

Mr. President, I am today introducing, for myself and Senators Cook, Dole, Goldwater, McGovern, Nelson, Packwood, Prouty, and Schweiker, a bill entitled "The Voluntary Military Manpower Procurement Act of 1969."

It was nearly 2 years ago that I introduced in the Senate a bill to institute a fully voluntary armed force. Last September I reintroduced the 1967 bill with some revisions. The bill I am introducing today is a further revision of the 1967 bill.

Step 1
Present a
generalization in lieu
of a case history.

In the past 2 years criticism of our present military draft system has grown, and substantial additional support has been indicated for the early transition to a fully voluntary military manpower procurement system.

Step 2
Show the
pervasiveness of the
problem.

President Nixon has endorsed the principle of a volunteer army; the Department of Defense has indicated through various spokesmen the advantages of this manpower procurement concept; and numerous political, social, religious, and educational organizations have indicated their agreement.

A certain amount of this support has resulted, of course, from the growing discontent with the Vietnam adventure and the large-scale drafting of men for this conflict. The young of the country on whom the draft falls so inequitably, especially for the maintenance of a war many of them feel is morally indefensible, are reflecting their dissent in ever more vocal numbers. The minorities are also restive under the draft. The nation is divided by the provisions of an act which require what so many patently do not believe in.

---

*This is the substance of a speech delivered by the Hon. Mark O. Hatfield on the floor of the United States Senate on January 22, 1969.

There also has been in the same time period, a growing concern in this country about infringement on our individual liberty and a desire for freedom from unjustified government intrusion.

The present draft system, in addition to its other drawbacks, is a drastic invasion of individual liberty. Conscription is involuntary servitude, plain and simple. It is the complete usurpation by the government of an individual's freedom of choice. The *Wall Street Journal* has stated editorially that it is "about the most odious form of government control we have yet accepted."

Step 3
Present the solution.

I firmly believe that each man has a moral obligation to serve his country, but he must be granted as much freedom as possible to choose what form this service shall take. Conscription must always be the last desperate resort in meeting military manpower needs, and not merely the easy way out, as it is now. There have been periods in our history when conscription was the only alternative to destruction, but circumstances have changed and forcing men into service is no longer the only alternative in meeting manpower requirements.

The draft also has numerous other drawbacks, including the fact that it is militarily inefficient, inherently inequitable to draft-age Americans, and productive of low morale in the Armed Forces. Let me point out now the practical aspects of the volunteer force and the provisions of this bill which would do away with these handicaps.

The volunteer service system would provide an efficient military force with emphasis on quality rather than quantity.

The present draft system is designed only to provide large numbers of men. This point was clearly emphasized in the 1957 Report of the Defense Advisory Committee on Military Personnel — the Cordiner Report:

> As the tools of modern defense and the technology of their use become more intricate and complex, men — the human element in defense — become more, not less important. . . . The Committee is firmly convinced that human beings are the most important component of all modern weapons systems. . . . If the armed forces are manned with personnel of minimum or marginal capability, they cannot achieve operational effectiveness in proportion to the technical capacity built into the materiel. . . . Greater numbers of men do not satisfy this need. Only marked increases in the level of competence and experience of the men in the force can provide for the effective, economical operation required by the changing times and national needs.

That report was published nearly 12 years ago, but little has been done to upgrade the skill and competence of our men. The sad fact is that draftees, who have been taken from civilian life against their wishes, spend their 2 years of military service counting the days until they get out. As soon as the required period is over, they inevitably return to civilian life. Their empty bunks are filled with other unwilling draftees and the cycle continues. Any personnel manager would be quick to agree that low morale and inefficiency are the obvious results.

The eagerness of draftees to return to civilian life also prevents specialized training and in-depth knowledge of the complex weapons systems of our country. With its emphasis on quantity rather than quality, the draft automatically produces a high turnover rate in personnel. At the present time, only about 7 percent of the young men drafted stay in the Armed Forces beyond their 2-year obligation.

This high turnover rate causes many of the services most experienced personnel to be tied down in training new recruits. Today, seven out of every 10 men in the Army have less than 2 years military experience. As one Pentagon military official has noted:

> As soon as we are able to operate as a unit, the trained men leave and we have to start all over again.

Step 4
Present the plan.

A major portion of the bill I am introducing is directed at upgrading the conditions and status of a military career—from increasing educational opportunities to improving the social, cultural, and recreational facilities for military men and their families. As military life becomes more attractive and as it enjoys a higher status, the number of young men entering the service freely would increase, with many considering a career in the military. The turnover rate of these willing enlistees would be dramatically reduced, making it necessary to recruit fewer men, and the services would have a higher percentage of skilled, motivated men.

Another provision of the bill would accelerate the substitution of civilians for noncombatant military personnel. This would effectively reduce the size of the armed services and would also reduce the number of new enlistees.

A third provision would help insure the recruitment of the necessary number of young men by accepting many who now try to volunteer and who would like a military career but who are currently rejected because of slight physical or educational deficiencies. Through additional and specialized training programs, these men could become productive members of the armed services.

Most important of all in attracting sufficient enlistees would be the improvement of military pay scales. We certainly cannot expect to recruit young men into military life when the salary offered them is at least one third less than what they could be earning as civilians.

It is difficult to project the costs necessary for the establishment of a volunteer force. Authoritative studies indicate that the pay increases needed to recruit the necessary number of volunteers would come to $5 to $7 billion more per year. The bill I am introducing calls for $100 per month pay raises for enlisted men with the price tag coming to about $3.7 billion at our present force level.

While this additional outlay in salaries would be significant it must be weighed against the substantial savings that would result under a volunteer force. Presently, it costs $6,000 just to train the average serviceman, making the total training cost for draftees now in uniform—those men who will leave the service the moment their 2-year hitches expire—about $3 billion. Many training centers that are expensive to maintain and operate could be closed. Other cost adjustments would result, such as the increase in tax revenue from civilians who otherwise would be drafted. Unfortunately, it is difficult to estimate the very real savings that would result because of the increased competence and efficiency of the armed services.

I do not think there is any question that the volunteer system could supply the necessary number of military personnel. The manpower pool is increasing with nearly 2 million new men attaining draft age each year. The total number of draft-eligible males in the 18 to 26 age category now stands at more than 12 million. To meet necessary personnel requirements the military needs to recruit only about 5 percent of this total each year. Certainly, sufficient inducement can be made to attract that many.

Step 6
Refute the major
objection to the plan.

The bill I am introducing also responds to the main point of criticism of the volunteer force—that the system lacks the necessary flexibility for meeting crises. It includes a special provision for the improvement of the Ready Reserve and the National Guard. I submit that the volunteer force would be more flexible and, in conjunction with a strengthened Reserve and National Guard, would be better able to respond to an emergency military situation than is the current draft system.

Even in the past, for such emergencies as the Korean conflict in 1950 and the Berlin crisis of 1961, the Defense Department relied largely on recall of trained reserves rather than draftees. Military emergencies being what they are in this day of speed and highly complex weaponry, they cannot be resolved by summoning large numbers of untrained men to boot camp. Competence, not compulsion, is the key to an effective national defense.

As recognized by the bill, the volunteer system could be phased in gradually. There already is a large base from which to start since draftees comprise only 15 percent of the enlisted members of the present Armed Force. In case of emergency during the transition or later, and the president determines that the military manpower needs of the country are not being met, the bill provides that the president shall recommend to Congress legislation calling for the involuntary induction of persons into the Armed Forces.

Step 7
Present the
conclusion.

    I feel strongly that a volunteer military manpower system will work. But for such a system to be given a chance to prove its merit, we must dispel the myth that the draft, however undesirable, is inevitable. We must be willing to accept the challenge of new realities and have the foresight and confidence to accept logic over habit and reason over the retarding security of tradition.

    I believe the volunteer force is a workable alternative, that it will remove the inequities of the old system which have caused tension and division, and that it will help restore unity to this nation.

    The major difference between the typical advantages mode and its *residues variation* is the step in the variation that considers one or two leading alternatives to the solution that the communicator intends to propose. Because a speaker generally faces time limitations, he should not attempt a complete attack on the alternatives. Rather, the speaker should bring against each alternative the major objection to it and thus reject the alternative for that reason. After the speaker considers any alternatives, he then presents the advantages of his solution.

    The following format indicates the steps that a speaker employs in following the residues variation:

Step 1: Employ a case history. ⎫ (Introduction)
Step 2: Show the extent of the problem. ⎭

Step 3: Consider alternative solutions. ⎫
Step 4: Present the solution. ⎪
    A. Affirm the solution in one sentence. ⎬ (Body)
    B. Present any machinery. ⎪
    C. Present arguments (advantages). ⎭

Step 5: *Urge* the adoption of the solution and *summarize* the reasons. (Conclusion)

    As has been pointed out, the various modes of communication represent approaches of the communicator toward adapting his thought to the hearer. Inasmuch as the communicator should be satisfied with nothing less than the most effective possible adaptation, he should modify a mode appropriately as circumstances warrant. The following text of a speech by Najeeb E. Halaby, president of Pan American World Airways, Inc., is an excellent example of adaptation. The statement that he supported was that the fourth major airport in the New Jersey–New York metropolitan area should be built at the Solberg site in New Jersey. Inasmuch as some persons strongly supported an alternative site at McGuire South, Mr. Halaby found it necessary not only to support his choice of site but also to give reasons for rejecting the McGuire site. In terms that should have been meaningful to the hearers — people, terrain, accessibility — Halaby provided a basis for identifying with the persons who favored the McGuire site. If Halaby had ignored the McGuire site, he would have permitted listeners to wonder why, thus diminishing the force of his argument.

Mr. Halaby also adapted to his hearers and to the other speakers in another way. He was aware that following his speech, two other speakers would present technical speeches that would develop the disadvantages of the McGuire site and the advantages of the Solberg site. He elected the best course of action by introducing the problem, stating his point of view, and briefly outlining the major arguments, without preempting any of the material of the speakers to follow. Thus, by being aware of his own role in relation to the total presentation, Halaby adapted to the other speakers on the program and therefore promoted the adaptation of both his presentation and those of the other speakers.

In Support of the Solberg Site*

I am pleased to be able to appear before you today to speak briefly in favor of the proposed major airport at Solberg. I intend to be brief, as it does not seem appropriate that I attempt an extended, technical presentation on detail best set forth by specialists who will testify.

Step 1
Illustrate the
problem.

There is, as you the responsible legislators know, an unfortunate but very real urgency in this matter. More than ten years ago it was recognized by the Port of New York Authority and various other agencies involved, including the airlines, that the New Jersey–New York Metropolitan area's three major airports were becoming insufficient to satisfy demand. To my knowledge, that projected insufficiency, now a reality, has not been denied by any public or private body. The great need is an undisputed need in fact. The breakdown in our vital air transportation system this past summer,

---

*Statement by Najeeb E. Halaby, president of Pan American World Airways, Inc., before the New Jersey Joint Legislative Committee, March 18, 1969.

Chapter Eleven

created by the crippling air traffic congestion at Kennedy International Airport, Newark Airport and La Guardia Airport, tells a story that requires no embroidery.

Step 2
Show the extent of
the problem.

We are not now, any of us, faced with a problem of justification, but rather with a problem of location. We are faced not with considering why, but with deciding where. In the context of now, we are too late. Without exaggeration, the governmental and business operations of the New Jersey–New York Metropolitan area directly or indirectly concerned with air transportation are destined to suffer severely restrictive procedures for the next five to seven years until a fourth major airport can be placed in operation.

There is existent an attriting of air commerce from this area. It is, to date, small but it is there and it is growing. Individual passengers and shippers are looking for routes that bypass the metropolitan area. Airlines have or will operate schedules to and from other areas that, under a nonrestrictive situation, would have originated and/or terminated in this area. The CAB is seeking to develop bypassing routes. The FAA has given notice of hourly flight number restrictions.

Step 3
Present criteria for
measuring the
solution.

The location of an airport is generally a compromise relating people, geography and time. A commercial airport must serve a population concentration . . . it must be on and within hospitable terrain . . . it must be quickly accessible by feeder transport means. In the New Jersey–New York Metropolitan area, the population concentration is centered on Manhattan, with a business center trend line running roughly through Jersey City to Newark. Two of the existing three major airports, Kennedy and La Guardia, are both on Long Island, east of Manhattan, separated by two rivers from New Jersey, and diametrically opposite to the Newark–Manhattan axis. The adjacent Connecticut and northern New York counties have neither the best suited terrain nor the population demand for service. New Jersey has the requirement and the terrain.

Step 4
Consider alternative
solutions.

Extensive surveys have narrowed the field of possible consideration to two areas, northwestern New Jersey and south central New Jersey, in particular the Solberg and what I shall designate here as the McGuire South sites. Without reviewing in detail the pros and cons of these two sites as you have the airlines position as a matter of record—

Step 5
Present the solution.
(Conclusion is
implied.)

I will state again for Pan Am that we strongly endorse the Solberg proposal and strongly oppose the McGuire South proposal. We believe, upon careful consideration, that McGuire South is too remote from the population to be served, it would require an astronomic investment in feeder transportation systems, and it would, if built, languish like a New Jersey memorial to the wrong airport at the wrong place at the wrong time. Solberg, on the other hand, best meets the conditions of people to be served, terrain and accessibility. It is the place, and this is the time.

Conclusion

The speaker ultimately must show his hearers that his proposal would benefit them. The advantages mode accomplishes this goal by integrating argument and evidence explicitly for the purpose of making both meaningful to the hearer. The difference between the advantages mode and the defects mode is one of emphasis, as revealed in Step 3 of both modes. Because of its positive emphasis, the advantages mode is more applicable to deliberative topics than is the defects mode.

In employing the advantages mode, one should follow this format:

Step 1: Employ a case history.

Step 2: Show the extent of the problem.

Step 3: Present the solution.
    A. Affirm the solution in one sentence.
    B. Present any machinery.
    C. Show arguments for the solution in terms of advantages.

Step 4: *Urge* the adoption of the solution and *summarize* the reasons.

If the speaker believes that his hearers may not find his solution to be meaningful until they are satisfied that another prominent solution will not work, then he should use the residues variation. Between Steps 2 and 3 of the regular advantages mode, the speaker using the residues variation should insert the Step: "Consider alternative solutions." This is the only step that distinguishes the standard advantages mode and the residues variation.

Suggested Readings

Dewey, John. *How We Think.* Boston: D. C. Heath & Co., 1910. Chap. 6, "The Analysis of a Complete Act of Thought." This chapter, particularly the segment on the steps in reflection, is a definitive statement of interest to all students of communication.

Monroe, Alan H., and Douglas Ehninger. *Principles and Types of Speech,* 6th ed. Glenview, Ill.: Scott, Foresman and Co., 1967. Chap. 16, "Adapting the Speech Organization to the Audience: The Motivated Sequence." Monroe's interest in adaptation has been long-standing, and this selection deserves careful reading by the serious student.

For additional references, see the suggested readings for Chapter 10.

Suggested Assignments

1. Select a topic in the advantages mode and do the following:
   a. Complete the statement "I want my audience to believe that . . ."
   b. Give a satisfactory answer to the question "Why do I want this audience to believe this specific point?"
   c. Give a satisfactory answer to the question "Why would the advantages mode of communication best enable me to adapt my specific thought to this group of hearers?"
2. Construct an advantages thought analysis for your speech in that mode.
3. Write your introduction and your conclusion.
4. Write a segment of your speech centered about any one division with its subdivisions.
5. Provide a written defense of your choice of the advantages mode over the defects mode.
6. Present a speech in the advantages mode or the residues variation.

The Classical
Mode

I discuss the classical mode last because it is the oldest and—it seems fair to state—the most famous approach to adaptation. In my brief account of the development of the classical format, I trust that you will be able to understand something of the development of the classical mode, as well as the relationship of classical principles to the defects and advantages modes.

The two speeches that I have included to exemplify the classical mode illustrate the flexibility of this mode in contemporary use. Christine Broslavick gave her speech to her fellow college students. On the other hand, Douglas MacArthur presented his speech on one of the most formal occasions possible: to a joint session of the Congress. However, you should consider the applicability of the classical mode particularly when you may not be known to your audience or when your audience may be opposed to your point of view on the topic.

Communicators have been employing classical principles of adaptation at least since the time of Corax.[1] Corax specifically designed his art of rhetoric to be used by citizens who were speaking in the law courts

---

[1]R. C. Jebb, "Rhetoric," *The Encyclopaedia Britannica*, 11th ed., Vol. 23 (Cambridge, Eng.: University Press, 1911), p. 233.

to reclaim land lost to tyrants in years past. He recommended that a speech be divided into five parts:

Part 1: Proem

Part 2: Narrative

Part 3: Arguments

Part 4: Subsidiary Remarks

Part 5: Peroration

Corax's pioneering work was a landmark in the development of the art of persuasion and its critical dimensions. However, it was Aristotle who wrote the first systematic treatise on the subject of rhetoric. Aristotle[2] argued that the only *essential* parts of a speech were (1) the statement and (2) the proof. And, in any event, he said, a speech could not have more than the following:

Part 1: Introduction

Part 2: Statement

Part 3: Argument

Part 4: Epilogue

The next major rhetorical theoretician was the author of the *Rhetorica ad Herennium*,[3] thought by some to be Cicero. Written about 86 B.C., this treatise lists six parts of an address:

Part 1: *Exordium*

Part 2: *Narratio*

Part 3: *Divisio*

Part 4: *Confirmatio*

Part 5: *Confutatio*

Part 6: *Conclusio*

Finally, in Cicero's *A Dialogue Concerning Oratorical Partitions*,[4] there were four divisions that are strongly suggestive of Aristotelian influence:

Part 1: Opening

Part 2: Narration

Part 3: Confirmation

Part 4: Peroration

---

[2] Aristotle, *Rhetoric,* 1414a30–1414b18.

[3] Lester Thonssen and A. Craig Baird, *Speech Criticism* (New York: Ronald Press Co., 1948), pp. 77–78.

[4] Thonssen and Baird, p. 91.

Considering the writings of Corax, Aristotle, the writer of the *ad Herennium*, and Cicero, one can derive the following steps for proceeding to adapt thought to the hearer by employing classical precepts. These principles are excellent, not because they are old but because they function from sound premises in relation to adapting to man's mind.

Step 1: *Exordium* (proem, introduction, opening) ⎫
Step 2: *Narratio* (narration of facts and statement) ⎬ (Introduction)

Step 3: *Confirmatio* (argument) ⎫
Step 4: *Confutatio* (refutation) ⎬ (Body)

Step 5: *Peroratio* (epilogue, *conclusio*) (Conclusion)

In the foregoing, if one believes that he needs to strengthen the image of the configuration of the speech to come, he may add the *divisio* (*partitio* — partitioning) between Steps 2 and 3 above.

This classical mode is particularly effective in deliberative discourse in which one argues for the adoption of a controversial solution before a group largely unfamiliar to the speaker. One should not use the classical mode when speaking before an audience with whom he is intimately acquainted or when speaking on a topic to which there has been little or no objection — for example while arguing "You should take your polio vaccine."

The first step, the *exordium*, has as its purpose assisting the speaker (1) to establish rapport and (2) to gain and hold the attention of the audience. Presumably, most speakers are friendly, and the *exordium* provides them with a convenient opportunity to reveal their congeniality at the same time that they establish a common bond with the hearers.

If the speaker establishes a common bond by telling the audience of a case history or by telling them a story that links them to him and to the problem he is going to discuss, then he has both established rapport and has captured attention. Regarding gaining attention, a speaker deludes himself, in most instances, if he thinks that his hearers are sitting on the edge of their seats eagerly awaiting his speech. It may be that a hearer's mind is on the roast left in the oven or on preparations for a trip to the country. In any event, the speaker should assume that nobody is thinking about his topic prior to the *exordium*, and he should use the *exordium* to attract the attention of the audience specifically to the thought he intends to communicate.

Among those phrasing a well-turned *exordium* was General of the Army Douglas MacArthur. On April 19, 1951, General MacArthur spoke to a joint session of the Congress of the United States, after having been relieved of his command by President Truman because of disagreement over policy in the conduct of the Korean conflict. MacArthur, with a reputation for having one of the most brilliant military minds in the history of the United States, could not help being aware that his presence before Congress pointed up dramatically the rift between himself and President Truman. He seemed fully aware of his audience and of his words as he said:

> Mr. President, Mr. Speaker, and distinguished Members of the Congress, I stand on this rostrum with a sense of deep humility and great pride—humility in the wake of those great American architects of our history who have stood here before me, pride in the reflection that this forum of legislative debate represents human liberty in the purest form yet devised. Here are centered the hopes and aspirations and faith of the entire human race.
>
> I do not stand here as advocate for any partisan cause, for the issues are fundamental and reach quite beyond the realm of partisan consideration. They must be resolved on the highest plane of national interest if our course is to prove sound and our future protected. I trust, therefore, that you will do me the justice of receiving that which I have to say as solely expressing the considered viewpoint of a fellow American. I address you, with neither rancor nor bitterness, in the fading twilight of life with but one purpose in mind—to serve my country.[5]

In his *exordium*, then, General MacArthur referred to his feelings upon being in the presence of Congress: humility toward himself, and pride in his country. Humbling himself and praising the Congress should have assisted MacArthur to project the image of a man of "goodwill" and of "good moral character." More explicitly, he established his ethos through the *meaning* $\longrightarrow$ *identification* $\longrightarrow$ *persuasion* sequence. What legislator would have failed to find meaningful such phrasing as "great American architects of our history who have stood here before me," "this forum of legislative debate represents human liberty in the purest form yet devised," and "with but one purpose in mind—to serve my country"?

The second step of the classical mode is the *narratio*. This step states the relevant facts of the problem sufficiently to establish, prima facie, a justification for speaking on the topic. Inasmuch as the *narratio* is always subservient to the whole, and since the whole involves a problem, therefore the *narratio* should establish facts concerning (1) the nature of the problem and (2) its extent.

The leaders of nations are confronted with a host of problems, and Sir Winston Churchill, Prime Minister of Great Britain in 1952, was no exception. He came to the United States and spoke to a joint session of the Congress on January 17, 1952, asking them "not for gold but for steel,

---

[5]*Representative Speeches of General of the Army Douglas MacArthur*, 88th Congress, 2nd Session, Senate Document No. 95 (Washington: U.S. Government Printing Office, 1964), p. 14.

---

not for favors but equipment . . ." The following *narratio* of Sir Winston's led up to his request:

I have not come here to ask you for money [laughter and applause] — to ask you for money to make living more comfortable or easier for us in Britain. Our standards of life are our own business, and we can only keep our self-respect and independence by looking after them ourselves.

During the war we bore our share of the burden and fought from first to last unconquered, and for a while alone, to the utmost limit of our resources. [Applause.]

Your majestic obliteration of all you gave us under lend-lease will never be forgotten by this generation of Britons or by history.

After the war, unwisely as I contended and certainly contrary to American advice, we accepted as normal debts nearly four thousand million pounds sterling of claims by countries we had protected from invasion or had otherwise aided, instead of making counterclaims which would at least have reduced the bill to reasonable proportions.

The thousand million loan we borrowed from you in 1946 and which we are now repaying was spent not on ourselves, but mainly in helping others. In all, since the war, as the late government affirmed, we have lent or given to European or Asiatic countries thirty hundred million pounds in the form of unrequited exports. This, added to the cost of turning over our industry from war to peace and rebuilding homes shattered by bombardment, was more than we could manage without an undue strain upon our life energies from which we shall require both time and self-discipline to recover.

Why do I say all this? Not to compare our financial resources with yours, for we are but a third of your numbers and have much less than a third of your wealth; not to claim praise or reward but to convince you of our native and enduring strength and that our true position is not to be judged by the present state of the dollar exchange or by sterling area finance.

Our production is half as great again as it was before the war; our exports are up by two thirds; recovery while being retarded has been continuous and we are determined that it shall go on. [Applause.]

As I said at Fulton, in Missouri, 6 years ago, under the auspices of President Truman, let no man underrate the abiding power of the British Commonwealth and Empire. Do not suppose we shall not come through these dark years of privation as we came through the glorious years of agony, or that half a century from now you will not see seventy or eighty millions of Britons spread about the world and united in defense of our traditions and way of life and of the world causes which you and we espouse.

If the population of the English-speaking Commonwealths be added to that of the United States we will all have such cooperation with all that such cooperation implies, in the air, on the sea, and all over the globe, and in science, industry and moral force, there will be no quivering precarious balance of power to offer its temptation to ambition or adventure. I am very glad to be able to say the same to you here today. [Applause.]

It is upon this basis of recovery in spite of burdens, that the formidable problem of the new rearmament has fallen upon us.

It is the policy of the United States to help forward in many countries the process of rearmament. In this we who contribute ourselves two thirds as much as the rest of Europe put together require your aid if we are to realize in good time the very high level of military strength which the Labor government boldly aimed at and to which they committed us. It is for you to judge to what extent the United States interests are involved. Whether you aid us much or little, we shall continue to do our utmost in the common cause. But, Members of the Congress, our contribution will perforce be limited by our own physical resources and thus the combined strength of our two countries and also of the free world will be somewhat less than it might be.[6]

During the foregoing narration, Churchill employed certain references that should have initiated several *meaning* ⟶ *identification* ⟶ *persuasion* sequences. Sir Winston's remark that "I have not come here to ask you for money" drew a response suggesting that the remark was meaningful to the audience of legislators. The Congress, during the period 1939–1945 and after the war, had loaned or granted considerable funds to aid war-torn nations. Thus, Churchill's humor presumably gave his reference to money the right touch. In addition, such phrases as "self-respect and independence" and "bore our share of the burden" should have been meaningful for the audience, a number of whom had voted to sustain Britain in the war against the Axis powers. References to Britain's recovery, if one may judge by the reaction of the Congress, were very meaningful to the members. Beyond the foregoing, Churchill's references to "in defense of our traditions and way of life and of the world causes which you and we espouse" and to the cooperation among English-speaking countries (including the United States) should have provided additional meaningful bases for identification.

The third step of the classical mode, the *confirmatio*,[7] is the major segment of the speech. It is here that the speaker presents the argument and evidence of his thought analysis to promote belief in the mind of the hearer. The speaker here presents the full thrust of his reasoning.

---

[6]*Memorial Addresses in the Congress of the United States and Tributes in Eulogy of Sir Winston Churchill*, 89th Congress, 1st Session, House Document No. 209 (Washington: U.S. Government Printing Office, 1965), pp. 237–239.

[7]See the two speeches later in this chapter for examples of the *confirmatio*. Inasmuch as the *confirmatio* represents the entire body of the speech, the author believes that it is a better use of space and the reader's time to refer him to the body of each full-length speech at the end of this chapter.

The fourth step of the Classical Mode, the *confutatio,* is designed to provide the speaker with an opportunity to refute objections that have been made against the proposal or idea that the speaker is advocating. As has been observed, the classical mode — with its provision for refutation — is particularly applicable to any speaking occasion upon which the speaker would wish to counter an objection to his proposal. The length of the *confutatio* varies considerably, much as does the length of the *narratio* — both depending upon the requirements peculiar to the subject. The two examples following, although showing a difference in style — perhaps because of the difference in time — illustrate the applicability of the *confutatio* segment of the classical mode.

On May 30, 1777, Lord Chatham (William Pitt the elder) spoke before the House of Lords on a motion for an address to the Crown to put a stop to hostilities between the American Colonies and the mother country. Approaching the conclusion of his speech, he said:

> My Lords, I shall no doubt hear it objected, "Why should we submit or concede? Has America done any thing on her part to induce us to agree to so large a ground of concession?" I will tell you, my Lords, why I think you should. You have been the aggressors from the beginning. I shall not trouble your Lordships with the particulars; they have been stated and enforced by the noble and learned Lord who spoke last but one (Lord Camden), in a much more able and distinct manner than I could pretend to state them. If, then, we are the aggressors, it is your Lordships' business to make the first overture. I say again, this country has been the aggressor. You have made descents upon their coasts; you have burned their towns, plundered their country, made war upon the inhabitants, confiscated their property, proscribed and imprisoned their persons. I do therefore affirm, my Lords, that instead of exacting unconditional submission from the colonies, we should grant them unconditional redress. We have injured them; we have endeavored to enslave and oppress them. Upon this ground, my Lords, instead of chastisement, they are entitled to redress. A repeal of those laws, of which they complain, will be the first step to that redress. The people of America look upon Parliament as the authors of their miseries; their affections are estranged from their sovereign.[8]

With regard to Lord Chatham's speech, one should exercise restraint in concluding that the *confutatio* was meaningful to his hearers, the House of Lords. Because American readers of the manuscript, past and present, would likely be in favor of the sentiment of Chatham's speech, it would be easy to overlook the critical question of what his hearers thought was meaningful. Admittedly, the *confutatio* is always difficult; for it refutes a

---

[8]Chauncey A. Goodrich, *Select British Eloquence* (New York: Harper & Brothers, 1852), pp. 133–134.

---

point that is probably held by at least some hearers. Thus, the speaker needs to refute the argument and still provide a meaning with which opposing hearers find it possible to identify.

The next example of an able employment of a *confutatio* is from the speech of General Douglas MacArthur to a joint session of the Congress of the Republic of the Philippines, July 5, 1961, in Manila, Philippine Islands. He had just suggested the desirability of outlawing global war.

> You will say at once that, although the abolition of war has been the dream of man for centuries, every proposition to that end has been promptly discarded as impossible and fantastic. But that was before the science of the past decade made mass destruction a reality. The argument then was along spiritual and moral lines, and lost. But now the tremendous evolution of nuclear and other potentials of destruction has suddenly taken the problem away from its primary consideration as a moral and spiritual question and brought it abreast of scientific realism. It is no longer an ethical equation to be pondered solely by learned philosophers and ecclesiastics, but a hard-core one for the decision of the masses whose survival is the issue.[9]

General MacArthur was subtle in refuting what his hearers may have thought about his proposal to outlaw war. He did not make his *confutatio* personal; rather, he talked about the *conception* of outlawing global war. MacArthur was careful to avoid a personal confrontation with his hearers.

The fifth step of the classical mode is the *peroratio*. Regardless of whether it includes a summary of the divisions of the *confirmatio,* the *peroratio* must include an appropriate appeal that focuses on the main idea the speaker is advocating. Whether there is a summary will depend partially upon the structure of the thought analysis as revealed in the body of the speech. If one has three major divisions he wishes the hearers to remember, then he should include a summary of those divisions immediately prior to his appeal. However, if the speaker has one point to which he directs his appeal, then he does not need the summary before the appeal.

The following *peroratio,* taken from the speech of General MacArthur just cited, illustrates the appeal without the summary. General MacArthur concluded as follows:

> We are in a new era. The old methods and solutions no longer suffice. We must have new thoughts, new ideas, new concepts. We must break out of the straitjacket of the past. We must have sufficient imagination and courage to translate the universal wish for peace — which is rapidly becoming a universal necessity — into actuality. And, until then, at whatever cost or sacrifice, we must be fully prepared — lest we perish.[10]

[9]*Representative Speeches*, p. 99.
[10]*Representative Speeches*, p. 100.

The following speech texts in the classical mode represent two variations in the classical approach to adaptation. On the one hand, Christine Broslavick, a student, spoke before a familiar audience; on the other, General MacArthur spoke to a special audience on a special occasion. Thus, the *exordium* of each text reflects the differences in audience and occasion. With regard to the *narratio,* the relationship between the topic and the audience determined both (1) what was said and (2) how much was said in both speeches. In particular, because he was a controversial figure, General MacArthur needed to provide Congress with considerable background information. Moreover, considering the difficulty of his subject, even if he had not been under fire, the general would have had to provide considerable contextual material. No such need faced the student. The relationship between the speaker's thought and the audience in the two speeches also determined the *confirmatio,* the *confutatio,* and the *peroratio* in each.

Programmed Teaching Machines*

Step 1: Exordium
Establish rapport; gain
and hold attention.

Recently, I saw a cartoon in a magazine picturing a young student about twenty feet tall bent over speaking to a teacher. The caption read: "Hi ma'am. I'm the future that you are supposed to shape." It took considerable thought before I realized what a tremendous assignment this student had given the teacher. But as capable as the teacher may be, he may fail this assignment if he can't be found in the classroom.

Step 2: Narratio
State the data that point
up the nature and extent
of the problem.

In September of 1966, the Chicago schools had 600 teacher vacancies on opening day. Cleveland hired 650 new teachers and still had 235 openings. It began hiring any college graduate even if he could teach only one period a day.

*This speech was composed and delivered by Christine Broslavick while a student in the basic public address course at Northern Michigan University, Marquette, Michigan.

In Kansas City, the director of personnel said that it takes fifty telephone calls to find five substitutes when one regular teacher becomes ill.

Now, there are reasons for this shortage of teachers, but reasons or not, the fact remains— we have a teacher deficiency and this, if left unchecked, will create a deficiency in our educational system. It is a threat such as this that prompts me to believe that programmed teaching machines should be incorporated into our school systems.

This, I feel, should be done for two reasons. First, programmed teaching machines would compensate for our teacher shortage. And second, programmed teaching machines would improve our educational system.

Let's consider these two points individually. Point one. Programmed teaching machines would compensate for our teacher shortage. These machines would enable the teacher to handle up to twice as many students. In Utah, the Salt Lake City *Tribune* published an article which read in part: "'Using 60 of these machines, one teacher can handle six classes of 60 students each or 360 students a day in algebra and trigonometry,' Supt. Bell said. 'Each of the two high schools in the district will be equipped with 120 machines, and two teachers in each school will thus be able to handle up to 720 daily.'"

These machines not only relieve the teachers of much time consuming paperwork, but they also provide the student with exercises for practice and drill. Thus, the teacher is relieved of providing simple rote instruction.

The teaching machine, in some cases, may substitute for a teacher. Fry, in his book *Teaching Machines and Programmed Instruction,* said: "No one, certainly, expects programmed learning to replace conventional teaching, for that is not its purpose. The program can, of course, be used to substitute for an instructor when local conditions dictate the need, as where the students are badly isolated or where staff limitations do not permit a course offering that can be had through programmed materials."

Clearly, then, programmed teaching machines may well prove to be the one singular rem-

(Statement)

Divisio
Foretell the divisions
to be discussed.

Step 3: Confirmatio
Prove the statement.

I. Programmed teaching machines would compensate for our teacher shortage.

A. Machines would enable the teacher to handle up to twice as many students.

B. Machines may, in some cases, substitute for a teacher.

edy for our teacher shortage in the next few decades.

Point two. Programmed teaching machines would improve our educational system. Teaching machines are flexible. They allow for a greater range of subject matter. If, for example, a junior high or senior high school student wished to pursue a language — say, Russian — and no instructor is available to teach this particular subject, the student could take the course through programmed teaching. The same could be done with any other course not offered in the school system.

More than this, the programmed teaching machines can cope with students of various levels of intelligence. Dull students can bring themselves up to the learning level of their average peers, while the advanced student can pace his learning at a more progressive rate.

Teaching machines improve the quality of instruction. First of all, they allow for more individualized help. Educators who have successfully used the teaching machine have thought of it as a liberating device which enabled them to work more with the individual student. Secondly, they provide for the highest quality of concepts and curriculum material. This is quality material not readily accessible to teachers by any means other than by machine programming. It would be particularly advantageous for students and teachers from smaller school systems.

Finally, the teaching machine requires thorough learning. One student who was involved in an experimental study which utilized the programmed teaching machine was asked if he liked using the machine method of instruction and if so, why. The student said that he liked using the teaching machine because "you can't get through the program unless you know it (the material) thoroughly."

Certainly, then, it should be evident that the use of the programmed teaching machine would greatly contribute to the improvement of our educational system.

However, there are, obviously enough, objections to such a proposal. First, some may feel that the cost of equipping our schools with these machines is too great to warrant their use. Not so. Beyond the initial cost of installation, it is estimated that ordinary classroom instruction with the systems available to us in the near future will cost thirty cents per student. On the other hand, tutorial instruction for special, remedial or vocational education is very, very much more expensive . . . $3 or $4.

Second, once the equipment is installed, how are we going to know whether the students will be receptive to this type of instruction? A survey of students working with experimental teaching machines found that 85–90 percent of these students preferred machine teaching to the conventional method of instruction. Moreover, at Roanoke, 31 percent of the eighth grade students completing a course in algebra by machine instruction surpassed the national average of ninth grade students completing the same course by conventional instruction.

Third, some fear that machine teaching will provide no teacher-student interaction, no reinforcement or rewards. But this contention is contrary to an article I read which states: "According to Skinner the traditional classroom situation does not provide reinforcement, or reward, often enough or strongly enough to meet the criteria of effective learning. The teaching machine offered a possible solution to the problem by providing immediate reward after each step in the completion of a program of learning." Skinner's view of an adequate teaching machine embodies this principle of reinforcement in terms of rewarding the student by permitting him to learn the validity of his answer as soon as he has given it.

Oddly enough, a fourth objection comes from book publishers who fear that such innovations in teaching would severely affect their book sales. In answer, I am certain that you, along with me, will agree with Dr. Everett, assistant superintendent for instruction in the New York Public Schools, when he said: "I happen to believe that books will be with us for a long time. I equate books with culture. With the advent of television there were gloomy predictions that reading would sharply decline. If anything, the reverse has been true."

Therefore, in conclusion I wish to restate that I firmly believe that programmed machine teaching should be incorporated into our school systems. This should be done for two major reasons. First, programmed machine teaching would compensate for our teacher shortage. Second, programmed machine teaching would improve our educational system.

Joint Meeting of the Two Houses of the U.S. Congress*

April 19, 1951   *Washington, D.C.*

Exordium

Mr. President, Mr. Speaker, and distinguished Members of the Congress, I stand on this rostrum with a sense of deep humility and great pride—humility in the wake of those great American architects of our history who have stood here before me, pride in the reflection that this forum of legislative debate represents human liberty in the purest form yet devised. Here are centered the hopes and aspirations and faith of the entire human race.

I do not stand here as advocate for any partisan cause, for the issues are fundamental and reach quite beyond the realm of partisan consideration. They must be resolved on the highest plane of national interest if our course is to prove sound and our future protected. I trust, therefore, that you will do me the justice of receiving that which I have to say as solely expressing the considered viewpoint of a fellow American. I address you, with neither rancor nor bitterness, in the fading twilight of life with but one purpose in mind—to serve my country.

---

*Speech by General of the Army Douglas MacArthur to the joint meeting of the Two Houses of the U. S. Congress, April 19, 1951, in *Representative Speeches of General of the Army Douglas MacArthur,* 88th Congress, 2nd Session, Senate Document No. 95 (Washington: U.S. Government Printing Office, 1964), pp. 14-20.

The issues are global and so interlocked that to consider the problems of one sector, oblivious to those of another, is but to court disaster for the whole.

While Asia is commonly referred to as the gateway to Europe, it is no less true that Europe is the gateway to Asia, and the broad influence of the one cannot fail to have its impact upon the other.

There are those who claim our strength is inadequate to protect on both fronts—that we cannot divide our effort. I can think of no greater expression of defeatism. If a potential enemy can divide his strength on two fronts, it is for us to counter his effort.

The Communist threat is a global one. Its successful advance in one sector threatens the destruction of every other sector. You cannot appease or otherwise surrender to communism in Asia without simultaneously undermining our efforts to halt its advance in Europe.

Narratio

Beyond pointing out these simple truisms, I shall confine my discussion to the general areas of Asia. Before one may objectively assess the situation now existing there, he must comprehend something of Asia's past and the revolutionary changes which have marked her course up to the present. Long exploited by the so-called colonial powers, with little opportunity to achieve any degree of social justice, individual dignity, or a higher standard of life such as guided our own noble administration of the Philippines, the peoples of Asia found their opportunity in the war just past to throw off the shackles of colonialism, and now see the dawn of new opportunity, a heretofore unfelt dignity, and the self-respect of political freedom.

Mustering half of the earth's population and 60 percent of its natural resources, these peoples are rapidly consolidating a new force, both moral and material, with which to raise the living standard and erect adaptations of the design of modern progress to their own distinct cultural environments. Whether one adheres to the concept of colonization or not, this is the direction of Asian progress and it may not be stopped. It is a corollary to the shift of the world economic frontiers, as the whole epicenter of world affairs rotates back toward the area whence it started. In this situation it becomes vital that our own country orient its policies in consonance with this basic evolutionary condition rather than pursue a course blind to the reality that the colonial era is now past and the Asian peoples covet the right to shape their own free destiny. What they seek now is friendly guidance, understanding, and support, not imperious direction; the dignity of equality, not the shame of subjugation. Their prewar standard of life, pitifully low, is infinitely lower now in the devastation left in war's wake. World ideologies play little part in Asian thinking and are little understood. What the peoples strive for is the opportunity for a little more food in their stomachs, a little better clothing on their backs, a little firmer roof over their heads, and the realization of the normal nationalist urge for political freedom. These political-social conditions have but an indirect bearing upon our own national security, but form a backdrop to contemporary planning which must be thoughtfully considered if we are to avoid the pitfalls of unrealism.

Of more direct and immediate bearing upon our national security are the changes wrought in the strategic potential of the Pacific Ocean in the course of the past war. Prior thereto, the western strategic frontier of the United States lay on the littoral line of the Americas with an exposed island salient extending out through Hawaii, Midway, and Guam to the Philippines. That salient proved not an outpost of strength but an avenue of weakness along which the enemy could and did attack. The Pacific was a potential area of advance for any predatory force intent upon striking at the bordering land areas.

All this was changed by our Pacific victory. Our strategic frontier then shifted to embrace the entire Pacific Ocean which became a vast moat to protect us as long as we hold it. Indeed, it acts as a protective shield for all of the Americas and all free lands of the Pacific Ocean area. We control it to the shores of Asia by a chain of islands extending in an arc from the Aleutians to the Marianas held by us and our free allies. From this island chain we can dominate with sea and air power every Asiatic port from Vladivostok to Singapore and prevent any hostile movement into the Pacific. Any predatory attack from Asia

Chapter Twelve

must be an amphibious effort. No amphibious force can be successful without control of the sealanes and the air over those lanes in its avenue of advance. With naval and air supremacy and modest ground elements to defend bases, any major attack from continental Asia toward us or our friends of the Pacific would be doomed to failure. Under such conditions the Pacific no longer represents menacing avenues of approach for a prospective invader—it assumes instead the friendly aspect of a peaceful lake. Our line of defense is a natural one and can be maintained with a minimum of military effort and expense. It envisions no attack against anyone nor does it provide the bastions essential for offensive operations, but properly maintained would be an invincible defense against aggression.

The holding of this littoral defense line in the western Pacific is entirely dependent upon holding all segments thereof, for any major breach of that line by an unfriendly power would render vulnerable to determined attack every other major segment. This is a military estimate as to which I have yet to find a military leader who will take exception. For that reason I have strongly recommended in the past as a matter of military urgency that under no circumstances must Formosa fall under Communist control. Such an eventuality would at once threaten the freedom of the Philippines and the loss of Japan, and might well force our western frontier back to the coasts of California, Oregon, and Washington.

To understand the changes which now appear upon the Chinese mainland, one must understand the changes in Chinese character and culture over the past 50 years. China up to 50 years ago was completely nonhomogeneous, being compartmented into groups divided against each other. The warmaking tendency was almost nonexistent, as they still followed the tenets of the Confucian ideal of pacifist culture. At the turn of the century, under the regime of Chan So Lin, efforts toward greater homogeneity produced the start of a nationalist urge. This was further and more successfully developed under the leadership of Chiang Kai-shek, but has been brought to its greatest fruition under the present regime, to the point that it has now taken on the character of a united nationalism of increasingly dominant aggressive tendencies. Through these past 50 years, the Chinese people have thus become militarized in their concepts and in their ideals. They now constitute excellent soldiers with competent staffs and commanders. This has produced a new and dominant power in Asia which for its own purposes is allied with Soviet Russia, but which in its own concepts and methods has become aggressively imperialistic with a lust for expansion and increased power normal to this type of imperialism. There is little of the ideological concept either one way or another in the Chinese makeup. The standard of living is so low and the capital accumulation has been so thoroughly dissipated by war that the masses are desperate and avid to follow any leadership which seems to promise the alleviation of local stringencies. I have from the beginning believed that the Chinese Communists' support of the North Koreans was the dominant one. Their interests are at present parallel to those of the Soviet, but I believe that the aggressiveness recently displayed not only in Korea, but also in Indochina and Tibet, and pointing potentially toward the south, reflects predominantly the same lust for the expansion of power which has animated every would-be conqueror since the beginning of time.

The Japanese people since the war have undergone the greatest reformation recorded in modern history. With a commendable will, eagerness to learn, and marked capacity to understand, they have, from the ashes left in war's wake, erected in Japan an edifice dedicated to the primacy of individual liberty and personal dignity, and in the ensuing process there has been created a truly representative government committed to the advance of political morality, freedom of economic enterprise, and social justice. Politically, economically, and socially Japan is now abreast of many free nations of the earth and will not again fail the universal trust. That it may be counted upon to wield a profoundly beneficial influence over the course of events in Asia is attested by the magnificent manner in which the Japanese people have met the recent challenge of war, unrest, and confusion surrounding them from the outside, and checked communism within their own frontiers without the slightest slackening in their forward progress. I sent all four of our occupation divisions to the Korean battlefront without the slightest qualms as to the effect of the resulting power vacuum upon Japan. The results fully justified my faith. I know of no nation more serene, orderly, and industrious — nor in which higher hopes can be entertained for future constructive service in the advance of the human race.

Of our former ward, the Philippines, we can look forward in confidence that the existing un-rest will be corrected and a strong and healthy nation will grow in the longer aftermath of war's terrible destructiveness. We must be patient and understanding and never fail them, as in our hour of need they did not fail us. A Christian nation, the Philippines stand as a mighty bulwark of Christianity in the Far East, and its capacity for high moral leadership in Asia is unlimited.

On Formosa, the Government of the Republic of China has had the opportunity to refute by action much of the malicious gossip which so undermined the strength of its leadership on the Chinese mainland. The Formosan people are receiving a just and enlightened administration with majority representation on the organs of government, and politically, economically, and socially they appear to be advancing along sound and constructive lines.

(Statement)

With this brief insight into the surrounding areas I now turn to the Korean conflict. While I was not consulted prior to the President's decision to intervene in support of the Republic of Korea, that decision, from a military standpoint, proved a sound one, as we hurled back the invader and decimated his forces. Our victory was complete and our objectives within reach when Red China intervened with numerically superior ground forces. This created a new war and an entirely new situation — a situation not contemplated when our forces were committed against the North Korean invaders — a situation which called for new decisions in the diplomatic sphere to permit the realistic adjustment of military strategy. Such decisions have not been forthcoming.

While no man in his right mind would advocate sending our ground forces into continental China and such was never given a thought, the new situation did urgently demand a drastic revision of strategic planning if our political aim was to defeat this new enemy as we had defeated the old.

Apart from the military need as I saw it to neutralize the sanctuary protection given the enemy north of the Yalu, I felt that military necessity in the conduct of the war made mandatory:

1. The intensification of our economic blockade against China;

2. The imposition of a naval blockade against the China coast;

3. Removal of restrictions on air reconnaissance of China's coastal areas and of Manchuria;

4. Removal of restrictions on the forces of the Republic of China on Formosa with logistical support to contribute to their effective operations against the common enemy.

For entertaining these views, all professionally designed to support our forces committed to Korea and bring hostilities to an end with the least possible delay and at a saving of countless American and Allied lives, I have been severely criticized in lay circles, principally abroad, despite my understanding that from a military standpoint the above views have been fully shared in past by practically every military leader concerned with the Korean campaign, including our own Joint Chiefs of Staff.

I called for reinforcements, but was informed that reinforcements were not available. I made clear that if not permitted to destroy the enemy buildup bases north of the Yalu; if not permitted to utilize the friendly Chinese force of some 600,000 men on Formosa; if not permitted to blockade the China coast to prevent the Chinese Reds from getting succor from without; and if there were to be no hope of major reinforcements, the position of the command from the military standpoint forbade victory. We could hold in Korea by constant maneuver and at an approximate area where our supply line advantages were in balance with the supply line disadvantages of the enemy, but we could hope at best for only an indecisive campaign, with its terrible and constant attrition upon our forces if the enemy utilized his full military potential. I have constantly called for the new political decisions essential to a solution. Efforts have been made to distort my position. It has been said that I was in effect a warmonger. Nothing could be further from the truth. I know war as few other men now living know it, and nothing to me is more revolting. I have long advocated its complete abolition as its very destructiveness on both friend and foe has rendered it useless as a means of settling international disputes. Indeed, on the 2d of September 1945, just following the surrender of the Japanese nation on the battleship *Missouri,* I formally cautioned as follows:

"Men since the beginning of time have sought peace. Various methods through the ages have been attempted to devise an international process to prevent or settle disputes between nations. From the very start, workable methods were found insofar as individual citizens were concerned, but the mechanics of an instrumentality of larger international scope have never been successful. Military alliances, balances of power, leagues of nations, all in turn failed, leaving the only path to be by way of the crucible of war. The utter destructiveness of war now blots out this alternative. We have had our last chance. If we will not devise some greater and more equitable system, Armageddon will be at our door. The problem basically is theological and involves a spiritual recrudescence and improvement of human character that will synchronize with our almost matchless advances in science, art, literature, and all material and cultural developments of the past 2,000 years. It must be of the spirit if we are to save the flesh."

But once war is forced upon us, there is no other alternative than to apply every available means to bring it to a swift end. War's very object is victory—not prolonged indecision. In war, indeed, there can be no substitute for victory.

Confutatio

There are some who for varying reasons would appease Red China. They are blind to history's clear lesson. For history teaches with unmistakable emphasis that appeasement but begets

new and bloodier war. It points to no single instance where the end has justified that means —
where appeasement has led to more than a sham
peace. Like blackmail, it lays the basis for new
and successively greater demands, until, as in
blackmail, violence becomes the only other
alternative. "Why," my soldiers asked of me,
"surrender military advantages to an enemy in
the field?" I could not answer. Some may say to
avoid spread of the conflict into an all-out war
with China; others, to avoid Soviet intervention.
Neither explanation seems valid. For China is
already engaging with the maximum power it can
commit and the Soviet will not necessarily mesh
its actions with our moves. Like a cobra, any
new enemy will more likely strike whenever it
feels that the relativity in military or other potential is in its favor on a worldwide basis.

The tragedy of Korea is further heightened
by the fact that as military action is confined to
its territorial limits, it condemns that nation,
which it is our purpose to save, to suffer the devastating impact of full naval and air bombardment, while the enemy's sanctuaries are fully
protected from such attack and devastation. Of
the nations of the world, Korea alone, up to now,
is the sole one which has risked its all against
communism. The magnificence of the courage
and fortitude of the Korean people defies description. They have chosen to risk death rather than
slavery. Their last words to me were, "Don't
scuttle the Pacific."

Conclusio

I have just left your fighting sons in Korea.
They have met all tests there and I can report to
you without reservation they are splendid in
every way. It was my constant effort to preserve
them and end this savage conflict honorably and
with the least loss of time and a minimum sacri-
fice of life. Its growing bloodshed has caused me
the deepest anguish and anxiety. Those gallant
men will remain often in my thoughts and in my
prayers always.

I am closing my 52 years of military service.
When I joined the Army even before the turn of
the century, it was the fulfillment of all my boyish
hopes and dreams. The world has turned over
many times since I took the oath on the plain at
West Point, and the hopes and dreams have long

since vanished. But I still remember the refrain of one of the most popular barrack ballads of that day which proclaimed most proudly that—

"Old soldiers never die; they just fade away."

And like the old soldier of that ballad, I now close my military career and just fade away—an old soldier who tried to do his duty as God gave him the light to see that duty.

Goodbye.

Conclusion

The classical mode is argumentative and may emphasize any kind of proposition; thus, it is widely applicable. However, it is particularly applicable to formal speaking situations. It is also especially useful in adapting to those audiences holding views that are different from those held by the speaker.

In contemporary terminology, one may view the classical mode as follows:

Step 1: *Exordium*
    A. Establishes rapport.
    B. Attracts and focuses the attention of the audience.

Step 2: *Narratio*
    A. States the nature of the problem.
    B. Shows the extent of the problem.

Step 3: *Confirmatio*
    A. Presents the proposition.
    B. Presents any machinery needed to implement the proposition.
    C. Presents (1) the arguments and (2) the evidence.

Step 4: *Confutatio*—Refutes the major argument(s) against the proposition.

Step 5: *Peroratio*
    A. Summarizes the major arguments.
    B. Appeals to the audience for acceptance of the proposition.

Suggested Readings

Baird, A. Craig. *Rhetoric: A Philosophical Inquiry.* New York: Ronald Press Co., 1965. Pp. 170–180. This reading is a splendid supplementary explication of the subject of organization/adaptation.

Thonssen, Lester, and A. Craig Baird. *Speech Criticism: The Development of Standards for Rhetorical Appraisal.* New York: Ronald Press Co., 1948. Chap. 14, "The Structure of Oral Discourse." Notwithstanding the similarity between this reading and the first item above, the differences make each one worth reading. This chapter centers about the act of criticism.

Suggested Assignments

1. Select a topic in the classical mode and do the following:
   a. Complete the statement "I want my audience to believe that . . ."
   b. Give a satisfactory answer to the question "Why do I want this audience to believe this specific point?"
   c. Give a satisfactory answer to the question "Why would the classical mode of communication best enable me to adapt my specific thought to this group of hearers?"
2. Construct a classical thought analysis for your speech in that mode.
3. Write your introduction and your conclusion.
4. Write a segment of your speech centered about any one division with its subdivisions.
5. Provide a written defense of your selection of the classical mode rather than (a) the defects or (b) the advantages mode.
6. Present a speech in the classical mode.

Style

I suspect that if you and your classmates were to be in disagreement over any subject in this book, it would be about style. I would suggest, therefore, that you read this chapter with special attention to the relationship between thought and style. As you read the chapter, keep this question in mind: "How do the qualities of thought assist me to adapt my thought to the hearers?"

The general conception of style refers to the qualities of thought as expressed in language.[1] Therefore, the qualities of thought are the qualities of style; and the qualities of style are concerned with the entire communicative gestalt (configuration), from the introduction through the conclusion. In short, the qualities of the style of any segment of a communication are meaningful only in relation to the entire communicative gestalt.

The major determinant of the shape of the communicative configuration is, of course, the thought analysis, which represents the logical

[1]For his definition and discussion of the definition of style, see Austin Phelps, *English Style in Public Discourse* (New York: Charles Scribner's Sons, 1883), pp. 1–9.

and psychological development of the thought and is therefore the key to understanding the style of any communication. Style, then, relates not to a fragmented study of words but rather to a critical analysis of the various aspects of thought as they impact on the minds of hearers. Although it may be possible that human beings will set down their ideas in language for purposes of catharsis or solely for their own future reference, it is incredible that language could have been created for either or both of those purposes by themselves. Language is first and foremost communicative; it focuses primarily not upon the communicator but upon the human being who is the intended perceiver of the communicator's thought. Therefore, communication has dynamic qualities of style.

The Dynamic Qualities of Style

What, then, are the qualities of style? The qualities of style include (1) *intentionality*, (2) *tone*, (3) *autone*, and (4) *feeling*. *Intentionality* arises because the hearer is "intended"; that is, the communicator acts purposefully toward the hearer. If the speaker has no purpose, then he can initiate no integrated communicative behavior.

Intentionality has its origin in the statement and reveals itself particularly in the predicate of the statement. After the speaker has formulated his statement, then in due course he selects the appropriate mode of communication by which to adapt his purpose to the audience. Thus, intentionality of style should permeate the entire mode of communication that the communicator selects. The statement's relationship to the thought analysis dictates that the predicative development of divisions and subdivisions must develop the intentionality inherent in the predicate of the statement. Since a communication without purpose cannot have unity, emphasis, and coherence, intentionality of thought becomes the first quality of style.

For example, assuming that one has formulated the statement "The president of the United States should be elected by a direct vote of the people," then he should check it over first to determine whether it embodies his specific intention. Then, assuming that he has made his intentionality clear in his statement, the communicator next should select his mode of communication. Because the intention of the foregoing statement centers on benefits, the speaker likely would elect to employ either the advantages mode or the residues variation as the best one. However, insofar as either mode is concerned — or any other, for that matter —

each segment of the configuration preliminary to the thought analysis must develop the intention of the predicate of the statement. That is to say, whether a segment is an *exordium* or a case history, a *narratio* or a quantification, it must move the *intentionality* of the statement forward in a straight line. *If the steps of the mode preliminary to the statement fail in this regard, then unity, emphasis, and coherence leading to the thought analysis will have been lost.*

Although these steps that precede the thought analysis are important, they are still preliminary. The substance of the thought of the communicator is in the thought analysis. Thus, in the divisions and subdivisions that develop the predicate of the statement, the communicator reveals full-blown the intentionality of his thought. The following statement, divisions, and subdivisions illustrate the way that intentionality reveals itself in the structure of the thought analysis:

Statement: The president // should be elected by a direct vote.
I. The direct election of the president // would institute the "one man–one vote" principle.
   A. It // would equalize the vote of the New Yorker and the Alaskan.
   B. It // would equalize the votes of all citizens.
   C. According to Senator ___, it // would make every man's vote equal to every other man's.
II. The direct election of the president // would eliminate the possibility of electing a "minority president."

By following the relationship in this illustration between the predicate of a division and the statement, and between the predicates of the subdivisions and the predicate of the division to which they relate, one should be able to see the intentionality of the style of the communicator. *Without this intentionality, or purpose, a speaker is unlikely to speak so as to stimulate the hearer to identify with his ideas.* An intentionless style, therefore, lacks persuasiveness.

In addition to purpose, the communicator also has an attitude in mind while speaking. The second quality of thought, *tone,*[2] refers to the attitude of the speaker toward the hearers. The possible meanings of tone are equal to the total possible attitudes that any man employing language may have. The communicator's concern is not with categorizing the various meanings of tone but rather with knowing how to develop a satisfactory tone.

First of all, the speaker must regard the hearer as one possessing basic human dignity. If the speaker looks down on the hearer, the hearer will detect it and will reject him rather than to identify with him. Second,

---

[2]See I. A. Richards, *Practical Criticism: A Study of Literary Judgment* (New York: Harcourt, Brace and Company, 1929), pp. 175–176.

---

one must have an active desire to help his audience — to be altruistic. One who has a positive attitude toward his hearers will inevitably gain some hearers.

The speaker should not underestimate the importance of tone in its power of persuasion. According to the biographer of W. J. Fox, Richard Garnett, Fox's power as a speaker lay in certain qualities:

> . . . a genuine humanitarianism, moral fervour and shrewd common sense, and these, combined with his power of hard-hitting and his preacher's knack of beginning the combat with Providence on his side, were irresistible. It is however in his moral boldness that Fox shines most.[3]

Fox's "genuine humanitarianism" and his "moral fervour" both represent conclusions drawn by listeners about his attitude toward the persons in his audience.

Any genuine humanitarian has the kind of tone that characterizes a persuasive style. Among the great speakers and humanitarians of America was Robert G. Ingersoll, whose address to farmers on the subject of farming demonstrated his strong feeling for the farmer. The following humorous excerpt from his speech reveals subtly, but clearly, Ingersoll's sympathetic attitude toward the farmer.

> It is not necessary in this age of the world for the farmer to rise in the middle of the night and begin his work. This getting up so early in the morning is a relic of barbarism. It has made hundreds of thousands of young men curse the business. There is no need of getting up at three or four o'clock in the winter morning. The farmer who persists in dragging his wife and children from their beds ought to be visited by a missionary. It is time enough to rise after the sun has set the example. For what purpose do you get up? To feed the cattle? Why not feed them more the night before? It is a waste of life. In the old times they used to get up about three o'clock in the morning, and go to work long before the sun had risen with "healing upon his wings," and as a just punishment they all had the ague; and they ought to have it now. The man who cannot get a living upon Illinois soil without rising before daylight ought to starve. Eight hours a day is enough for any farmer to work except in harvest time. When you rise at four and work till dark what is life worth? Of what use are all the improvements in farming? Of what use is all the improved machinery unless it tends to give the farmer a little more leisure?[4]

---

[3] Richard Garnett, *The Life of W. J. Fox, Public Teacher and Social Reformer 1786–1864*, concluded by Edward Garnett (London: John Lane, 1910), pp. 263–264.

[4] Robert Green Ingersoll, *Great Speeches of Col. R. G. Ingersoll* (Chicago: Rhodes & McClure Publishing Co., 1885), p. 13.

Chapter Thirteen

The third quality of style, also attitudinal, is *autone*, the attitude of the speaker toward himself.[5] One can have just as many attitudes toward himself as he can toward others. However, if for no other reason than there is only one of him, it would appear that the speaker's attitude toward himself is more stable than his attitude toward others. For example, although the speaker's attitude toward men in general might be altruistic, he might also have an active dislike or disrespect for a certain group or organization. His autone, on the other hand, is likely to be more stable.

Perhaps the one word that best represents the proper autone is humbleness. One of the great masters of communication during the twentieth century, President Franklin D. Roosevelt, was well aware of the importance of this quality. In his Inaugural Address, March 4, 1933, he epitomized what he thought that the citizen's attitude toward self ought to be; and, at the same time, he suggested where he thought his own meaning lay.

> Happiness lies not in the mere possession of money; it lies in the joy of achievement, in the thrill of creative effort. The joy and moral stimulation of work no longer must be forgotten in the mad chase of evanescent profits. These dark days will be worth all they cost us if they teach us that our true destiny is not to be ministered unto but to minister to ourselves and to our fellow men.
>
> Recognition of the falsity of material wealth as the standard of success goes hand in hand with the abandonment of the false belief that public office and high political position are to be valued only by standards of pride of place and personal profit; and there must be an end to a conduct in banking and in business which too often has given to a sacred trust the likeness of callous and selfish wrongdoing. Small wonder that confidence languishes, for it thrives only on honesty, on honor, on the sacredness of obligations, on faithful protection, on unselfish performance; without them it can not live.[6]

The fourth quality of style, again attitudinal, is *feeling* — one's attitude toward the subject (topic).[7] If the speaker does not feel that the subject is important, then he has no reason to expect his audience to believe that it is important. Someone has said that nothing great is ever accomplished without enthusiasm. Although there are undoubtedly some exceptions to that statement, it has the ring of truth. As one looks at the great speeches of the world, he cannot escape the conclusion that feeling is an important quality of style.

---

[5]See Chapter 1, Philosophy of Human Communication, on finding one's meaning outside of self.

[6]*Inaugural Addresses of the Presidents of the United States from George Washington 1789 to Lyndon Baines Johnson 1965*, 89th Congress, 1st Session, House Document No. 51 (Washington: U.S. Government Printing Office, 1965), p. 236.

[7]See Richards, p. 175.

To take one example, in "His Speech to the Court at His Trial," November 2, 1859, John Brown said:

> This court acknowledges, as I suppose, the validity of the law of God. I see a book kissed here which I suppose to be the Bible, or at least the New Testament. That teaches me that all things whatsoever I would that men should do to me, I should do even so to them. It teaches me, further, to "remember them that are in bonds, as bound with them." I endeavored to act up to that instruction. I say I am yet too young to understand that God is any respecter of persons. I believe that to have interfered as I have done—as I have always freely admitted I have done—in behalf of His despised poor was not wrong, but right. Now, if it is deemed necessary that I should forfeit my life for the furtherance of the ends of justice, and mingle my blood further with the blood of my children and with the blood of millions in this slave country whose rights are disregarded by wicked, cruel, and unjust enactments—I submit; so let it be done![8]

At this point, the communicator might inquire as to how he reveals the three attitudinal qualities: (1) tone, (2) autone, and (3) feeling. In general, the speaker may employ several means of communicating his attitudes effectively. *First*, he expresses attitudes through his choice of reasons in his divisions, and in some subdivisions. *Second*, he communicates his attitudes by his choice of evidence through the case history and through expert opinion. *Third*, he reveals his attitudes through his choice of language. *Fourth*, he reveals his attitudes through voice, in particular through intonation. *Fifth*, he shows his attitudes through bodily action.

The Descriptive Qualities of Style

Inasmuch as the qualities of thought always imply attitudes of some kind, any discussion of the descriptive qualities of style must be premised upon the dynamic qualities of style. The descriptive qualities of style include (1) *precision,* (2) *clarity,* (3) *energy (force),* and (4) *propriety.*

Precision reveals itself first, and most obviously, in the statement. Precision also manifests itself in the segments of the communicative gestalt. Finally, precision shows itself in the thought analysis.

In formulating the statement with precision, the communicator

---

[8]William Jennings Bryan, ed., *The World's Famous Orations,* Vol. 9 (New York: Funk and Wagnalls Co., 1906), pp. 187–188.

should employ specific nouns and specific verbs. Because adjectives and adverbs tend toward imprecision, the speaker should examine carefully each modifier that he contemplates using. To take an example, a communicator formulated the statement that "The United States // should guarantee all citizens greater freedom of speech." What is "greater" freedom? What is meant by "The United States"; did the speaker mean only the collection of the fifty states, or did he mean the federal government? What is meant by "guarantee"? This statement failed to be precise. Assuming that the speaker wished to consider the general topic above, he might formulate the statement more precisely, as follows: "The Congress of the United States should pass legislation guaranteeing every citizen's right to speak except to urge violent overthrow of the federal government."

To make sure that all segments of the communicative gestalt are precise, the communicator should select those introductory segments of the communicative gestalt that point precisely to the statement. For example, if the speaker selects a mode that calls for him to open with a case history, then he must select the case history that points to the statement. A case history always is a case history of something; an opening case history is always a case history pointing precisely toward the statement.

In a similar manner, all other segments introductory to the statement must aim toward the statement. For instance, the quantification following an opening case history should amplify that case history in one way or another, thus magnifying the precise point of the case history.

In the following excerpt, the case history precisely points up the nature of the problem, and the following paragraph shows the pervasiveness (a form of quantification) of the problem. Both the case history and the quantification lead progressively and precisely to the speaker's statement regarding the need for new laws regulating oil pollution.

Oil is the life blood of our modern industrial society. It fuels the machines and lubricates the wheels of the world's production.

But when that vital resource is out of control, it can destroy marine life and devastate the environment and economy of an entire region. The costs of the *Torrey Canyon* disaster, for example, are still being counted. 100,000 birds and millions of fish were killed. Over 100 miles of Cornish coast were soaked in an oily slime that further washed across the Channel to ruin French beaches. Vacation seasons and tourist economies were decimated. The cleanup costs to the British Government alone were about $8 million in addition to the expenditures incurred by local government and private business.

The plain facts are that the technology of oil—its extraction, its transport, its refinery and use—has outpaced laws to control that technology and prevent oil from polluting the environment. In short, oil is largely out of legal control. It is out of legal control in the United States and around the world.[9]

The next step for the communicator to take is to formulate precise divisions and subdivisions in support of the statement. Clearly, the principles applicable to the statement apply equally well to divisions and subdivisions.[10] After the speaker has formulated the divisions and sub-divisions of the analysis, he should organize the divisions and subdivisions so that their movement and development of the statement is precise. Since organization is a mental process, precision of organization is another aspect of precision of thought and, therefore, of style.

The second descriptive quality of style, *clarity,* relates directly to the audience. As has been observed, the audience cannot understand imprecise ideas; therefore, *precision is the essential antecedent of clarity.*

Like precision, clarity must characterize the entire communicative gestalt. Inasmuch as the etiology of the various modes previously discussed in this text derives from the adaptive function inherent in the communicative act, each segment of each mode therefore must be clear. In particular, because thought moves progressively from beginning to end, the segments of any mode preceding the thought analysis must be not only independently clear but also cumulatively clear. Similarly, just as the statement, divisions, and subdivisions must be precise, so also they must be clear. Further, if the communicator is going to reach the hearer effectively, then he must organize his message in terms of divisions and all subdivisions.

Ultimately, of course, the communicator must wrestle with words — sometimes individually. Among words that are perfectly precise, there are a good many that are not clear to a general audience. In particular, terms peculiar to the professions come under this heading. For example, many terms associated with space travel and rocketry are precise and clear to physicists and astronomers but are not intelligible to many laymen. The term "vacuum welding" is a case in point. Basically, the communicator should (1) select precise words, (2) select common words, and (3) employ short words to promote clarity *as the words are uttered.*

In relation to precise words, the communicator's friends are specific nouns and specific verbs. He should avoid pronouns, adjectives, and adverbs unless using them is essential. Common words refer, of course, to words that the speaker frequently uses, or at least to appropriate working members of his vocabulary. As for length of words all other things being equal, the shorter the words the less attention the hearer needs to give to what he is hearing. If both a speech and the words in the speech are long,

[9]Remarks by Max N. Edwards, Assistant Secretary for Water Pollution Control, U.S. Department of the Interior, Washington, D.C., before the International Conference on Oil Pollution of the Sea, Rome, Italy, October 8, 1968, Department of the Interior news release, October 8, 1968.

[10]See Chapter 6 regarding the development of the statement, divisions, and subdivisions.

then some hearers may tire to the extent of "tuning out" the speaker.

In the following illustration, the words used were precise, but they were not common to the vocabulary of the recipient of the communication:

One of the reasons we sometimes back away from the word "research" is the jargon that research people use. It's like the story of the plumber who wrote to a government agency, and said that he had found that hydrochloric acid quickly opened drain pipes. And he asked if this was all right to use. A scientist at the agency replied that "the efficacy of hydrochloric acid is indisputable, but the corrosive residue is incompatible with metallic permanence."

The plumber wrote back, thanking him for assurance that hydrochloric acid was all right. Disturbed by this turn of affairs, the scientist showed the letter to his boss—another scientist—who then wrote to the plumber saying "we cannot assume responsibility for the production of toxic and noxious residue with hydrochloric acid and suggest you use an alternative procedure."

The plumber wrote back that he agreed that hydrochloric acid worked fine. Greatly disturbed by this misunderstanding, the scientists took their problem to the top boss. He cut out the research jargon and wrote to the plumber. "Don't use hydrochloric acid. It eats hell out of the pipes."[11]

Lest the communicator think that the foregoing illustration is an isolated and atypical story, he should read the following excerpt from the *CA Newsletter* [College of Agriculture], Washington State University:

The error, common to us all, of assuming that everybody places the same meanings on words is strongly underlined in a study of the understanding of insecticide labels recently reported by a couple of University of Wisconsin ag. editors.

The study pinpoints the necessity to lean over backward in explaining the meanings of what often seem to be simple terms.

The study included farmers, homemakers, and high school vo-ag. students.

About 16 percent of the farmers thought "agitate" meant to apply spray quickly. About 70 percent of the farmers and 96 percent of the homemakers were right on "antidote." Most popular wrong definition was that it meant a printed warning that the material is poisonous. Only 22 percent of the farmers knew what "herbicide" means. Twenty per cent of the farmers and 14 percent of the homemakers thought it had something to do with fertilizer.

Homemakers and students did well on "hazardous." Ten percent of the farmers thought it meant that something is poisonous to insects but safe for people.

---

[11]"Lighter Side" by Gene Brown, Oneonta *Star*, June 15, 1964. Reprinted by permission.

Most homemakers had the right scoop on "foliage" but 17 percent of the farmers and students missed. Many farmers thought foliage meant the ground around plants. Students favored the idea that foliage was a certain form of the insect.

A common term on labels is "avoid prolonged contact." All homemakers knew what this meant, but only three fourths of the farmers and less than half the students did. Favorite wrong choice by farmers had to do with the length of pipe on spraying equipment.[12]

The communicator will find it difficult to overemphasize clarity; the tendency is more often in the other direction. Few, if any, American speakers had a style any more effective than Abraham Lincoln, and one characteristic of his speaking was its clarity. In particular, his Gettysburg Address was characterized by a beauty of precision, simplicity, and conciseness seldom, if ever, surpassed. There was no single word that should have been unintelligible to his audience; nor were any words vague or imprecise. In this address, approximately 75 percent of his words were monosyllabic. And of the remaining approximately 25 percent, only about two fifths were three syllables or longer—about 7 percent of the total.

The third descriptive quality of style, *energy,* refers to the impact on the human mind of the ideas symbolized in language. *Both precision and clarity are essential to energy;* for, obviously, if an idea is incomprehensible, then it cannot have impact on the minds of the hearers. If, therefore, the preliminary segments of a communicative gestalt are precise and clear, then the introduction to that particular mode has energy. And if, in turn, the statement, divisions, and subdivisions of the thought analysis are precise and clear, then the body of the communicative configuration has energy.

More specifically, in order to communicate with energy, one should consider at least the following: (1) specific nouns, (2) specific verbs, (3) conciseness, (4) point of view, (5) voice of verbs, (6) sentence structure, and (7) transitions.

Specific nouns are superior to either common or general nouns and to pronouns because specific nouns leave a more definite impression. The more definite the impression a word leaves the more rhetorical force (energy) it has. For example, the place in which one lives may be called an abode, but it might be a one-room shack or a castle. There is also a rhetorical difference between a dog and a Great Dane or a Dachshund. In a manner similar to nouns, specific verbs leave a more definite impression than general verbs. It is one thing to say "I *ran* home"; it is another to say "I *went* home." It is one thing to *disagree,* another to *object,* and a third to *protest.*

The third way to promote energy is conciseness, and it involves using as few words as possible to create the effect that the communicator de-

[12]*CA Newsletter* for the Faculty and Staff of the College of Agriculture, Washington State University, 15 (December 2, 1965), 7.

Chapter Thirteen

sires. Conciseness relates especially to energy by reducing the degree of attention that the hearer needs to sustain while comprehending the meaning as he hears the words. A master of conciseness was Winston Churchill. For example, his statement to Congress "Here we are together" was a model of a concise statement full of meaning for both the speaker and the Congress. This is not to say that all sentences should be so short as the foregoing; it *is* to say that concise sentences conduce to energy. They are powerful—have energy—because no words are wasted. Thus, concise sentences are short; but, more particularly, they pack together as much meaning as possible into the words.

Further, in relation to energy, the communicator should keep to a point of view. As minimum requirements, he should (1) keep to the same subject, (2) keep to the same person throughout the communication, and (3) use verb tense consistently throughout the communication. The underlying assumption behind these suggestions is that keeping to a point of view aids the hearer in giving his full attention to the development of the idea contained in the statement. If the communicator switches subjects, person, or tenses, he then requires the hearer to adjust his attention accordingly, and he may even confuse the hearer. For example, in the following excerpt, the communicator changed point of view from the "story of the United States' expansion" to "we"—a change of both subject and person, and from "is" to "spread"—a change in tense.

> For an equally large number of people, the story of the United States' expansion is distorted and fragmented. From our small settlements on the Atlantic Coast, we spread westward across North America.

In relation to the voice of verbs, one should use the active voice to create a strong impression. For instance, instead of saying that "paraphrasing the Declaration of Independence was also used," the speaker should say that "Mr. ___ paraphrased the Declaration of Independence." Or, in place of "the Secretary of State was seen by Mr. Lincoln," the speaker should say "Mr. Lincoln saw the Secretary of State." Generally, the only time that one desires to use a passive voice verb and create a weak impression is while communicating bad news or disappointment, or when delivering a eulogy.

By carefully regulating sentence structure to create the greatest attention, one also may improve his energy of style. In particular, in order to create and sustain maximum attention, the speaker may use *periodic structure*. A periodic structure suspends its sense until the grammatical close, thus sustaining the attention of the hearer until the completion of the structure. However, the communicator should use periodic structure with discretion. If one speaks only in rhetorical periods, then he is going to be artificially uniform and will lose the benefits of a judicious employment of periodic structure.

In general, one should use periodic structure when two assertions are tangentially related, either causally or conditionally. This example should illustrate the dynamic advantages of periodic structure over its opposite — loose structure:

> Periodic: After the Lunar Module and the Command Module have redocked, then the astronauts will prepare to return to earth.
>
> Loose: The astronauts will prepare to return to earth after the Lunar Module and the Command Module have redocked.

Note that there is a natural sequence of events — a subordinate relationship between the first clause in the periodic structure and the following main clause in that structure. When such a natural sequence exists, the communicator should utilize its strengths. On the other hand, the loose structure above reverses the natural sequence of "After — then." All other factors being equal, the sentence structure *that commands the maximum attention will create the most energetic impact on the mind of the hearer.*

Finally, from the standpoint of the communicative gestalt as a whole, one may increase the energy by using adequate transitions. Transitions are rhetorical bridges between ideas both great and small. Just as a bridge over a stream enables traffic to go from one precise point to another without either impediments or detours, so also a transition enables the speaker to move an idea easily and in a straight line precisely from point A to point B.

The communicator should supply transitions at these points:

1. Between the segments of the mode of communication.
2. Between the statement and divisions.
3. Between the divisions and subdivisions.
4. Between separate levels of subdivisions.
5. Between paragraphs.

Although each person probably will develop his own style of transition, he should find it helpful to be familiar with the different types commonly employed. The rule of thumb that the communicator should follow is that each transition should be appropriate to the subject matter that it relates.

First, speakers may employ the dismissive-introductive transition, "not only — but also." For example, "Communicators must be not only precise but also clear."

Second, one may employ some variation of the enumerative transition, as in these paragraphs designating the transitions. Some variations of the enumerative transition are "finally," "in addition," "initially," or "to conclude." For instance, "Finally, after the speaker has composed his speech, he then should practice delivering it."

Third, one may employ some form of contrast as a transition. One should not use this kind of transition unless the subject matter involves a genuine contrast—for example, between paragraphs. The speaker may introduce such a contrasting paragraph (or sentence) with "but," "on the other hand," "by contrast," or "by comparison." To illustrate, "In contrast with the defects mode, the eulogy employs the passive voice."

Although the foregoing kinds of transition are only illustrative, they do suggest effective ways to make a transition. The communicator who develops facility in their use should be able to construct his own variations as the particular characteristics of his communication dictate.

The last descriptive quality of style is *propriety*.[13] Propriety, however, is not a quality in the sense that precision and clarity are. Propriety is not so much an objective judgment of an attribute as it is a value judgment involving badness or goodness, or acceptability and unacceptability.

The speaker may be precise, clear, and forceful, and his speech may have all of the favorable attitudes implicit in those qualities of style; but if the audience deems his communication to lack propriety, then all of the other qualities will be relatively ineffective. Thus, the ultimate test that the speaker must make is a judgment regarding what the audience will think of his speech in terms of propriety. In making his judgment regarding propriety, the speaker must consider himself, his subject, and the occasion in relation to his audience.

Conclusion

The speaker should remember, first of all, that style refers to the qualities of thought in a speech. Therefore, when preparing to communicate, one should develop his style from the inside out by making certain of his (1) intentionality, (2) tone, (3) autone, and (4) feeling. In addition, one may develop an effective style by paying particular attention to the descriptive qualities: (1) precision, (2) clarity, (3) energy (force), and (4) propriety. These last have to do with the selection and arrangement of words; therefore, the speaker can manage these qualities by giving close attention to his thought and its symbolization.

---

[13]In Chapter 2, see the criteria for propriety in the selection of a topic.

Suggested Readings

Blankenship, Jane. *A Sense of Style: An Introduction to Style for the Public Speaker*. Belmont, Calif.: Dickenson Publishing Co., 1968. This entire volume should prove to be most helpful to the undergraduate student of human communication.

Spencer, Herbert. *Philosophy of Style: An Essay*. New York: D. Appleton and Co., 1873. This early volume by an outstanding scientist is as valid now as when it was written, and it deserves perusal by the serious student.

Strunk, William, Jr., and E. B. White. *The Elements of Style*. New York: Macmillian Co., 1959. This delightful little manual is full of excellent advice for both writers and speakers.

Suggested Assignments

1. Locate a speech embodying the "dynamic qualities of style." Write out a segment of the speech and explicate adequately your position that the segment possesses those "dynamic qualities."

2. Analyze the style of a speech in terms of the "descriptive qualities" of style. Be certain to show the interrelationships among (1) precision, (2) clarity, (3) energy, and (4) propriety throughout the entire speech.

Delivery

I do not wish to present so many "do's and don'ts" about delivery that you become like the thousand-legged worm who, when asked how he managed to coordinate his legs in walking, suddenly became paralyzed. If you wish to become effective in delivering your speeches, rest assured that you can.

You will find that there are very few essentials to effective delivery. As you read this chapter, you should pay special attention to the discussion of natural manner and of conversational quality; for they are the foundation of successful delivery.

Alfred North Whitehead stated the obvious when he said that "Speech is human nature itself, with none of the artificiality of written language."[1] Insofar as is known, Aristotle, author of the first systematic treatise on the subject of oral communication,[2] was the first person to comment on delivery. Although he would have preferred that men judge a speaker's

---

[1] Alfred North Whitehead, *Modes of Thought* (New York: Capricorn Books, 1958), p. 52.

[2] Aristotle, *Rhetoric.*

ideas on their own merit, Aristotle said that because of the defects of hearers, the communicator should study delivery. Notwithstanding Aristotle's judgment that delivery "affects the success of a speech greatly,"[3] he did not discuss delivery beyond providing a very cursory treatment of volume, modulation, and rhythm.

Since Aristotle's time, delivery has experienced much emphasis — perhaps undue emphasis. The elocutionists of seventeenth and eighteenth century England represent for modern readers the extreme emphasis of the physical aspects of delivery. Examples of such elocutionary works are Gilbert Austin's *Chironomia,* Albert Bacon's *Manual of Gesture,* and John Walker's *Elements of Elocution.*[4]

Although modern communicators devote varying amounts of attention to delivery, it would not seem unfair to state that if there is a change, then it would be away from an elocutionary view of delivery. Among scholars in the area of human communication there seems to be a consensus in favor of moderation.

One of the characteristics of the contemporary approach to delivery is the conversational manner. This approach to delivery, although emphasized in present theory and practice, was born in Greece. It had its origin with one of the Attic orators, Lysias, who was born around the middle of the fifth century B.C., although the exact date is uncertain. During a period of better than 20 years, Lysias wrote speeches for delivery by others in the law courts. He is said to have been the master of the "plain" style. When he wrote a speech for delivery by another, he attempted to write it so that the speech, *as delivered,* would *sound like that person.* His ability to compose speeches that sounded as if they came from the minds of the speakers was the secret of his success.

Without attempting to trace the thread of conversational manner in delivery from Lysias to the modern era, it is sufficient to point out that the nineteenth century witnessed significant progress in relation to the development of the theory of delivery. In his *Elements of Rhetoric,* published first in 1828, Richard Whately gave substantial attention to delivery. He opened Part 4, "Of Elocution," by stating:

> On the importance of this branch, it is hardly necessary to offer any remark. Few need to be told that the effect of the most perfect composition may be entirely destroyed, even by a Delivery which does not render it unintelligible; — that one, which is inferior both in matter and style, may produce, if better spoken, a more powerful effect than another which surpasses it in both those points; and that even such an Elocution as does not spoil the effect of what is said, may yet fall far short of doing full justice to it.[5]

---

[3] *Rhetoric,* 1403b21–22.

[4] For further information about delivery, readers may consult Lester Thonssen and A. Craig Baird, *Speech Criticism,* Chap. 16 (New York: Ronald Press Co., 1948).

[5] Richard Whately, *Elements of Rhetoric* (New York: Sheldon & Co., 18–), p. 389.

In discussing delivery in terms of reading a manuscript and of speaking, Whately emphasized what he called the "natural manner." As a move to counter the common practice of his time of emphasizing voice, Whately urged speakers to concentrate entirely on their thought as the means of achieving an effective delivery. In terms of benefit, Whately stated:

> The advantage of this natural manner—*i.e.*, the manner which one naturally falls into who is *really speaking*, in earnest, and with a mind *exclusively* intent on what he has to say—may be estimated from this consideration; that there are few (as was remarked in the preceding chapter) who do not *speak* so as to give effect to what they are saying. Some, indeed, do this much better than others. Some have as I observed above, in ordinary conversation, an indistinct or incorrect pronunciation,—an embarrassed and hesitating utterance, or a bad choice of words: but hardly any one fails to deliver (when speaking earnestly) what he does say, so as to convey the sense and the force of it, much more completely than even a good reader would, if those same words were written down and read. The latter might, indeed, be more *approved;* but that is not the present question; which is, concerning the *impression* made on the hearers' minds. It is not the polish of the blade that is to be considered, or the grace with which it is brandished, but the keenness of the edge, and the weight of the stroke.[6]

Of course, there can be no static concept of natural manner. What would be one person's natural manner would not necessarily be another's. At the same time, such personal differences do not *in themselves* mean that one person's delivery makes him more effective than another. For instance, during the campaign against the English Corn Laws in 1839–1846, the Anti-Corn Law League had the services of John Bright, Richard Cobden, and William J. Fox. Historian G. M. Trevelyan said that "The League had the fortune to possess in its three chief speakers the three requirements of effective oratory. Cobden was argument, Bright was passion, Fox was rhetoric."[7] In short, each was effective in his own way.

What were some of the characteristics of Bright's delivery? Trevelyan states that ". . . his characteristic and vital contribution was the passion with which he reinforced reason, and the high tone of moral indignation and defiance which he infused into his listeners."[8] Further, in his *The Life of Richard Cobden,* John Morley reveals some of Bright's qualities that may help to explain why it was a part of his manner to be passionate.

> Bright had all the resources of passion alive within his breast. He was carried along by vehement political anger, and, deeper than that,

---

[6]Whately, pp. 415–416.

[7]George Macaulay Trevelyan, *The Life of John Bright* (Boston: Houghton Mifflin Co., 1913), p. 98.

[8]Trevelyan, p. 97.

---

there glowed a wrath as stern as that of an ancient prophet. To cling to a mischievous error seemed to him to savour of moral depravity and corruption of heart.[9]

With regard to Cobden's power as a speaker, Morley claims that, although Cobden was not lacking passion, his secret was persuasiveness:

> Still, it was not passion to which we must look for the secret of his oratorical success. I have asked many scores of those who knew him, Conservatives as well as Liberals, what this secret was, and in no single case did my interlocutor fail to begin, and in nearly every case he ended as he had begun, with the word *persuasiveness*. Cobden made his way to men's hearts by the union which they saw in him of simplicity, earnestness, and conviction, with a singular facility of exposition. This facility consisted in a remarkable power of apt and homely illustration, and a curious ingenuity in framing the argument that happened to be wanted. Besides his skill in thus hitting on the right argument, Cobden had the oratorical art of presenting it in the way that made its admission to the understanding of a listener easy and undenied. He always seemed to have made exactly the right degree of allowance for the difficulty with which men follow a speech, as compared with the ease of following the same argument on a printed page which they may consider and ponder until their apprehension is complete. Then men were attracted by his mental alacrity, by the instant readiness with which he turned round to grapple with a new objection. Prompt and confident, he was never at a loss, and he never hesitated. This is what Mr. Disraeli meant when he spoke of Cobden's "sauciness." It had an excellent effect, because everybody knew that it sprang, not from levity or presumption, but from a free mastery of his subject.[10]

Whether one uses "passion," "simplicity," "earnestness," a "singular facility of exposition," or a "remarkable power of apt and homely illustration," to describe Cobden's oratory, one cannot avoid the conclusion that these terms characterized a natural delivery by Cobden, stemming from a preoccupation with his thought.

But, what of William J. Fox? Some critics might be inclined to describe Fox's delivery as florid, and thus by implication to deny that his delivery came within the definition of natural manner. However, it appears that Fox's approach to delivery was appropriate to him, that audiences responded to him, and that he gave preeminence to his subject matter. One able critic and speaker who heard Fox speak was George J. Holyoake. Holyoake states:

---

[9] John Morley, *The Life of Richard Cobden,* Vol. 1 (New York: Macmillan Co., *n.d.*), p. 194.

[10] Morley, pp. 194–195.

Mr. W. J. Fox, a Unitarian minister, and subsequently M.P. for Oldham, surpassed all the orators of the League of that day in brilliance of speech. Shorter and more rotund than Charles James Fox, he, notwithstanding, produced effects of rhetoric transcending those of his great namesake. The term "brilliant" does not entirely describe them. You no more thought of his appearance while he was speaking than you did of Thiers's insignificant stature. His low, clear, lute-like voice penetrated over the pit and gallery of Covent Garden Theatre.[11]

Perhaps one of the most useful comments on Fox comes from the historian Augustus Mongredien, who not only describes Fox's delivery but also makes a brief reference to that of both Cobden and Bright. Mongredien describes Fox as follows:

There then came forward a round-faced, obese man, of small stature, whom (if you avoided looking at his eyes) you might take to be a person slow of comprehension and slow of utterance—a sleek, satisfied, perhaps sensual person—a calm, patient, and somewhat lethargic man. The only thing remarkable about him (always excepting his eyes) was a mass of long, thick, black hair, which waved over his neck and shoulders. This man spoke, and the vast audience was thrilled by his wonderful eloquence. It was W. J. Fox, the Unitarian Minister, and afterwards member for Oldham. The moment he began to speak he seemed another man. His large brown eyes flashed fire, and his impressive gestures imparted dignity to his stature. His voice displayed a combination of power and sweetness not surpassed even by the mellow bass tones of Daniel O'Connell in his prime. His command of language seemed unlimited, for he was never at a loss, not only for a word, but for the right word. Not argumentative and persuasive like Cobden, or natural and forcible as Mr. Bright, his *forte* lay rather in appealing to the emotions of his audience, and in this branch of the oratorical art his power was irresistible.[12]

The foregoing discussion leads to the conclusion that *a speaker's unique manner of delivery depends largely upon (1) his personality, (2) his relationship to his topic, (3) his relationship to his audience, and (4) generally accepted standards of propriety for human conduct.* Whereas Whately's concept of natural manner seemed to focus on the relationship between the communicator and his message as the means of producing the optimum impact on the hearer, James A. Winans, in the early twentieth century, wrote his famous essay focusing on "conversational quality," that is, on the communicator's relationship to his audience. Winans

---

[11]George Jacob Holyoake, *Sixty Years of An Agitator's Life,* Vol. 2 (London: T. Fisher Unwin, 1906), p. 227.

[12]Augustus Mongredien, *History of The Free-Trade Movement in England,* new ed., with introductory and supplementary chapters by the Rev. Dr. H. de B. Gibbins (London: Cassell & Co., 1897), p. 96.

---

was, of course, absolutely correct in saying "Do not understand that this is some new thing . . ." On the other hand, like Aristotle centuries before, and Whately of the preceding century, Winans was a penetrating observer; and he formulated his observations into a perceptive statement of truth. The following introduction to Winans' chapter entitled, "The Problem of Delivery—Conversing with an Audience," accurately describes the nature of delivery:

> Imagine all memory of speech-making to be blotted out, so that there is no person in the world who remembers that he has ever made a speech or heard a speech. Imagine, too, all speeches and all references to speeches in literature, to be blotted out; so that there is left no clue to this art. Is this the end of speech-making? Here comes a man who has seen a great race, or has been in a great battle, or is on fire with enthusiasm for a cause. He begins to talk with a friend he meets on the street; others gather, twenty, fifty, a hundred. Interest grows intense; he lifts his voice that all may hear. But the crowd wishes to hear and see the speaker better. "Get up on this cart!" they cry; and he mounts the cart and goes on with his story or his plea.
>
> A private conversation has become a public speech; but under the circumstances imagined it is thought of only as a conversation, as an enlarged conversation. It does not seem abnormal, but quite the natural thing. When does the talker or converser become a speechmaker? When ten persons gather? Fifty? Or is it when he gets on the cart? Is there any real change in the nature or the spirit of the act? Is it not essentially the same throughout, a conversation adapted as the talker proceeds to the growing number of his hearers? There may be a change of course, if he becomes self-conscious; but assuming that interest in story or argument remains the dominant emotion, there is no essential change in his speaking. It is probable that with the increasing importance of his position and the increasing tension of feeling that comes with numbers, he gradually modifies his tone and his diction, and permits himself to launch into a bolder strain and a wider range of ideas and feelings than in ordinary conversation; but the change is in degree and not in kind. He is conversing with an audience.[13]

In connection with conversing with an audience, Winans refers to the great Bostonian reformer Wendell Phillips as a person commonly associated with that manner of communication. One of the most revealing descriptions of Phillips' manner of conversing with an audience is a citation in Albert J. Beveridge's *The Art of Public Speaking*. Beveridge cities Elbert Hubbard within the context of his own advice to be conversational.

---

[13]James Albert Winans, *Public Speaking* (Ithaca, N.Y.: Sewell Publishing Co., 1915), pp. 17–18.

Elbert Hubbard, when a boy of twelve, heard Wendell Phillips, and thus describes him and his manner of speaking:

"One man arose and spoke. He lifted his hands, raised his voice, stamped his foot, and I thought he was a very great man. He was just introducing the Real Speaker.

"Then the Real Speaker walked slowly down to the front of the stage and stood very still. And everybody was also quiet . . . Phillips just stood there and told us about the lost arts; he stood still with one hand behind him or resting on his hip or at his side and the other hand motioned a little—that was all.

"We expected every minute that he would burst out and make a speech, but he did not—he just talked . . . and I understood it all.

"I remember the presence and attitude of the man as though it were but yesterday. The calm courage, deliberation, beauty and strength of the speaker—his knowledge, his gentleness, his friendliness! I had heard many sermons, and some had terrified me.

"This time I had expected to be thrilled too. . . . And here it was all just quiet joy—I understood it all. I was pleased with myself; and being pleased with myself I was pleased with the speaker. He was the biggest and best man.I had ever seen—the first real man."

There is your model. No prancing about, no striding to and fro like a caged and hungry lion, no stamping of foot or pounding with fist or shaking the same at high heaven, no tossing of arms as if in agony or rage, no shouting or bellowing nor yet tremolo tones and whispering; especially no grimacing or facial contortions.

Merely be quiet and at ease and talk like a human being—a friendly person conversing with friends, a kindly but intelligent teacher telling with clearness and force what you have to say.[14]

Beveridge also mentions hearing Robert G. Ingersoll, whom he describes as "a real orator, a master of the art . . ." Beveridge's description of Ingersoll is just as suggestive today as it has ever been.

In the first place he was perfectly attired, freshly shaved, well-groomed, neatly turned out in every particular. He came to the front of the platform in the most natural manner and, looking us in the eye in a friendly fashion, began to talk to us as if he were conversing with each of us personally.

He stood still, made no gestures for a long time, and when they came at last, they were, seemingly, so spontaneous and unstudied that we scarcely noticed them, so much a part of his spoken word did they appear to be. His gestures added to the force of his remarks. Only once did he show emotion, and then it was so appropriate, so obviously sincere, gestures so well expressing the physical reaction of his sentiments, that even this outburst was engaging.

In short, everything about Colonel Ingersoll was pleasing, noth-

---

[14] Albert J. Beveridge, *The Art of Public Speaking* (Boston: Houghton Mifflin Co., 1924), pp. 52–54.

---

ing was repellent—a prime requisite to the winning of a cordial hearing from any audience big or little, rough or polite.[15]

Since the time of Ingersoll, the trend toward conversational quality in oral communication has progressed steadily and would appear to be irreversible. One of the most notable examples of a speaker who "conversed" with an audience was Franklin D. Roosevelt, whose "fireside chats" were the essence of what Winans advocated. His delivery was clear, warm, personal, and seemed to encourage a 1-to-1 relationship with the President. His phrase "fireside chats" was a happy one too. It suggested enthymematically the President was "talking things over" with two or three persons before a friendly crackling fire in his living room.

It is impossible to leave the field of political oratory without mentioning two other contemporary persons of uncommon ability to converse with an audience: Senator J. William Fulbright and the late Senator Everett M. Dirksen. Although each one's natural manner differed radically from the other, both demonstrated at the ballot box over the years the ability to converse with audiences.

Historically, since the days of both Moses and St. Paul, the pulpit has been involved with communication and, seemingly affected by various rhetorical winds, has had its fancies. But now the conversational manner in preaching seems to be widely evident. Although Bishop Sheen and Norman Vincent Peale are by no means the only fine examples, their speaking does illustrate accurately the art of "conversing with" congregations.

If one takes a moment to reflect upon the idea of conversing with an audience, he observes that all such dialog must be premised upon attitudes acceptable to one's hearers:

1. The speaker must believe that his message is important to the hearers.
2. The speaker must believe that the hearers are worthy of respect.
3. The speaker's attitude toward himself should be appropriate.

Then, if a man has both a natural manner and a conversational quality in his delivery, he does well. However, the speaker must also adapt his message to his hearers by using his voice, which may be discussed in terms of (1) *loudness,* (2) *articulation,* and (3) *pitch.*

With regard to *loudness,* one should, of course, speak loudly enough to be heard. Each speaker needs to judge for himself how loud that will be. The variables of size of room, acoustics, number of persons present, as well as the vocal qualities (particularly resonance) of the speaker's voice make it essential that the speaker learn to sense his own volume. If one is quite unsure of himself, he can go with a knowledgeable acquaint-

---

[15] Beveridge, pp. 12–13.

---

ance to the site of his speech and test out the room in the deadest spots. Although the speaker might need to increase his loudness to compensate for the size of the audience, he still would have some notion of how well he could be heard in that particular room.

It is doubtless true that a century or so ago some people overemphasized *articulation*. However, at times one might wish for a bit more emphasis today. One does not need an "antiseptic" or "high-fidelity" articulation, but he should speak so as to make clear instantly what he is talking about. In order to make certain of his articulation, one should record his speech and play it back. During the replay, the student would find it advantageous to have a knowledgeable acquaintance or his teacher present.

The nonpathological problems of articulation center about the consonants and, in particular, the final consonants. Upon occasion, the unpracticed speaker also will fail to attack properly an initial consonant. Since vowels are by nature voiced, they ordinarily take care of themselves. Therefore, if the speaker will make certain to sound all consonants clearly, particularly the final and initial ones, then he should have acceptable articulation.

Finally, one should attempt to develop his ability to use his optimum *pitch*.[16] Beginning speakers, in particular, may have a pitch above the optimum level. One can encourage the development of a suitable pitch by relaxing the entire body; for it is fruitless to attempt to relax one's voice without relaxing the body generally.

One of the best ways to relax is by deep breathing. If one forces air into the lungs, that action itself tends to relax the related muscles in the thoracic and abdominal areas. In addition, the added oxygen has a relaxing effect. One should remember, however, that deep breathing is not a gimmick to influence pitch on impulse, and the only way that it will work to improve pitch for a lifetime is for one to breathe properly for a lifetime.

One should coordinate the deep-breathing sequence with the release of tension in and about the neck.[17] The reason for such coordination is that the vocal ligaments and associated muscle groupings (*intrinsic* laryngeal musculature) cannot *consciously* be relaxed. Therefore, the best that one can do is to relax the neck muscles (*extrinsic* laryngeal musculature) around the vocal apparatus.

Two other factors influence pitch. First, the faster one speaks, the higher the pitch tends to rise. Second, the more volume, the higher the pitch tends to go. Thus, if one needs to lower his pitch in order to obtain its optimum, then he may do so by (1) relaxing his body, (2) speaking slowly enough, and (3) avoiding excessive loudness.

Another important factor in adapting to hearers is the speaker's *rate*

---

[16] For a detailed discussion of pitch, see Arthur J. Bronstein and Beatrice F. Jacoby, *Your Speech and Voice* (New York: Random House, 1967), pp. 222–234.

[17] See Richard Luchsinger and Godfrey E. Arnold, *Voice-Speech-Language: Clinical Communicology* (Belmont, Calif.: Wadsworth Publishing Co., 1965), pp. 75–77.

---

of speaking. The speaker can determine easily whether he is speaking too rapidly by observing whether he is enunciating perfectly the sounds of his words. If he is slurring over or even omitting a few sounds, then he is speaking too rapidly. One way to correct a rapid rate is to enunciate distinctly all initial and final consonants — an impossibility for those speaking too rapidly. One advantage of this approach is that *it inherently takes into account the variables of one's vocal equipment.*

Of course, one may fall into the opposite error of speaking too slowly. However, the problem of slowness can be corrected easily. If one (1) selects a topic in which he has a vital interest, (2) selects a topic that he thinks is vital to the listener, (3) becomes absorbed in his topic, and (4) practices giving his speech, then he should be able to eliminate the problem of a slow rate.

The only purpose of delivery is to adapt the speaker's message so that it is meaningful to hearers. Since extempore delivery facilitates such adaptation, it is, in general, the best approach to delivery. First, the speaker has better eye contact built into this approach. Even if the speaker employs an outline in delivering his extemporaneous speech, he is in an inherently superior position to establish and maintain eye contact as compared with other approaches. (The only possible exception would be the memorized delivery.)

Second, and perhaps more important, the speaker can adapt his materials to his audience by adjustment during the presentation of the speech. If, while using an illustration to make a point, the speaker notices frowns on the brows of persons in the audience, then he has the flexibility to inject another illustration in order to clarify a particular point. When the frowns disappear, then the speaker may continue with his planned development.

Extempore delivery also avoids certain disadvantages. First, both reading the manuscript and delivering from memory require considerable additional labor beyond preparing the subject matter. If one is to be successful at reading a manuscript, then he must make certain while writing (1) that it is written in oral style, (2) that the words and phrases fit together in terms of sound, and (3) that the words are readily pronounced. Further, he must make sure that he has adequate time to prepare to read the manuscript. The alternative to the foregoing would be a failure to make one's speech meaningful to hearers.

Similarly, if one wishes to prepare a manuscript for memorizing, then he must prepare it in the same way as if he were to read it. However, the speaker must go one step beyond and expend extra labor in memorizing the manuscript. By speaking extempore, one avoids much of the foregoing added labor that could better be spent concentrating on the message.

The second major disadvantage that the extempore speaker avoids is the nagging fear of forgetting the precise wording of a memorized script. Thus, the extempore speaker is not preoccupied with recalling the words of a text, only to discover that his apprehension is hindering his eye contact and his ability to adapt to the audience.

Conclusion

The primary function of delivery is to facilitate the speaker's effort to adapt his message to the minds of the hearers. In attempting to lead hearers to believe his message, the speaker should, first of all, employ the natural manner. He should become so full of his subject that he can discuss it in an easy, natural way.

Second, the speaker should adopt the conversational manner. The speaker should present his ideas as though he were engaging in a personal conversation with each member of the audience.

Third, through his use of voice, the speaker promotes the adaptation of his message. He should speak audibly and as distinctly as possible without being artificial.

Finally, in presenting his message, the speaker should employ the extempore approach to delivery. The extempore approach is closest of all to the conversational manner.

Suggested Readings

St. Onge, Keith R. *Creative Speech*. Belmont, Calif.: Wadsworth Publishing Co., 1964. Part Four, "Delivery." This imaginative approach should be interesting to read, and it should also provide the student with valuable information, particularly regarding voice and diction.

Wilcox, Roger P. *Oral Reporting in Business and Industry*. Englewood Cliffs, N.J.: Prentice-Hall, 1967. Part Four, "Presenting the Report." This entire section is full of sound advice that is presented in a clear and straightforward manner. Although the book's orientation is toward business administration majors, the material has wide application.

Winans, James Albert. *Public Speaking: Principles and Practice*. Ithaca, N.Y.: Sewell Publishing Co., 1915. Chap. 1, "The Problem of Delivery—Conversing with an Audience." Because of the truth the essay contains, Winans' chapter on delivery remains as a relevant, clear statement for modern readers.

1. Prepare to deliver three separate divisions (with subdivisions), each in a different manner as follows (the best way to accomplish this assignment is to use divisions from the same speech, if possible):
   a. Division I: Deliver from manuscript.
   b. Division II: Deliver from memory.
   c. Division III: Deliver extempore.
2. Write a brief paper about the delivery of a speaker whose speeches (recorded and/or written) are available for examination. In the paper, you should attempt (a) to isolate the qualities of his delivery, and (b) to measure the effectiveness of the speaker's delivery.

Index